MILITARY ENCOUNTERS

WITH

Extraterrestrials

"Frank Joseph is a thorough researcher and a great writer. He is offering a new chapter for ufologists to learn more about military confrontations between humans and extraterrestrials. I support his quality of research and the verifiable evidence that he has discovered."

BRUCE WIDAMAN, FORMER STATE DIRECTOR OF
THE MISSOURI MUTUAL UNIDENTIFIED
FLYING OBJECTS NETWORK (MUFON)

"By equal measures, intriguing and terrifying. If just one of these incidents occurred as described in *Military Encounters with Extraterrestrials,* our history books will need to be rewritten."

NICK POPE, U.K. MINISTRY OF DEFENSE (RETIRED),
INVESTIGATOR OF UFO SIGHTINGS FOR
SECRETARIAT (AIR STAFF) DIVISION,
1991 TO 1994

MILITARY ENCOUNTERS

WITH

Extraterrestrials

The Real War of the Worlds

Frank Joseph

Bear & Company
Rochester, Vermont

Bear & Company
One Park Street
Rochester, Vermont 05767
www.BearandCompanyBooks.com

Bear & Company is a division of Inner Traditions International

Library of Congress Cataloging-in-Publication Data

Names: Joseph, Frank, author.
Title: Military encounters with extraterrestrials : the real war of the
  worlds / Frank Joseph.
Description: Rochester, Vermont : Bear & Company, [2018] | Includes
  bibliographical references and index.
Identifiers: LCCN 2018000628 (print) | LCCN 2018002077 (ebook) |
  ISBN 9781591433248 (pbk.) | ISBN 9781591433255 (ebook) |
Subjects: LCSH: Unidentified flying objects—Sightings and
  Encounters—History. | Human-alien encounters—History. | Military history.
Classification: LCC TL789 .J68 2018 (print) | LCC TL789 (ebook) |
  DDC 001.942—dc23
LC record available at https://lccn.loc.gov/2018000628

Printed and bound in the United States by Versa Press, Inc.

10 9 8 7 6 5 4 3 2 1

Text design and layout by Debbie Glogover
This book was typeset in Garamond Premier Pro with Titular, Moho OT, Gill
Sans MT Pro and ITC Avant Garde Gothic Std used as display typefaces.

To send correspondence to the author of this book, mail a first-class letter to the
author c/o Inner Traditions • Bear & Company, One Park Street, Rochester, VT
05767, and we will forward the communication, or contact the author directly at
www.ancientamerican.com.

Contents

Entering the Cosmic Arena

John E. Brandenburg, Ph.D.

> *Two possibilities exist: Either we are alone in the universe,*
> *or we are not. Both are equally terrifying.*
> ARTHUR C. CLARKE[1]

Unidentified flying objects have been fixtures of public discourse since the Second World War. They must be viewed, however, as part of a larger, more perilous drama concerning our journey of discovery through the universe. If we accept the extraterrestrial hypothesis—namely, that our species has been and still is in a relationship of some kind with intelligent beings from beyond our world—then a major part of this discussion includes involvement and confrontations between its armed forces and ours.

As author Frank Joseph shows, public sightings of UFOs represent the proverbial "tip of the iceberg" in a multifaceted collision between human and nonhuman cultures. His *Military Encounters with Extraterrestrials* focuses on just such a fundamental issue, which, as it turns out, is the most secret and perhaps most significant part of this covert, ongoing, if unacknowledged conflict. The harsh truth is, despite our best intentions and hopes, a major feature of the UFO phenomenon continues to be destructive and sometimes deadly clashes with off-world intruders penetrating our airspace at will.

This realization was already foreshadowed by my 2015 book, *Death on Mars*. In it, I present evidence of isotopic traces from an annihilating atomic attack launched against the Red Planet in the very distant past. In a universe we already know to possess many threats to intelligent life—supernovas, gamma ray bursts, comet and asteroid impacts—Mars tells us we must now add the threat of other intelligent life. Like our own war-torn world, the rest of the universe may be a cosmic arena for the execution of terrible evil on occasion, as the fate of Mars illustrates. Accordingly, encounters between the armed forces and UFOs are key to understanding how government authorities approach and handle UFO phenomena, not just in the United States, but internationally.

It is, therefore, fundamentally important for us to grasp that, as we make our way through the universe, it is neither simple nor always friendly. Indeed, Frank Joseph explores a wealth of relevant reports with the goal of educating readers about this vital aspect of the UFO situation. His *Military Encounters with Extraterrestrials* describes the most concealed, challenging aspect of humankind's continuing cosmic journey. Such awareness promises to become ever more necessary the further we venture from Earth, with all the limitless possibilities of space travel, because it replaces our vulnerable naïveté with realistic awareness. Given the often-harrowing accounts presented in this book, that perception alone may someday be more decisive than we presently dare to imagine.

JOHN E. BRANDENBURG, PH.D., is a theoretical plasma physicist and science worker in defense, energy, space, and astrophysics. In addition to his acclaimed *Death on Mars: The Discovery of a Planetary Nuclear Massacre* (Kempton, IL: Adventures Unlimited Press, 2015), he published *The GEM Unification Theory: Extending the Standard Model to Include Gravitation* (Frankfurt, Germany: LAP LAMBERT Academic Publishing, 2016), which predicts gravity modification by electromagnetism for human space flight.

INTRODUCTION

Close Encounters
of the Eighth Kind

Now I am become Death, the destroyer of worlds.
KRISHNA IN THE *BHAGAVAD-GITA*,
FIFTH CENTURY BCE[1]

The publication of this book nearly coincides with the one hundredth anniversary of the most important conflict in the entire history of mankind—the first shots fired against otherworld opponents. From its opening salvo, fired by early military aviation's preeminent warrior, to present-day "peacekeeping" operations in the Middle East, the undeclared, unreported, ongoing struggle is unknown to most, suspected by few, and familiar almost exclusively to those individuals engaged in it. It is, in effect, the Silent War. Although both sides have suffered undetermined numbers of casualties, and combatants are involved from almost all armed forces on Earth, the objectives of their commanding officers are classified and virtually nothing is disclosed about the enemy, whose own agendas are even more enigmatic.

This most important conflict is not an armed confrontation among nations or peoples, but between earthly humans and unearthly nonhumans—a true War of the Worlds. That concept originated in the visionary brain of H. G. Wells, whose 1897 novel of that title is the earliest published story about a global struggle pitting human-kind against beings from another planet. Wells depicted the aliens as more technologically advanced than the defenders of Western civilization, which was nearly lost in a seemingly inexorable conquest of our planet by outside forces, until a natural virus, harmless to humans, but to which the invaders lacked immunity, fortuitously wiped them out. While the tale's denouement is both satisfying and credible, Wells's characterization of alien military superiority has been borne out by the last hundred years of extraterrestrial confrontations.

Exactly fifty years after the prescient book's first publication, unidentified flying objects (UFOs) became an international sensation when the American aviator Kenneth Arnold made the first widely reported observation of them. He reported seeing nine large vehicles "shaped like a pie plate" flying in tandem near Mount Rainier, Washington, on June 24, 1947.[2] Since then, a burgeoning number of UFO sightings and experiences from around the world have led to their classification into seven major categories:

Close Encounters of the First Kind: visual sightings of an unidentified flying object

Close Encounters of the Second Kind: interference by a UFO in the functioning of an earthly vehicle or electronic device, or leaving behind other kinds of physical evidence

Close Encounters of the Third Kind: a human in the presence of an extraterrestrial

Close Encounters of the Fourth Kind: a human abducted by extraterrestrials

Close Encounters of the Fifth Kind: direct communication between extraterrestrials and humans

Close Encounters of the Sixth Kind: death of a human or animal associated with a UFO or extraterrestrial sighting

Close Encounters of the Seventh Kind: Creation of a human/alien hybrid being, either by direct sexual reproduction or by artificial scientific methods

This book embraces most of these categories, while adding another one—Close Encounters of the Eighth Kind: military confrontations between human combatants and extraterrestrials.

This category is necessitated by the long history of armed encounters with off-world belligerents since 1917, the year first shots were fired by soldiers against a UFO. The evidence goes far beyond hearsay. Meanwhile, the warning sounded by U.S. Army general Hugh S. Johnson to millions of his fellow Americans in a nationwide radio broadcast near the outbreak of World War II is even more appropriate at this time, given the orders of most air forces to shoot extraterrestrial vehicles on sight:

> We are utterly, tragically unready for war or defense today. Until we are ready, acts of war committed by us can force an attack on us, whether a probable future enemy desires it or not—or desires it now or not. Many recent acts of ours are acts of war. They are not prudent statesmanship. They are a sort of reckless shooting craps with destiny for the stake of our democracy.[3]

Although General Johnson was referring to international conflicts, his words are no less applicable to interstellar encounters in our time. Indeed, the stakes could be as high as they can get, as a world-class scholar suggests. John E. Brandenburg, Ph.D., is a plasma physicist at Orbital Technologies in Madison, Wisconsin, where he researches microwave electrothermal plasma thrusters for propulsion in space. Previously he investigated air plasmas and plasma propulsion at Florida Space Institute at America's Kennedy Space Center. Earlier associated with the Aerospace Corporation, Brandenburg was an independent consultant on space-missile defense with directed energy weapons at Mission Research Corporation and Sandia National Laboratories, in Albuquerque, New Mexico.

Brandenburg's book, *Dead Mars, Dying Earth,* coauthored with Monica Rix Paxson, won the Silver Medal in the Ben Franklin Awards for books on science and environment.[4] Accordingly, Brandenburg's

John E. Brandenburg, Ph.D.

deductions from Martian geology and topography are not the fantasies of a science-fiction writer, but academically rigorous conclusions reached by one of the most important scholars in the world today.

Brandenburg presents compelling evidence that the Red Planet is more appropriately named after the Roman god of war than previous generations suspected. Brandenburg's discoveries comprise the most astounding, even the most alarming news we could ever hope to learn: that a nonhuman civilization flourished on Mars more than a quarter of a billion years before our species evolved on Earth. This civilization was deliberately annihilated, and all life on its world was eradicated by some inconceivably powerful entity wielding atomic weapons. In a May 2013 interview with Australia's *New Dawn* magazine, I asked him what first suggested a nuclear attack on Mars during the remote ancient past:

> A comment by a nuclear physicist at Sandia Labs, where I worked, in 1984. I mentioned to him the excess in Mars's atmosphere of xenon 129 [an isotope, the radioactive form of a chemical element]. He became curious, and looked at the data, and then commented flatly: "someone nuked Mars." He then refused to discuss the matter any further. It took a long time for me to reconstruct the reasons for him saying this from the "open literature."

Brandenburg was particularly intrigued by:

the spectrum of krypton and xenon isotopes found in the Mars atmosphere, particularly xenon 129 and krypton 80. Both are produced by nuclear explosions, the xenon 129 directly from fission of uranium 238, and thorium by high-energy fusion neutrons, and the krypton 80 by intense neutron bombardment of the soil. The Mars meteorites, which are samples of subsurface rock form Mars, are depleted in Uranium, Thorium, and Potassium, all radioactive elements, relative to Earth rocks. But gamma rays from the surface of Mars measured by Russian and American probes show much higher levels spread over the Mars surface, radiation from two hot spots. Thus, space craft measurements of Mars's atmosphere, and surface radioactivity, plus measurements of meteorites from Mars show this evidence.

The fission of Uranium 238 and Thorium can only be done by fusion neutrons from a hydrogen bomb reaction, so, in my opinion, this cannot be explained naturally. Data taken by the Mars Science Laboratory's Radiation Assessment Detector (RAD) from Curiosity's interplanetary journey to Mars shows large exposures to radiation, as confirmed and published in *Science Magazine* in the 31 May 2013 issue.[5] A thin layer of radioactive substances including uranium, thorium and radioactive potassium covers the Martian surface in a pattern radiating from a hot spot, as indicated by recent maps showing gamma rays in a radiating debris pattern. What may have been an air-burst the equivalent of one million, one-megaton hydrogen bombs occurred over the northern *Mare Acidalium* region of Mars, where there is a heavy concentration of radioactivity.

The terrible truth: Mars was actually Earthlike for most of its geologic history. Mars held a massive and evolving biosphere, but was wracked by a mysterious and astonishing nuclear catastrophe. The possible archaeology at *Cydonia Mensa* and *Elysium* on Mars looks like a primitive civilization. It appears, from examining several, possibly archaeological locations, that the destroyed culture was roughly equivalent to our Western European Bronze Age that began during the late 4th Millennium BCE, and ended around 600 BCE. But that is only an impression from orbit. We must land there and find out. We have seen, in space-probe images at several places, what looks like artificial ruins. I think we must dispatch astronaut teams to Mars as soon as possible to dig at the principle [*sic*] sites, that is the best way to maximize knowledge of what happened and when it happened. It was long ago, perhaps two hundred to three hundred million years ago. Not even dinosaurs were present then. Only long-lived and stable isotopes record this event.[6]

I asked how Brandenburg's colleagues in the scientific community reacted to his evidence concerning an artificial nuclear event on Mars. He replied:

I have shown this to many experts in defense nuclear science. They agree with my interpretation, but cannot be quoted publicly. The reaction of my colleagues at the STAIF II meeting [the second Space Technology and Applications International Forum, held April 16–18, 2013, in Albuquerque], where I presented this work was astonishment. However, none disagreed with my basic analysis.[7]

If it is correct, Brandenburg's analysis verifies the existence of extra-terrestrial civilizations, at least in the remote past. It also suggests the Earth's vulnerability to some outside attack like the one that obliterated life on Mars.

Many more hard facts establish the existence of military operations conducted by our species against off-world opponents since 1917. Could this war escalate into the kind of global annihilation that befell our planetary neighbor? If such an event did indeed take place long ago, was it a precedent for what we risk in the future? Yesterday, Mars; tomorrow, Earth?

What might the alternatives be? Attempted negotiation with non-humans, or defeating them? Communication with our closest relatives, chimpanzees, continues to elude us, so expectations for useful dialogue with creatures from another world seem to be unjustified. And, given their apparently huge technological edge, attempting to overcome them militarily seems dangerously ill-advised. Our minds balk at the very notion of such questions. Indeed, as recently as October 2016, the *Christian Science Monitor* reported that "a team of international scientists was able to create a 3-D map, and now calculates there are at least two trillion galaxies in the universe."[8]

An average galaxy, such as our own, has an estimated one hundred billion planets. Multiply this number by two trillion, and the existence of civilized beings capable of intergalactic travel jumps from theoretical possibility to statistical inevitability. That these beings continue to violate our airspace is no less certain, as affirmed by the abundant evidence that I will present in the following history. Unlike other volumes in the vast and growing library of ufology, this work concentrates exclusively on the military aspect of the extraterrestrial problem.

This book relies upon evidence provided by armed-forces personnel, and often by highly competent airmen, the world's most dead-serious eyewitnesses. The lives of these professional observers, and those of their comrades, depend on keen awareness of their surroundings in every detail. No-nonsense accuracy is expected of them in filing written reports to their superior officers. Thus these reports affirm the reality of the existence of UFO controversies in a way unlike any other body of supporting facts. Accordingly, their testimonies amount to exceptionally trustworthy evidence far more reliable than the recollections of untrained civilians.

Readers familiar with my previous work, which deals primarily with alternative archaeology, may want an explanation for this untypical subject change. They may be unaware that I have published four military titles as a kind of unpremeditated preparation for this effort. More decisively, a chance encounter with material unrelated to my earthbound research set me on this alternate path nearly a quarter of a century ago.

During September 1993, I was at the Cairo Museum studying the life of Pharaoh Thutmose III. As the sixth monarch of the Eighteenth Dynasty, he was king of Egypt for fifty-four years, beginning in

1479 BCE. Among his documents I was allowed to inspect was an English-language translation of the Tulli Papyrus. Hoping to learn something about the pharaoh's connection with ancient Egyptian seamanship, I was surprised to read instead how, during the "sixth hour of the day" (1:00 p.m.) on an unspecified day in February, during "the twenty-second year" of Thutmose's reign (1457 BCE), multiple persons observed "a disc [or ring] of fire coming in the sky. Its body was one rod [about one hundred fifty feet] long, and one rod wide. It had no voice." (Most modern UFO sightings are described as noiseless.)

Eyewitnesses were terrified. "Their hearts became confused, then they laid themselves on their bellies." Afterward "they went to the King to report it." His Majesty ordered an investigation. "Now, when some days had passed over these things—it was following supper—they [the fire discs returning in additional numbers] were more numerous than anything. They were shining in the sky more than the sun to the limits of the four supports of heaven [the four cardinal directions]. Powerful was the position of the fire discs. The army of the king looked on, and His Majesty was in the midst of it [Thutmose put the country on high

Portrait statue of
Pharaoh Thutmose III
at the Kunsthistorisches
Museum, Vienna,
circa 1450 BCE.

alert]. Thereupon, they [the fire discs] went up higher, directed toward the South," and vanished. The objects represented "a marvel that never occurred since the foundation of this land. And it was [ordered] that the event [be recorded for] His Majesty in the Annals of the House of Life [to be remembered] forever."[9]

While most Egyptologists have nothing to say about the Tulli Papyrus, some assume that it describes a kind of meteorological occurrence they are otherwise at a loss to define. A few still argue that the document is a hoax perpetrated by ufologists. These skeptics are apparently unaware that the original was found in 1933, fourteen years before flying saucers became public knowledge, by the director of the Egyptian section in the Vatican Museum—hardly someone fitting the profile of a swindler. Alberto Tulli never profited from his discovery. In fact, for the rest of his life he kept it secret among his personal papers, where it was only discovered after World War II by Boris de Rachewiltz (1926–97) an Italo-Russian Egyptologist whose dozen books about Nile civilization are still sought as classics. Étienne Drioton of the Egyptian Museum in Cairo transcribed the text from the original hieratic script into more familiar hieroglyphics. De Rachewiltz then translated it into English and published it in 1953. The quality of his translation is considered acceptable. Moreover, the transcribed Egyptian text that survives stands up to scrutiny, and does not appear to be an obvious hoax. Drioton was not only on staff at the Cairo Museum, he was also an authority in his own right, and is routinely referenced by others in the field.

More recently, anthropologist R. Cedric Leonard, a national associate of the Smithsonian Institution, completed his own redaction of the Tulli Papyrus, which elucidates de Rachewiltz's translation but does not differ significantly from it.

The academic credentials of every scholar associated with the Tulli Papyrus, combined with its own textual evidence, confirm the record's authenticity. Indeed curators at the Egyptian Museum, the foremost institution of its kind in the world, do not admit suspect materials into their collections, especially concerning one of ancient Egypt's most important leaders. The Tulli Papyrus not only describes history's earliest

Illustration of Timoleon from *Promptuarii Iconum Insigniorum,*
a mid-sixteenth century iconography book.

known sighting of UFOs, but is also the first documented encounter between such craft and military forces. It was not, however, the only incident of its kind recorded by ancient sources.

In book 16 chapter 66 of his *Bibliotheca Historica* (Historical library), Diodorus Siculus, writing in the first century BCE, told how the Greek general Timoleon was at sea with his fleet during the summer of 343 BCE in an invasion of Sicily, when he and his men saw "a torch in the sky" that stayed with their ships until they hit the beaches.[10]

The earliest recorded extraterrestrial intervention in mankind's military affairs took place in 74 BCE, when an army commanded by Rome's redoubtable general Lucius Licinius Lucullus was about to attack the assembled forces of Mithridates VI, the Persian king of what is today northern Turkey. "But presently," Plutarch described in his *Lives,* "as they were on the point of joining battle, with no apparent change of weather, but all on a sudden, the sky burst asunder, and a huge, flame-like body was seen to fall between the two armies. In shape,

Engraving of stone bust depicting
Lucullus (Hermitage Museum,
Saint Petersburg, Russia).
Image by Janmad.

Roman marble sculpture from the first
century CE portraying Mithridates VI
as Hercules. This statue has been part
of the Louvre collections since 1860.
Photograph by Eric Gaba.

it was most like a *pithos* [a large wine jar], and in color, like molten silver. Both sides were astonished at the sight, and separated."[11]

A somewhat similar instance was later documented by the *Annales Laurissenses maiores* (Royal Frankish annals). These are year-by-year histories of the French monarchy from the mid-eighth to the early ninth centuries CE, and remain, in the words of Wikipedia,

Plate from the medieval
Annales Laurissenses maiores.

"a crucial source on the political and military history of the reign of Charlemagne."[12] The annals record how his soldiers were defending Germany's Sigiburg Castle, overlooking the Ruhr River, when besieging Saxon forces fled from "the likeness of two, large, flaming shields, reddish in color," that began hovering overhead, in 776 CE.[13]

Well-documented encounters such as these establish that the UFO phenomenon was not sparked by mid-twentieth-century hysteria, as skeptics insist. It goes back not decades, but millennia. It was only after man learned how to fly and carry his weapons into the sky that he could challenge the frightening "fire discs," as will be seen in the following pages.

PART ONE

Sightings from the World Wars

1
Engagement with Extraterrestrials in World War I

UFOs are real. Too many good men that don't experience hallucinations have seen them.

CAPTAIN EDDIE RICKENBACKER,
LEADING U.S. FIGHTER ACE OF
THE FIRST WORLD WAR.[1]

After sunrise, March 13, 1917, one of military aviation's most famous pilots took off at the controls of his pursuit biplane from the Jasta 11 fighter-squadron field in western Belgium. Twenty-five-year-old Baron Manfred von Richthofen, better known as the Red Baron, was accompanied in the air only by his younger wingman, Peter Waitzrik. Their dawn patrol flew routinely for almost an hour through the clear skies of early morning until a large metallic disk, ringed at its perimeter by undulating orange lights, appeared without warning directly in front of them. In a later interview, Waitzrik recalled:

> We were terrified, because we'd never seen anything like it before. The thing was maybe forty meters [136 feet, compared to the 28-foot-ten-and-one-quarter-inch wingspan of their own pursuit planes] in diameter. The Baron immediately opened fire, and the

thing went down like a rock, shearing off tree limbs, as it crashed in the woods. Then, two little, baldheaded guys climbed out and ran away. The Baron and I gave a full report on the incident back at headquarters, and they told us not to ever mention it again. And except for my wife and grandkids, I never told a soul. But it's been over eighty years, so what difference could it possibly make now?[2]

Throughout much of the rest of the twentieth century, silence had been imposed on Waitzrik by his decades-long career as a flight captain for Lufthansa, whose directors, like chief airline executives almost everywhere, forbade their employees, especially their pilots, from making public pronouncements about encounters with extraterrestrial vehicles.

Waitzrik continued: "The U.S. had just [about] entered the war, so we assumed it was something they'd sent up." Instead, it looked "just like those saucer-shaped spaceships that everybody's been seeing for the last 50 years. So there's no doubt in my mind now that that was no U.S. reconnaissance plane the Baron shot down, that was some kind of spacecraft from another planet—and those little guys who ran off into the woods weren't Americans, they were space aliens of some kind."[3]

Figure 1.1.
Baron Manfred von Richthofen, also known as the Red Baron, who accompanied Waitzrik on his flight.

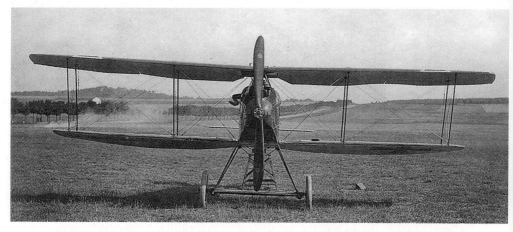

Figure 1.2. A Halberstadt pursuit plane of the type von Richthofen flew in March 1917, when he was alleged to have shot down a UFO.

Since Waitzrik's story was first published in 1999, historians have pointed out its fundamental inconsistencies. Writer Joe Berger told how von Richthofen shot down the UFO while flying his famous red triplane, a characterization perpetuated more recently in the cover art of British author Nigel Watson's 2015 book, *UFOs of the First World War*.[4] According to skeptics, the Baron's aircraft in mid-March was not a triplane, but an entirely different Albatros D.III 789/17 biplane.

While it is true that the Fokker model would not make its debut until the following August, half a year after the alleged event, the baron flew neither it nor an Albatros, but a Halberstadt D.II from March 9 until the end of the month. The little pursuit model was powered by a 120-hp, six-cylinder, in-line Mercedes engine and had a maximum speed of about 93 mph, not much compared with an interplanetary vehicle.

Skeptics scoff at the notion that a vessel capable of traveling from another world could have fallen so easily to the 7.92-millimeter rounds of a single Spandau machine gun fired by the baron. It is true that metallic fragments retrieved from the exteriors of extraterrestrial spacecraft are typically described as almost tissue-thin and extraordinarily light, resembling tinfoil used for chocolate-candy wrappers. Yet the UFOs often seem immune to armed attack (as will be described in later chapters), perhaps because they protect themselves with some kind of undetectable shield that appears to depend on the crew's awareness for its effectiveness. The "two little baldheaded guys" operating "the thing" destroyed by von Richthofen might have been so preoccupied with observing events on the ground below that they failed to notice his approach—which would have been difficult enough to detect under normal combat conditions, because head-on, the spindly Halberstadt fighter he was flying was almost invisible, even at close range.

Berger's article was illustrated with an authentic World War I era photograph (Ref. *Bundesrarchiv Bild* 183-2004-0430-501) of the Baron seated in his aircraft. Taken on May 23, 1917, it shows him with ten other Jasta 11 pilots. The last man on the right, *Leutnant* Otto Brauneck, is incorrectly identified in a circle as "Peter Waitzrik." Berger writes that Waitzrik was "a German Air Force ace," although no one by that name is listed in the annals of *Deutsche Luftstreitkräfte* fliers credited with at least five victories. It was not unusual, however, for von Richthofen to set out on routine patrols with rookie airmen to whom he preferred to offer the personal benefit of his experience and expertise rather than with fellow officers. Peter Waitzrik appears to have been just such a fledgling pilot.

Historical errors or exaggerations of detail like these are hardly unknown in newspaper articles but are generally and relatively unimportant if they do not significantly detract from the core report. What actually hurt Waitzrik's credibility was the fact that his story was published by *Weekly World News*. His appearance in a notorious American tabloid was enough for most historians to dismiss him as the perpetrator of an obvious hoax.

What the debunkers did not know was how Waitzrik and his family had failed to interest mainstream newspaper editors or even ufologists in Germany, particularly in his hometown of Bonn, in his most cherished wartime memory. Increasingly desperate to see his long-kept secret in print before he passed away, his children finally approached the only periodical willing to release it. As such, his words should be judged on their own merits, within the historical context of

World War I, despite the venue of their publication. We may someday be grateful to the *Weekly World News,* because had its editors followed the more respectable broadsheets in ignoring Waitzrik's secret, it would have died with him.

If the last statements of a dying old flier were true—a man whose professional career as a pilot spanned most of the previous century—then the opening shot in our planet's real War of the Worlds was fired one hundred years ago by military aviation's most renowned airman flying a cloth-covered biplane near the Belgian border with France, where the alien intruders suffered their first loss. Although this may seem absurdly incredible, it does not lie beyond the realm of possibility. In 1979's epic film *Apocalypse Now,* a crew chief steers his U.S. patrol boat equipped with state-of-the-art electronics and machine guns up a river through enemy territory in wartime Vietnam when he is struck down by a primitive javelin hurled from shore by a native hiding in the jungle. As the captain lies mortally wounded on deck, he utters his last words in astonished disbelief: "A spear!" The contrasting irony between the lethal victory of that Stone Age weapon over the modern warship was so extreme that it dominated the final moment of the character's life.

Scientific advances in armaments may have granted modern man domination over less well-developed societies, but it has not rendered him invincible. So too, our extraterrestrial visitors appear to have mastered forms of technology that are beyond present human understanding. But unfavorable circumstances and enemy vigilance are potentially fatal chinks in the armor of every warrior. Baron von Richthofen's reflex instinct took advantage of a fleeting opportunity to fire at the UFO. Thus, an inconceivably superior vehicle, capable of traveling between star systems, was brought down by a fragile airplane of laminated cloth and wood, with a maximum range of 156 miles, mounting a pathetic little machine gun. In that moment, the chasm of difference between each craft was overcome by the decisive action of one man.

Neither the wreckage of the disk von Richthofen shot down nor its two surviving operators are mentioned in any contemporaneous German Army field reports. For millennia before, unknown thousands of eyewitnesses around the globe observed profuse varieties of UFOs. But not until March 13, 1917, was one of them brought down. None of this was appreciated or understood at the time, because the baron, his neophyte wingman, and their *Luftstreitkräfte* (German Air Force) superiors never considered an extraterrestrial explanation for the strange disk. They could only conclude that it must have been the latest example of American weapons technology—with some reason, because the United States, while still officially neutral, was momentarily expected to join the European fray.

SIGHTINGS IN THE STATES

Interestingly, the date of von Richthofen's uncredited victory over a UFO lends some credibility to Waitzrik's account. Precisely one month and a day after their otherworldly encounter, and just a week following Congress's declaration of war against Imperial Germany, three servicemen from Company L of the 6th Massachusetts National Guard were in position near Maine's Portsmouth Naval Shipyard, described by encyclopedist Michael David Hall as "the most important military facility then on the East Coast."[5] About 2:30 on the brightly moonlit morning of April 14, 1917, they observed an unidentified vehicle flying slowly in their direction at low altitude over the Piscataqua River.

Remarkably in these early days of aviation, when all airplane engines were loud enough to be heard for miles around, the approaching craft was utterly silent. When it dove toward the bridge at which the soldiers were stationed, they opened fire with their M1903 Springfield rifles. The craft abruptly accelerated no less noiselessly at a terrific speed, vanishing away almost instantly into the night. The Massachusetts National Guard conducted a thorough investigation of the incident, concluding that neither civilian nor military aircraft, American or foreign, had been involved. Indeed only a tiny handful of domestic pilots even existed in New England at the time, none of them qualified for flight after dark. The possibility of a German warplane operating at night anywhere in the United States was even more unlikely, especially

Figure 1.3. Maine's Portsmouth Naval Shipyard in 1917.

given the unidentified object's rapid acceleration, which was utterly beyond the capabilities of early twentieth-century aviation.

The credibility of the Company L guardsmen began to be called into question until additional reports were filed over the following days by military and civilian eyewitnesses describing similar vehicles sighted in the immediate vicinity of the skies above the shipyard. These later observations included one of an airborne vehicle adorned with a pair of green lights (which no known aircraft carried before 1920), and, in a daylight sighting, something resembling "a toy balloon surrounded by a circle of smoke"—hardly the description of a contemporaneous Curtiss Jenny or Gotha bomber.[6]

Although the Piscataqua River engagement was the first of its kind in the United States, it was preceded by the premier bombardment of earthly targets by off-world aggressors. On January 10, 1916, fifteen months before the Maine occurrence, a glazing house for sealing explosives in travel-protected glass containers manufactured by the DuPont gunpowder factory at Carneys Point, New Jersey, was demolished by a powerful explosion. Though America had not yet entered World War I, many Americans sensed a need to prepare. Watson describes Carneys Point as "an important munitions factory that had quickly expanded to meet the needs of the war effort, and at this time employed twenty-five thousand workers."[7]

The following morning, nine miles across the Delaware River, DuPont's Hagley Yard munitions plant in Wilmington, Delaware, experienced two blasts that obliterated several powder mills. Within twenty-four hours, the same plant was hit by a third detonation, destroying another powder mill.

On January 14, 1916, an acid house at DuPont's Gibbstown, New Jersey, factory blew up. Two weeks later, disaster again struck Carneys Point, when five buildings were burned to the ground. Fire erupted in a photographic studio at the same plant on February 4. Forty-eight hours later, DuPont's Tacoma, Washington, munitions works exploded. No less than thirty-nine mysterious conflagrations suddenly and simultaneously raged across Philadelphia for sixteen hours, beginning on the night of February 14—during late winter, a season known for its low fire hazard. The next day, destruction returned to the Gibbstown factory, when a distillation house was destroyed by fire. Carneys Point was yet again ravaged by fires on February 17 and 24, while DuPont's Deep Water Point station for shipping explosives blew up on February 22.

In his *UFOs of the First World War*, author Nigel Watson remarks that "so many explosions in DuPont factories making gunpowder for the Allied forces in such a short space of time, and within such a small area" (except for the Tacoma, Washington plant), was extraordinary.[8] Readers might assume that such accidents could result from the dangers endemic to munitions manufacture, especially during an era that was less technologically developed than our own. But the series of disasters that beset the gunpowder factories and the city of Philadelphia, compressed into six weeks and four days, was unprecedented.

In fact, DuPont prided itself on its well-deserved reputation for safety. None of the company's infrastructure had suffered any mishaps for the previous nine years, and, even then, a 1907 explosion had been limited to a single building at one plant—not, as would transpire later, recurring at four separate factories in three different states.

At the time, foreign saboteurs were strongly suspected, even though America was still more than a year away from going to war with the Germany of Kaiser Wilhelm II. But the Germans were unlikely to carry out sabotage in the United States, because they were desperately striving to keep the Americans out of the European conflict, aware as they were that President Woodrow Wilson would side with Great Britain.

If enemy sabotage and industrial accidents are unlikely causes for early 1916's factory explosions and fires, then we could infer that they were connected with an outstanding number of UFO sightings associated with the conflagrations. Multiple eyewitnesses observed one of the objects above downtown Wilmington, near the DuPont offices, while a railroad worker "saw an airplane flying over the power plant along the Brandywine [Valley]" following the Hagley Yard detonation; no civilian or military planes even existed in western New Jersey at the time.[9] The airborne machine appeared again over the city on February 13, 1916, when its return was reported in the local press. After the fire there six days before, an unknown craft hovering over the ashes "was clearly visible," according to Watson, "and it began to display a light just before it flew out of view."[10]

Another strange vehicle was seen circling at altitude without a sound over the Gibbstown plant on January 31, shortly after the factory exploded, by numerous residents of nearby Paulsboro, New Jersey. Among them was Albert J. Parsons, a U.S. Marine Corps veteran and captain of DuPont's security police at Carneys Point. He described how around 8:45 p.m., "a white light appeared suddenly over the Deep Water Point section of the plant. It shone steadily at an estimated height of fifteen hundred feet . . . [and] moved at times, and then appeared to be still, and then it seemed to be going up and down, or moving in a semi-circle."[11]

This strange motion is similar to the so-called "falling-leaf" movement sometimes associated with UFOs. These otherworld vessels focused their attention on war factories across the United States, such as a rifle-manufacturing works in Eddystone, New Jersey, or the DuPont gunpowder yard at Coatsville, Pennsylvania, both on February 4, 1916. At the same time, wrote the *Philadelphia Inquirer,* "some foreign war contrivance never before seen on this side of the Atlantic" was seen suspended directly above the Italian freighter *Bologna* as she was loading explosives at the Deep Water Point.[12] In the early dawn of February 13, a vehicle aloft bearing red and white lights, but larger by far than any known aircraft, was observed to noiselessly and carefully probe New Jersey's Ingersoll-Rand, Edison Cement, and Taylor-Wharton companies.

Four days later, at 8:30 a.m., a lookout manning the Ellis fire tower outside Ashland, Wisconsin, reported a large, bright light that flew low around the Barksdale DuPont plant, the largest munitions manufacturer in the state, employing twenty-three hundred workers. In addition to producing dynamite, Barksdale supplied the U.S. Army with the more powerful triton explosives. Watson's observation that "sightings of aircraft were concentrated around industrial and military locations" characterizes the veritable wave of UFOs seen by thousands of persons within a remarkably brief period.[13]

Although these "aircraft" were sighted after each conflagration, they were never identified. But the devastation they wrought at five explosives plants, sometimes repeatedly, suggests that intruders from a civilization not of this Earth violently opposed the United States' participation in World War I. No other combatant nation suffered similarly destructive raids on its munitions manufacturing, while close passes executed over America's most important explosives factories suggest that they were being closely monitored by nonhuman reconnaissance.

While extraterrestrial explanations may seem plausible alternatives to hypotheses arguing for German sabotage or coincidental accidents, none of the many observers in January and February 1916 claimed to have observed a UFO actually attack any of the DuPont plants; at most, "some foreign war contrivance" was seen flying in their immediate vicinity following each blaze.[14] As such, documentation of direct cause and effect is lacking. Bridging that gap with logical assumptions, no matter how apparently credible, remains insufficient to confirm connections between events on the ground and observations in the sky, if only because it ignores other perhaps still unknown possibilities, such as undiscovered meteorological phenomena interfacing catastrophically with unstable chemical compounds.

For example, what Watson describes as "a skyquake" shook buildings in Cincinnati, Ohio, on January 12, between the Carneys Point and Gibbstown explosions: "This incident might indicate that some geophysical mechanism could have been at work in a variety of localities on that day or series of days."[15] A UFO was observed by multiple eyewitnesses from Glenolden, Pennsylvania, to Philadelphia on February 3, about six and a half hours after an earthquake with an epicenter in Schenectady, New York, shattered windows for twenty-five miles around. Critics might argue that these two were the only sightings associated with extraordinary natural conditions, while the Barksdale plant in Wisconsin and the Tacoma factory were too far removed from events in New Jersey, Delaware, or Pennsylvania to have been similarly affected.

Moreover, alien interference with American war production in early 1916 was hardly the last such series of incidents, as the following chapters illustrate. Most eyewitness accounts of the DuPont and other related explosions match typical descriptions of UFOs observed from the late 1940s until the present, when first nuclear facilities, then missiles with atomic warheads, were attacked or sometimes destroyed, thereby lending greater probability to extraterrestrial explanations.

There survives at least a hint that some of World War I's most prominent Americans were aware that their country's munitions plants were being systematically targeted for demolition by "some other species from some other planet."[16] As recorded in a document from the era at Washington, D.C.'s Carnegie Endowment for International Peace, famed philosopher, psychologist, and educational reformer John Dewey addressed a visiting Japanese delegation in 1917. Dewey's peculiar open-

Figure 1.4. The Lehigh Valley pier after destruction of the Black Tom facility on July 30, 1916. Witnesses before the explosion, heard as far away as Philadelphia, reported seeing a peculiar-looking "silver aeroplane" hovering silently over New Jersey's major munitions depot just before the blast, which was equivalent to an earthquake measuring 5.5 on the Richter scale.

ing words suggest he knew more than he could say: "The best way to cause all the people of the world to come together in one world government and end war forever would be if we were attacked by some other species from some other planet."[17]

2

Allies and ETs in World War II

The special committee on non-terrestrial science and technology [is] coming to grips with the reality that our planet is not the only one harboring intelligent life in the universe.

PRESIDENT FRANKLIN D. ROOSEVELT,
TOP-SECRET MEMO ON WHITE HOUSE STATIONERY,
WASHINGTON, D.C., FEBRUARY 22, 1944[1]

In September 1942, Albert Lancashire was on duty at Cresswell radar base near Newbiggin-by-the-Sea, on England's northeast coast. Scanning the afternoon skies, the twenty-seven-year-old observer spotted a luminous sphere moving noiselessly behind a wispy cloud. As he was about to sound the alarm, the object shot down a foot-wide beam of bright yellow light that struck him in the face. Albert threw up his hands and felt "a floating sensation" before quickly losing consciousness. Seconds or minutes later, he awoke, unharmed, a few yards from where he had suddenly and inexplicably fallen asleep. The luminosity in the sky was gone, and he resumed his duties. Lancashire did not report the incident and virtually forgot about it until well into his seventies when he recollected having "walked up a beam of light and been taken aboard a craft by a pygmy-sized man."[2] His brief capture was the only published account of its kind from World War II, but it occurred nearly twenty years before the famous Betty and Barney Hill incident, a classic UFO abduction case.

Three months before Lancashire's abduction, a confrontation far more typical of such encounters experienced by Royal Air Force crew members was reported by Lieutenant Roman "Ray" Sabinski, serving with a division of Polish volunteers attached to the RAF.

On the night of June 25, 1942, Sabinski was the commander of a twin-engine Vickers *Wellington* long-range medium bomber during its return flight from a mission to Germany's Ruhr Valley. As he crossed the border over Holland in clear weather, his tail gunner alerted him of an approach to the stern by "a very bright light"—an enemy fighter equipped with a searchlight, as both men naturally assumed. But as the interceptor gained on them, it did not resemble an aircraft so much as an amorphous, copper-colored sphere. When it came within firing range, all four of the *Wellington's* Browning machine guns blazed streams of .303-caliber ammunition at the target.

"To the crew's surprise," writes military historian Keith Chester, "the rounds were simply entering the object and not coming out the

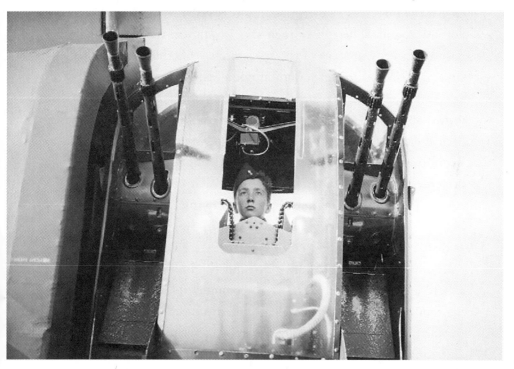

Figure 2.1. Rear turret of a *Wellington* bomber.

opposite side. The bullets were neither falling towards the ground, nor were they passing through the object; they simply entered the ball of light and disappeared. Remarkably, with so many apparent hits on the object, the crew could see no visible damage, no effect whatsoever."[3]

As the tail gunner continued to fire on it, the sphere "suddenly changed position," Sabinski observed, "and, at a terrific speed, moved over to the port side, almost at the same distance, about two hundred yards from the wing." Now the nose gunner opened with his quartet of machine guns, catching the target in a crossfire that would have shredded any other aircraft, but not this one. They ceased firing only when Sabinski personally took over the controls to execute emergency evasive action. "And while I was doing quite violent maneuvers," he said, "moving the wings up and down, uh, this object stayed exactly at the extension of the wing, which means you would have to, at that distance, develop tremendous speed to catch up and keep formation with my aircraft."[4]

When not even these exertions could shake off their unwelcome escort, the bomber's eight Brownings resumed firing on it, again without any results. The sphere then shot around to momentarily hold a position directly in front of the nose gunner, who pumped it with long streams of 7.7-millimeter rounds at point-blank range. It then "took off at a fantastic speed," according to Sabinski, flying "at least a forty-five degree angle, and just disappeared between the stars."[5] After landing back at base, he learned that a fellow *Wellington* commander, participating in the same mission and flying some distance behind Sabinski, had been identically confronted by the same kind of harmless interceptor.

On November 28 of the same year, an Avro *Lancaster* heavy bomber of the 61st Squadron flew out of its base in Syerston, Lincolnshire, to raid the northern Italian city of Turin. After completing the target run around an exceptionally clear and bright midnight, every man aboard beheld a two hundred- to three-hundred-foot-long object sporting four pairs of red lights spaced equal distances along its body. They watched the craft proceed on a course level with their own altitude at an estimated speed of five hundred miles per hour, ten to fifteen miles southwest of Turin, where it vanished. Five minutes later, the object reappeared at fourteen thousand feet, cruising in a southwesterly direction just over the mountaintops of the Alps. Captain Lever remarked that he had seen similar craft three months earlier during operations over Amsterdam.

In his meticulously compiled *The UFO Files: The Inside Story of Real-Life Sightings,* British author David Clarke describes a document relating to this incident in the "Royal Air Force files at the National Archives stamped 'Secret.' At the time [1942], it was judged to be of such significance that details were sent directly to the RAF Bomber Command with a covering letter from the Air Vice Marshal of No. 5 Group, RAF, which read, 'Herewith a copy of a report received from a crew of a *Lancaster* after a raid on Turin. The crew refuses to be shaken in their story in the face of the usual banter and ridicule.'"[6]

On September 10, 1944, while "a reconnaissance plane and its crew were returning from a mission over occupied Europe, on the English coast, possibly near Cumbria, their aircraft was approached by a metallic UFO, which shadowed them," according to the August 5, 2010, issue of Britain's *Telegraph* newspaper. "Later, during discussions about the unexplained incident, the two men were claimed to have become so concerned by the incident that Churchill ordered it remain secret for fifty years or more."[7]

For the previous five years, the British prime minister had occasionally received reports of sightings of unconventional aircraft made by his airmen, but had always dismissed them as the results of fatigue, fear, mistaken visions of the moon and stars, meteorological phenomena, or some such rational cause. This latest RAF encounter, however, was different: "Photographs of the object, which the crew claimed had 'hovered noiselessly' near the plane, were taken by the crew."[8]

Impressed by the visual evidence, Churchill immediately called together a secret meeting of scientists and military commanders to discuss the incident and similar ones that preceded it. There were the usual speculations about Germany's advanced arms technology until "a weapons expert dismissed suggestions the object was a missile, as the event was 'totally beyond any imagined capabilities of the time.'"[9]

Figure 2.2. Air Marshal Lord Hugh Dowding.

"Of course the flying saucers are real," Air Marshal Lord Hugh Dowding, commander-in-chief of the Royal Air Force Fighter Command, later confirmed, "and they are interplanetary. More than 10,000 sightings have been reported, the majority of which cannot be accounted for by any 'scientific' explanation. . . . I am convinced that these objects do exist, and that they are not manufactured by any nation on Earth. . . . I can, therefore, see no alternative to accepting the theory that they come from some extraterrestrial source."[10]

"Another person at the meeting," the *Telegraph* article continues, "raised the possibility of a UFO, at which point, Churchill ordered the report [together with flight crew photographs of the object] to be classified for at least half a century, and reviewed by the Prime Minister to stop 'panic' spreading."

"This event should be immediately classified," he insisted, "since it would create mass panic among the general population and destroy one's belief in the Church."[11]

From September 17 to 19, Churchill conferred in Washington, D.C., with President Franklin Roosevelt, who had already been briefed "on non-terrestrial science and technology" seven months before. After their visit, Churchill "made the orders [suppressing public information about UFOs] during a secret war meeting with U.S. general Dwight Eisenhower, then commander of the Allied Forces, at an undisclosed location in America."[12] Churchill's recognition of unidentified flying objects was nothing new to Eisenhower, who had already known about them for the previous three years.

APPLICATIONS OF
EXTRATERRESTRIAL TECHNOLOGY

By the 1940s, UFO sightings and crashes were being reported across America. Around 9:00 p.m., April 12, 1941, Reverend William Guy Huffman Sr. was telephoned by local police concerning an airplane crash that evening outside Cape Girardeau, a small Missouri city on the Mississippi River, 115 miles southeast of St. Louis. The caller asked if the Baptist minister might be available immediately to administer last rites to any dead and dying victims.

Figure 2.3.
Rev. William Guy Huffman.

As a neighbor drove Huffman to the disaster site at a farmer's field some twelve miles away, police and fire department assistance had already been dispatched. The crash may have involved a military aircraft from the nearby Harvey Parks Airport, about thirty miles to the south, in Sisketon, where United States Army Air Corps flight cadets were in training. Accordingly, Cape County sheriff Reuben R. Schade likely notified his brother, Ben, a purchasing agent at Sisketon's Missouri Institute of Aeronautics, by telephone. This would explain the appearance of Army personnel at the site shortly after Huffman arrived there. What he saw, however, was no conventional airplane.

It was a badly damaged, shiny, silvery disc, well under one hundred feet across, surrounded by broken fragments reflecting the last moments of a contained blaze that was being damped down by firefighters. The minister stepped closer. He found no propellers, struts, cables, or recognizable engine parts, but, through a gaping space, the flickering light of the conflagration enabled him to see a sparse interior of some dials or buttons on a kind of control panel, where three child-size seats had been removed earlier. Apparently occupied by a trio of "little people," someone had pulled the seats from the vessel and laid them out on the ground several yards from the crash.[13]

Two of the creatures had already died; the third, somewhat apart from them, took a few shallow breaths before expiring. They were all alike, no more than four feet in length, with grey, wrinkled skin; thin, elongated torsos and limbs; three fingers, without nails, plus a long thumb on each hand; a pair of dots for nostrils; a horizontal slit for a mouth; and two, huge, black, teardrop-shaped eyes on the otherwise featureless faces of oversized, bulbous heads. All of this took place a quarter of a century before the Barney and Betty Hill abduction case made gray aliens internationally known.

A newspaperman posed and photographed one of the humanoid corpses between a pair of reporters. A troop of U.S. Army personnel arrived to cordon off the smoldering crash and confiscate all exposed film, personal notes, and souvenirs. Before their expulsion from the site, the two dozen or so civilians were sworn to lifelong secrecy in the name of national security. This took place at a time quite different from our own, when government authority was universally respected and an American's word was his or her bond. Soldiers returned to the Sikeston Air Base with the wrecked disk, related debris, and three cadavers; the following week all the remains were transported to Washington, D.C., and secured in a secret subterranean storage room beneath the basement level of the Capitol building.

Some months later, Secretary of State Cordell Hull escorted Turner H. Holt to the underground holding area. Thanks to Hull's influence, Holt had been appointed to an important advisory position in the Roosevelt administration. In consideration of his friend's recent promotion, plus Holt's celebrated reputation as a pastor of the Church of Christ, Hull "desired to gauge his reaction [to the Missouri artifacts] from a religious or spiritual man's point of view."[14] On display was the crashed "vehicle," as Holt described it, plus its three former occupants, the "little people," who were suspended each in its own glass jar of formaldehyde like frogs in a high school biology class.

Bound by an oath pledging secrecy for the sake of national security, Holt broke his secret only to his wife and daughters, pledging them to say nothing about his peculiar visit to anyone. But he did urge them to go public with the story after he died, because "it was simply too important for history to just forget."[15]

Even after their father's passing in 1993, Holt's two daughters refrained from discussing his unforgettable experience as long as their mother, Vina, who "didn't even approve of such talk," was still living. Not until April 2009 did Allene and Lucille share their father's account with noted Canadian researcher Grant Cameron. Such a fantastic tale could be easily dismissed as a hoax were it not for the indefatigable investigation of this case by Paul Blake Smith, himself a resident of Cape Girardeau, near the site of the 1941 crash. He supports his meticulous reconstruction of events with revealing source materials, such as a personal statement written in 1999 by retired Central Intelligence Agency and U.S. Army counterintelligence officer Thomas Cantwheel, who told of an "aerodyne [a generic term for any artificial flying object] recovered in 1941 that crashed in southwestern [*sic:* actually south*eastern*] Missouri."[16]

Cantwheel's statement was underscored by a letter written in the early 1980s by theoretical physicist Edward Teller, known colloquially as "the father of the hydrogen bomb," in which he mentioned "1939, two years before a captured UFO"—an obvious allusion to the Cape Girardeau event—to President Ronald Reagan.[17] Earlier, in September 1947, in part 5 of a classified "National Security Structure" report, U.S. Air Force general Nathan Twining, assigned by President Harry S. Truman to investigate UFOs, similarly referred to "the recovery case of 1941."[18]

During World War II, ten months after the Missouri crash, President Franklin Roosevelt addressed the Army Chiefs of Staff in a confidential memorandum "on the issue of finding out practical uses for the atomic secrets learned from study of celestial devices."[19] Two years later, in a "double top secret" White House "memorandum for the Special Committee on Non-Terrestrial Science and Technology," he agreed "that application of non-terrestrial know-how in atomic energy must be used in perfecting super weapons of war to [e]ffect the complete defeat of Germany and Japan. In view of the cost already incurred in the atomic bomb program, it would, at this time, be difficult to approve without further support of the Treasury Department and the military. I therefore have decided to forego such an enterprise."[20]

In point of fact, Roosevelt's Air Force scientists had not exactly failed to back-engineer the object retrieved from a Missouri farmer's field. U.S. physicists early recognized an atomic component in the Cape Girardeau specimen. They strove to apply it somehow, if not by replicating the craft itself, then by including some aspects of its technology in America's ongoing atom-bomb project, as Roosevelt himself indicated in his memorandum cited above. Cantwheel writes:

> The AAF [Army Air Force commanders] hoped to introduce this craft [their duplication of the Missouri original] in war, but money resources were not available. Funding was not available to R&D

until 1946. . . . The "S" [saucer] craft could take off vertically and reach altitudes as high as ninety thousand feet at supersonic speeds. The craft was so complicated that test pilots had great difficulty in high performance at very high altitudes. Several test pilots were killed as a result of decompression, and ejection capsule or escape cylinders were not designed for high altitude ejections. As a result, one "S" craft was lost. The materials used in the construction by Hughes Aircraft Company failed to protect the test pilots in maximum throttle settings and exposed them to high dose radiation, which resulted in serious illness and death. Test pilots continued over the WSPG [White Sands Proving Grounds, in New Mexico] in early 1947 at Kirkland AAF and at Alamogordo AAF Tularosa Range with better results to flight performance, but exposure to the radiation from the atomic engine continued. In 1947, the "S" craft was modified to carry atomic weapons over long distances, but high altitude flight simulations and pilot survivability was still a problem. . . . At least a dozen "S" craft were built and test flown. Three were lost due to mechanical failure and pilot error. Two more "S" craft were lost along with five fatalities that caused the AAF to cancel the project indefinitely.[21]

But what became of the alien wreckage and bodies that Secretary of State Hull and Pastor Holt saw deep beneath the Capitol building? Smith writes:

My best guess is that the materials were distributed during perhaps late 1941 and the following year to three different locales. First, scientist Dr. Vannevar Bush and his Scientific Research and Development Board apparently worked in some offices within Washington, D.C.'s Fort Belvoir, where George Marshall had some sway. I should imagine that is where the hardware was taken, scrutinized and photographed carefully, and slowly synthesized and weaponized.

Second, the legendary Wright Field (later Wright-Patterson AFB), near Dayton, Ohio, had metallurgical labs, aeronautical engineers, and developed more sites as World War II raged, to keep up with captured enemy aircraft. And third, the military airbases and labs, such as Sandia, in New Mexico, likely got their hands on the technology and its replicated or reverse-engineered copies, some of which were tested in the desert there, according to former Army CIC and CIA man, Thomas Cantwheel. These are educated guesses. I can't imagine FDR and Marshall hoarding the materials for more than a year in the bowels of the Capitol Building. Once "the heat wore off'" in the months after the crash—and there were no alien recriminations—they likely got that ET stuff out of there to start utilizing it for the war effort, especially after December 7th. America was in deep trouble in the early months and years of the war, and every effort and resource had to be expended to dig us out of a major hole. So I think it is long gone.[22]

Although MO41 (as the Cape Girardeau vehicle was called) may have vanished piecemeal between various Air Force bases, its crash was by no means the last one.

3

The Battle of Los Angeles

Regarding the air raid over Los Angeles. . . . This Headquarters has come to the determination that the mystery airplanes are, in fact, not earthly, and, according to secret intelligence sources, they are in all probability of interplanetary origin.

GENERAL GEORGE C. MARSHALL, CHIEF OF STAFF[1]

While President Roosevelt's scientists were desperately struggling to transform the Cape Girardeau disk into an invincible wonder weapon, conventional Japanese warplanes wiped out the U.S. fleet at Pearl Harbor on December 7, 1941. Over the weeks and months that followed, news went from bad to worse for the Americans, as their forces were beaten into retreat across the vast Pacific theater. They had entered the war with an outmoded, poorly equipped armed forces.

An unbroken string of defeats overseas engendered public anxiety at home, where even the West Coast was shelled with impunity by the deck-gun crew of a Japanese submarine floating a few hundred yards off California, ten miles down the coast from Santa Barbara. While FDR was droning on in a nationwide radio broadcast about the iniquities of Imperial Japan, I-17 lobbed 5.5-inch shells at the Ellwood oil fields, destroying a derrick and pump house. Putting a bold face on their humiliation, Pentagon spokesmen publicly ridiculed Kozo Nishino for the relatively minor damage he inflicted. The wily commander had nevertheless landed twenty-five rounds on the mainland of the United States, then leisurely cruised away after more than twenty minutes. "The 4th [USAAC] Interceptor Command, although aware of the sub's attack," observed Paul T. Collins in a *Fate* magazine article, "ordered a blackout from Ventura to Goleta, but sent no planes out to sink it. Not one shot was fired at the sub."[2] The unwillingness of American defenses to confront, much less interfere with, the submarine attack stressed already-low civilian and military morale.

Naturally, no one was prepared for the events that started at 3:16 in the morning of February 25, 1942, when the two million residents of Los Angeles were jolted from their sleep by the eruption of every artillery piece in the metropolitan area, accompanied by wailing choirs of air-raid sirens. A total blackout went into immediate effect, from L.A. to the Mexican border and inland to the San Joaquin Valley, as thousands of civil-defense wardens grabbed their white helmets, and colossal luminous beams, projected heavenward by more than twenty searchlights, swept the clear night sky for enemy aircraft.

Pilots assigned to the 4th Interceptor Command, which had recently refrained from going airborne against Commander Nishino's submarine, were similarly alerted, but yet again stood down, leaving protection of the entire urban area exclusively in the hands of flak gunners on the ground. They fired something under fifteen hundred shells by 4:14, though the all clear was not sounded or the blackout order lifted until 7:21. Dawn revealed several buildings and vehicles damaged by shell fragments, and five persons lay dead of heart failure and automobile accidents amid the chaos.

But there was less panic than exhilaration at the Fourth of July–type display. For all the excitement, no bombs had been dropped, no warplanes shot down. Speaking at a press conference shortly afterward, Secretary of the Navy Frank Knox dismissed the event as a "false alarm." Less than three months had passed since Pearl Harbor, he explained, resulting in frayed "war nerves." Public-relations officials for the United States Army Coast Artillery Association added that the shooting must have been triggered by some errant weather balloon mistaken for a Japanese bomber, a conclusion that would later be repeated by the U.S. Air Force Historical Research Agency.

These statements were vigorously opposed by Lieutenant General John L. DeWitt, in charge of the Army's Western Defense Command, who insisted that the early-morning blackout and antiaircraft action had been triggered by unidentified targets sighted over the beach area. He was supported in this by squadron pilots of the inert 14th Interceptor Command, claiming they were ordered to man their planes and await flight orders that never came, after unknown intruders were reported flying over the coastline.

In two official statements issued while Secretary Knox was attributing the allegedly nonexistent raid to mass hysteria, senior officers at the U.S. Army command in San Francisco confirmed and reconfirmed the presence of unidentified aircraft over the Southland. Cannoneers at the 37th Coast Artillery Brigade likewise affirmed that they had begun firing 0.50-caliber machine-gun bullets and 12.8-pound antiaircraft shells into the air after sighting a solid target hit at least twice, without effect.[3] Their fire was joined by the 65th Coast Artillery Regiment, in Inglewood, and the 205th Artillery Regiment (Antiaircraft), based in Santa Monica.

"Overhead, silently, a glowing object was moving slowly," reported Bill Henry of the *Los Angeles Times,* "as antiaircraft batteries focused by spotlights began to take aim. I was far enough away to see the object without being able to identify it. I would be willing to bet what shekels I have that there were a number of direct hits scored on the object."[4]

A fellow *Times* reporter, Marvin Miles, described in his article "Chilly Throng Watches Shells Bursting in Sky" that "the object in the sky slowly moved on, caught in the center of the lights like the hub of a bicycle wheel surrounded by gleaming spokes. The targeted object inched along high, flanked by the cherry-red explosions."[5]

"A *Los Angeles Herald Express* staffer," writes Collins, "said he was sure many shells hit it directly. He was amazed it had not been shot down. The object proceeded at a leisurely pace over the coastal cities

THURSDAY MORNING.   **Los Angeles Times**   **   FEBRUARY 26, 1942.   **B**

Searchlights and Anti-aircraft Guns Comb Sky During Alarm

SEEKING OUT "OBJECT"—Scores of searchlights built a wigwam of light beams over Los Angeles early yesterday morning during the alarm. This picture taken during black-out shows nine beams converging on an "object" in sky in Culver City area. The blobs of light which show at apex of beam angles were made by anti-aircraft shells.
See Story on Page 1, Part 1.

MARKINGS—Hugh Landis of 1738 W. 43rd Place points to holes made in his car, as it stood in garage, by fragments of anti-air-

Figure 3.1. *Los Angeles Times,* February 26, 1942.

between Santa Monica and Long Beach, taking about thirty minutes of actual flight time to move twenty miles; then it disappeared from view."[6]

Collins wrote later of the event, "Eyewitness reports from thousands searching the skies with binoculars under the bright lights of the coast artillery verified the presence of one, enormous, unidentifiable, indestructible object."[7]

A boy at the time he and his family witnessed it, Ralph Blum saw how "the white, cigar-shaped object took several direct hits, but continued on its eastward flight."[8]

Another young eyewitness recalled that he, together with his mother and father, "observed the entire episode through the large bay window of our home, facing west. I remember distinctly the convergence of searchlights reflecting off the bottom of some kind of slow moving objects, apparently flying in formation. They seemed to be completely oblivious and impervious to the shells exploding around them. I was quite the aviation buff back then, as I am now, but I must admit that I had a devil of a time trying to identify the objects. We were looking through our room bay window, which gave us an unobstructed panorama of view facing the northwest, west and southwest. We then went to our south-facing kitchen and porch windows to observe the action, where it culminated in the south. Ergo, the action followed the coast-line. I strongly remember the searchlights converging on the bottoms of the reddish objects flying in formation."[9]

In fact, a coast artillery colonel spotted twenty-five planes at twelve thousand feet over Los Angeles. As soon as the blackout went into effect, "the information center was inundated with phone calls from patriotic citizens reporting enemy planes in the sky . . . the Army issued a War Department report, which indicated that between one and five unidentified objects had flown over L.A."[10]

On second thought, embarrassed that American antiaircraft gun-ners could not shoot down slow-moving weather balloons at low altitude over nearly an hour, and afraid that such a public display of incompetence would further damage already depressed civilian morale, government authorities now gave out that the defenders of Los Angeles had been deceived by a meteorological phenomenon of some kind. They were, however, emphatically contradicted by War Secretary Henry Stimson, who declared that approximately fifteen "planes" had doubtless

Figure 3.2. The Battle of Los Angeles was officially dismissed as war hysteria, but War Secretary Henry Stimson knew otherwise.

violated southern California airspace. He knew but could not speak publicly about the state's still-classified radar installations, which had tracked unknown targets approaching about twelve thousand feet over the sea, one hundred twenty miles off the West Coast, on February 25, at 2:15 a.m.

Within four minutes after the alarm was sounded, "ground observers were reporting an enormous, luminous object," writes Kevin D. Randle, a retired U.S. Army colonel and intelligence officer with a master's degree in military science.[11] Their sighting was confirmed by nonmilitary witnesses, some using binoculars. According to reporter Dirk Vander Ploeg, they observed "a large orange object that moved slowly over the coast between Santa Monica and Long Beach. The object traveled the twenty miles in approximately thirty minutes, and then disappeared."[12]

Eight-year-old C. Scott Littleton resided with his family "in Hermosa Beach, right on the beach. We thus had a grandstand seat. While my father went about his air-raid warden duties, my late mother and I watched the glowing object, which was caught in the glare of searchlights from both Palos Verdes and Malibu/Pacific/Palisades, and surrounded by the puffs of ineffectual antiaircraft fire, as it slowly flew across the ocean from northwest to southeast. It headed inland over Redondo Beach, a couple of miles to the south of our vantage point, and eventually disappeared over the eastern end of the Palos Verdes hills, what's today called Rancho Palos Verdes. . . . In any case, I don't recall seeing any truly discernable configuration, just a small, glowing, slight lozenge-shaped blob light—a single blob, BTW [by the way]. We only saw one object, not several, as some witnesses later reported."[13]

"I could clearly see the V formation of about twenty-five, silvery planes overhead," wrote Peter Jenkins, editor of the *Los Angeles Herald Examiner,* "moving slowly across the sky, toward Long Beach."[14]

Police Chief J. H. McClelland, the police chief there, "watched what was described as the second wave of planes from atop the seven-story Long Beach City Hall. . . . An experienced Navy observer with powerful Carl Zeiss binoculars said he counted nine planes in the cone of the searchlight. He said they were silver in color. [During World War II, all Japanese aircraft wore camouflage colors; none were silver.] The [UFO] group passed along from one battery of searchlights to another, and under fire from the anti-aircraft guns, flew from the direction of Redondo Beach and Inglewood on the land side of Fort MacArthur, and continued toward Santa Ana and Huntington Beach. Anti-aircraft fire was so heavy we could not hear the motors of the planes."[15]

In his authoritative *UFO Encyclopedia,* Jerome Clark recounts the testimony of an air-raid warden, who counted "six to nine luminous, white dots in triangular formation . . . visible to the northwest. The formation moved painfully slowly."[16]

Others moved very differently. "The eerie lights were behaving strangely," Collins quotes an eyewitness. "They seemed to be navigating mostly on a level plane at that moment—that is, not rising up from the ground in an arc or trajectory, or in a straight line, and then falling back to earth, but appearing from nowhere, and then zigzagging from side to side. Some disappeared, not diminishing in brilliance or fading away gradually, but just vanishing instantaneously into the night. Others remained pretty much on the same level and we could only guess their elevation to be around ten thousand feet, but some of them dived earthward, only to rise again, mix and play tag with about thirty to forty others moving so fast that they couldn't be counted accurately."[17]

Perhaps the most compelling sighting made during the Battle of Los Angeles belonged to a young Hollywood interior decorator, who gave only her first name. At the time, Katie lived on the west side of Los Angeles, not far from Santa Monica, where, after the attack on Pearl Harbor, she volunteered to become an air-raid warden. Around 2:30 on the morning of February 25, she was rung up by the district civil-defense supervisor, notifying her of the alert. He also told her to keep a sharp lookout for an enemy warplane supposedly flying near her neighborhood. Katie rushed to the window. Gazing upward into the night sky, which was already alive with exploding shells and the crisscrossing beams of busy searchlights, she beheld a singular craft:

> It was huge. It was just enormous. And it was practically right over my house. [The cigar-shaped object appeared over Culver City and Santa Monica, both neighborhoods on the west side of town, and closer to the Pacific Ocean.] I had never seen anything like it in my life. It was just hovering there in the sky and hardly moving at all. It was a lovely, pale orange, and about the most beautiful thing you've ever seen. I could see it perfectly, because it was very close. It was big. They [USAAC commanding officers] sent fighter planes up, and I watched them in groups approach it, and then turn away. They were shooting at it, but it didn't seem to matter. I'll never forget what a magnificent sight it was. Just marvelous! And what a gorgeous color![18]

Contrary to Katie's observation, the 14th Fighter Squadron was supposedly grounded throughout the action. Her sighting was nevertheless seconded by Scott Littleton, who, as mentioned above, watched with his family as the strange object slowly moved out of view: "And very quickly afterward, I saw—we all saw—a flight of planes following the track of the object going overhead; anywhere from three to five interceptors, clearly, piston-driven, U.S. planes. No one has ever admitted that those planes were in the sky."[19]

One day later, in a CBS Radio News broadcast, Byron Palmer reported, "U.S. Army planes quickly took to the dark sky, but whether they contacted the object has not been announced." He said activity of the previous night had been observed by "watchers on the roof-top of the Columbia Broadcasting Building, in the heart of Hollywood." Interestingly, Palmer was the first announcer in broadcast history to use the term "unidentified flying object." It must have come naturally to him.[20]

In any case, federal government authorities clearly lied about the Battle of Los Angeles from its beginning. Neither Katie's account nor that of any other eyewitness to the events of February 25, describe known weather balloons, meteorological phenomena, or even aircraft, ours or theirs. To be sure, six months later, a Yokosuka E14Y reconnaissance aircraft, launched just off the Pacific Northwest coast by Japanese Navy submarine I-25, dropped 680 pounds of incendiaries on Oregon in two separate sorties (September 9 and 29, 1942), aimed at starting massive forest fires near the city of Brookings. Although local woodlands were too damp from rains to catch fire, these two raids comprised the only bombing of the continental United States by aircraft during World War II. Postwar examination of Japanese military records revealed that no such attacks or attempted missions were undertaken against the U.S. mainland before the Yokosuka seaplane flights over Oregon. A few hundred out of nine thousand free balloons armed with time bombs did crash across North America, but these were not launched from Japan until 1944.

Nonetheless, some eyewitnesses that night in February 1942 saw a silvery object resembling a balloon or blimp incongruously carrying red flares as it hovered over Santa Monica. Palmer himself observed "the unidentified object, which some sources thought might be a blimp."[21] Many UFOs before and since have been described as oblong, cigar-shaped, tubular, or resembling a dirigible or blimp. Littleton similarly recalled, "What captured our rapt attention was a silvery, lozenge-shaped 'bug,' as my mother later described it, whose bright glow was clearly visible in the searchlight beams that pinpointed it. Although it was a clear, moonlit night, no other details were visible, despite the fact that, when we first saw it, the object was hanging motionless almost directly overhead."[22] The Japanese operated no zeppelins or blimps: military powers everywhere had long before discarded these as bombers following their disastrously unsuccessful performance during World War I. In any case, millions of observers of the "unidentified object" over Los Angeles that night did not see a conventional aircraft.

"Still others," Dirk Vander Ploeg writes, "reported seeing flares falling from the sky."[23] None were dropped or shot heavenward by the California defenders. Rense writes that "observers reported lighted objects, which were variously described as red-and-white flares in groups of three red and three white, fired alternately, or chain-like strings of red lights, looking something like an illuminated kite."[24]

Most descriptions of the Battle of Los Angeles overlook the fact that the metropolitan area had been put on alert at 7:18 p.m., February 24, the night *before* the shooting started and the blackout was imposed, when air-raid wardens reported "strange, blinking lights and flares" in the sky nosing around the city's defense plants. The presence of such unaccountable objects in the immediate vicinity of America's weapons-producing infrastructure was reminiscent of similar encounters at the DuPont munitions factories in 1916. It also foreshadowed their reappearance over atomic-bomb facilities from the close of World War II into the present century. Many sightings from numerous civilian, military, and professional observers were at odds with official explanations of weather balloons, meteorological conditions, or "war nerves."

An angry editorial on the front page of the *Los Angeles Times* took such unconvincing interpretations to task: "According to the Associated Press, Secretary Knox intimated that reports of enemy air activity in the Pacific Coastal Region might be due largely to 'jittery nerves.' Whose nerves, Mr. Knox? The public's, or the Army's? . . . it seems to *The Times* that more specific public information should be forthcoming from government sources on the subject, if only to clarify their own conflicting statements about it."[25]

Other southern California newspapers were similarly confused. "There is a mysterious reticence about the whole affair," the *Long Beach Independent* charged, "and it appears that some form of censorship is trying to halt discussion on the matter. Although it was red-hot news, not a single national radio commentator gave it more than passing mention. This is the kind of reticence that is making the American people gravely suspect the motives and the competence of those whom they have charged with the conduct of the war."[26]

Even the staid *New York Times* "expressed a belief that the more the incident was studied, the more incredible it became." A February 28 editorial wondered, "If the batteries were firing at nothing at all, as Secretary Knox implies, it is a sign of expensive incompetence and jitters. If the batteries were firing on real planes, some of them as low as nine thousand feet, as Secretary Stimson declares, why were they completely ineffective? Why did no American planes go up to engage them, or even to identify them?"[27]

Prompted by the gathering controversy to call for a congressional investigation into the Battle of Los Angeles, Representative Leland Ford of Santa Monica declared, "None of the explanations so far offered removed the episode from the category of 'complete mystification' . . . this was either a practice raid, or a raid to throw a scare into two million people, or a mistaken identity raid, or a raid to lay a political foundation to take away Southern California's war industries." In any case, he could not accept federal public relations' attempts at explaining away the February 25 event as a "false alert."[28]

Later that same day, the *Los Angeles Times* published a large photograph taken by one of its own reporters during the height of the battle, as searchlights converged on and illuminated something entirely unlike any warplane known in the world at that time. Hovering at nine thousand feet, with no wings, tail, fuselage, or propeller, it resembled a bowl topped by another, inverted dish, and joined at their rims, surmounted by an upside-down cup, with flak bursting harmlessly around the craft. The newspaper caption reads, "Seeking Out Object" [an "object," not an aircraft or balloon, because the caption writer could not identify it]. "Scores of searchlights built a wigwam of light beams over Los Angeles early yesterday morning during the alarm. This picture was taken during blackout; shows nine beams converging on an object in sky in Culver City area. The blobs of light which show at apex of beam angles were made by antiaircraft shells."[29] According to Rense, "the object was clearly locked in the focus of dozens of searchlights for well over half an hour, and seen by hundreds of thousands of people."[30]

It resembles nothing if not a stereotypical vehicle that, starting years after the war, was associated with extraterrestrial visitations. When the image was taken, no one so much as considered a nonearthly identity for the sighting. It has since been seized upon by ufologists as photographic proof of a "flying saucer" from outer space. Wikipedia writes, "Some ufologists and conspiracy theorists . . . assert that the photo was heavily modified by photo retouching prior to publication, a routine practice in graphic arts of the time intended to improve contrast in black and white photos."[31] But Wikipedia does not explain why a newspaper graphic artist in early 1942, other than trying "to improve contrast" in a black-and-white shot, should have modified it "by photo retouching" so as to depict a characteristic UFO in an era when such things were unknown to the vast majority of Americans.

To answer this objection, Bruce Maccabee obtained a print made directly from the original unretouched negative of the *Los Angeles Times* photograph for close analysis. Maccabee worked on optical data processing, generation of underwater sound with lasers, and various aspects of the Strategic Defense Initiative (SDI) and Ballistic Missile Defense (BMD) using high-power lasers. As such, Maccabee was eminently qualified to assess the controversial image:

> The fact that the beams [of the spotlights appearing in the photograph] basically do not get past the "object" (there is some faint evidence of beams above the object), whatever was at the beam convergence must have been optically quite dense. . . . The beams are quite bright before they reach the "object" and zero or nearly zero afterward. Just how much optical density of smoke this requires I do not know. However, certainly a solid metallic object would be sufficient to block the beams. . . . How large is the "object"? . . . I would hazard a guess that the width of the illuminated "object" is on the order of 100 feet or more in size.[32]

Steven Lacey, another photo analyst, "was able to clear up the image into something that clearly shows a classic saucer shaped craft right in the center of where all those searchlights are aimed. I enlarged the picture and I adjusted the brightness and contrast using the levels tool. The picture clearly shows a saucer shaped craft."[33]

Elsewhere in General George C. Marshall's statement excerpted at the head of this chapter, he said how "it was learned by Army G2 that Rear Admiral Anderson recovered an unidentified airplane off the coast of California . . . with no bearing on conventional explanation."[34] The rear admiral he mentions was Walter Stratton Anderson (1881–1981), who was indeed the senior commander of U.S. Navy operations in the waters off Southern California during the Battle of Los Angeles. Littleton, later an anthropology professor at California's Occidental College, tells of popular speculation during the days that followed: "The rumor is that it [the 'unidentified airplane' Marshall mentioned] finally crashed in the water, and was recovered by Navy divers. So, maybe it was wounded, and it crashed."[35] If so, then the U.S. government obtained its second off-world vehicle in less than a year.

As a retired anthropology professor, Littleton submitted the object he and his parents saw in 1942 to the same scientific rigor used when teaching his students: "By a process of elimination, the most efficient— and I say this as a scholar—the most efficient explanation is that it was what we would call today a UFO, something not of this world, something that belonged to another technology. If that's true, then this event was one of the largest UFO sightings in history. Over a million people saw it."[36]

Chapter 4
Foo Fighters

I have also known men who have seen pink elephants.

GENERAL CARL SPAATZ,
U.S. AIR FORCE CHIEF OF STAFF,
REFERRING TO PERSONS CLAIMING TO HAVE
SIGHTED UNIDENTIFIED FLYING OBJECTS[1]

An American veteran of the Normandy invasion on D-Day recalled his service aboard a B-17 heavy bomber, one of thirteen thousand Allied warplanes operated against the European continent by the U.S. 8th Air Force before the landings got under way in the early morning hours of June 6, 1944. "Our target was a railroad depot. I was the right-side waist-gunner looking inside of our formation before we left on our raid. About ten minutes after we crossed the coast [around 1:00] a.m., I heard one of our [fighter-pilot] escorts over the radio call out, 'bandits 6 o'clock high and low!' Now, after I heard this, I went to cock my weapon, and it jammed. I tried my best to check the jam. It appeared normal," but remained inoperative.[2]

Just then the distressed waist-gunner saw the "bandits" swiftly approaching, but they resembled no fighter planes with which he was familiar. The luminous spheres bore no national insignia, and their intentions were hardly less uncertain. "One of the objects appeared in between our formation, and I went to cock my weapon." Its jamming coincided with the failure of electrical systems aboard the aircraft, as the radio went dead and "our number four engine stalled out."[3]

Unable to communicate and losing power, the defenseless *Flying Fortress* could not keep up with its formation and dropped out of place to become an easy target for enemy interceptors. As the mysteriously stricken B-17 gradually fell behind, the objects sped off at exceptionally high speed. Fifteen minutes later, the waist-gunner's .50-caliber Browning unjammed itself, radio communication flickered on, and the previously dead Wright Cyclone engine sputtered back to life. The shaken crew had met with a "foo fighter," one of the "pink elephants" General Spaatz mentioned in order to laugh off such imaginary nonsense.

But for too many of his airmen who experienced similar encounters, these confrontations were no laughing matter. *Foo fighter* was a pun on *feu,* the French word for *fire,* as it derived from the then-popular *Smokey Stover* comic strip: "Where there's foo, there's fire." The term was colloquially applied by USAAF flight crews to unknown metallic spheres, disks, lights, boomerangs, cigar shapes, or fireballs that mostly escorted, sometimes buzzed, occasionally threatened, and infrequently skirmished with Allied airmen. Evidently, the D-Day heavy bomber had been singled out for an electromagnetic attack by the spherical intruders, which did not disturb any of the other bombers. But its airmen were more fortunate than their comrades aboard another B-17 the previous year.

During a September 6, 1943, mission to raid Stuttgart, the 384th Group found itself proceeding between two thousand and three thousand feet beneath and a little behind perhaps five Luftwaffe aircraft. Before any engagement could occur, a "cluster . . . composed of small, round objects, silvery in color," simply fell out of the sky, as witnessed by two different American crews. "As to its shape, it was a mass of material, kept a good pattern, did not dissipate, as it streamed down and fell comparatively slow. . . . In one instance, the cluster appeared to be about eight feet in length and about four feet wide as it streaked down. Another observation stated it was about seventy-five feet long and twenty feet wide. These dimensions in length being the size from

Figure 4.1. Burned B-17.

top to bottom, as it fell." There was no connection between the mass of silver spheroids and the German interceptors. "These enemy aircraft were not seen to drop the material out. It came from above our aircraft," from a clear sky. "In all instances, the objects fell in the path of our aircraft. Some was observed to fall on the wing of a B-17 belonging to our Group. The wing immediately started to burn," and the *Flying Fortress* fell to earth like a comet. "This aircraft did not return."[4] Its ten crew members were the first human fatalities in the twentieth century's War of the Worlds.

Lethal attacks by UFOs on Allied or Axis warplanes were rare. More typically, pilots and crews on both sides of the conflict were approached in flight by the foo fighters, which kept pace with the warplanes (often despite extreme evasion maneuvers) before vanishing away at high speeds. Such encounters were by no means dubious tales brought on by battle fatigue, fear, disorientation, altitude sickness, weather conditions, misidentification of conventional aircraft, or glimpses of enemy secret weapons. These presumed causes were more often used by Air Force brass to explain away, rather than to actually explain, what their men were experiencing. Many hundreds reported remarkably similar experiences in all combat theaters, the majority occurring in the last two years of the war. How many more Air Force witnesses never reported what they saw for fear of losing their flight privileges, or even of being classified as "Section Eight" (military language for "insane"), to say nothing of ridicule from fellow fliers, cannot be ascertained.

While B-17 crews were encountering foo fighters over Europe, their Communist allies eighteen hundred miles away in the east were seeing the same kinds of inexplicable craft. On July 4, 1943, just as the pivotal Battle of Kursk was about to commence, a huge, silvery disk hovered over the opposing forces, but did not intervene in the fighting, and vanished after a few minutes. "The Soviet High Command feared that the object was Hitler's much-vaunted 'secret weapon,'" writes Russian-born Paul Stonehill, an expert on Soviet affairs. Although no photographs of it survive, "a drawing of the object was made, and several Soviet colonels, who later took part in the battle, signed it."[5]

On August 26, three days after the battle, Red Army senior lieutenant Gennady Zhelaginov reported having seen "a sickle-shaped" craft fly at extraordinary speed—far faster than any Russian or German warplane—over an area of Kursk targeted by his artillery. Before it vanished into the southwest, he noticed that the boomerang-like vehicle was dark blue overall, but with a bright orange center section.

More typical was a sighting made over Poland by Lev Petrovitch Ovsischer, the bombardier-navigator of a Petlyakov Pe-2 medium bomber. In November 1944, he, the pilot, and rear gunner observed an immense, excessively bright object passing slowly over a front-line Soviet airfield, near Warsaw, at approximately sixteen hundred feet. On the ground, Red Army lieutenant-colonel A. Kovalchuk observed that the five-hundred-foot-long craft roughly resembled and moved like a dirigible, although it made not a sound and lacked fins, outboard engines, propellers, gondolas, portholes, guy-wires, insignia, or external details of any kind.

Stonehill writes, "Air defense units fired on it with cannons and machine guns" to no effect, as the uniformly dark apparition gradually disappeared over the northern horizon. The encounter was authoritatively documented by retired Soviet Army colonel Gherman Kolchin in a 2000 issue of *New Literary Observer,* "the oldest Russian independent magazine specializing in philology, cultural history and historical anthropology."[6]

Like their British and American comrades, the Russians never gave a thought to extraterrestrial possibilities, but consistently referred to such vehicles as "German disks." Kent Courtney shared their conclusion. While ferrying a transport plane from Brazil to Morocco, in February 1943, at ten thousand feet over the South Atlantic, several lights flew at him head-on, narrowly avoiding a collision, then turned back to buzz his aircraft before speeding away into the night. After landing safely in Casablanca, he made his report. "We were advised by the Army and Air Force to keep it to ourselves," the former USAAF captain told Alexandria, Louisiana's *Daily Town Talk*. "The official view of the Air Force was to quell the investigation, to stop it cold." Courtney "talked with numerous World War II pilots who had seen UFOs."[7]

"The boys were afraid they'd be grounded if they reported the lights, so they kept still about them," Harre Cowe, a USAAF fighter pilot stationed in France on November 8, 1944, recalled three years later for an interview with the *Seattle Daily Times*. "But the following night, another crew saw the same thing, and reported it. After that, all the crews in the squadron, with the exception of two, had the same experience."[8]

Night fighter crews in the squadron to which Cowe was attached reported seeing the strange lights while flying over the Rhine Valley. So many sightings and their repeated commonalities constitute powerful proof of the reality of the phenomenon. Skeptics may deprecate the value of such observations, but they forget that eyewitness testimony, particularly if it is consistent and offered by persons unknown to each other, is admissible in a court of law as corroborative evidence.

Cowe went on to describe something more than a sighting his squadron experienced: "The first crew to see them noticed that the lights seemed to be flying right with the airplane [a Northrop P-61 *Black Widow* night fighter]. The boys didn't know what they were, and tried evasive action, but the lights seemed to stay right with them. Finally, one of the boys decided to shoot at one of the lights to see what would happen, and he blasted away [with four 20-millimeter Hispano cannons, plus another quartet of .50-caliber Browning machine guns firing from an upper turret]. There was an explosion that rocked the plane and bent the Plexiglas dome on it."[9]

Figure 4.2. A Northrop P-61 *Black Widow.*

FOO FIGHTERS IN THE PACIFIC

A somewhat similar confrontation took place the night of August 10–11 that same year on the other side of the world, but with different results. First Officer Russell Watson was piloting a B-29 *Superfortress,* number 6362, on its return flight from a combined raid of the 20th Air Force on the Pladjoe oil refinery at Palembang, Sumatra. In his report to the 20th Bomber Command's air-intelligence section, he stated that his and "several bomber crews" observed what they believed was

> a bizarre and confusing type of new weapon. . . . One aircraft was under continuous attack for 1 hour and 10 minutes, beginning 10 minutes after leaving the target area. Reddish-orange balls about the size of baseballs suddenly appeared "out of nowhere" on the starboard beam; a momentary flash or trail about 6 inches long preceded the red-ball effect and this was followed immediately by an explosion.
>
> The balls appeared to break up into 4 or 5 fragments that flew in all directions, and appeared in fours, threes, twos, and singly, but never more than 4 appeared at the same time. There was usually

about an interval of about ten seconds between volleys. The crews estimated that they observed a total of 250–300 separate bursts during the attack. The explosions were always off the right beam, never closer than 400 yards, never father away than 700 yards, and always accurate as to altitude.

The aircraft was flying at 16,000 feet over an under-cast at 10,000 feet varying from 5/10 to 10/10 [of a mile]. Lateral visibility was estimated as 30 miles except for occasional scattered clouds, but no enemy aircraft were sighted. There were no ground flashes observed when the ground was visible. Bursts were not observed when the aircraft flew through clouds, but reappeared when the clouds were passed.

On one occasion, the course was altered sufficiently to allow tail guns to bear in the direction of the bursts, but 20-mm and 50-cal. fire from the B-29 had no visible effect. . . . The B-29 was not damaged.[10]

This was not the only occurrence of alien pursuit in the Pacific Theater. On November 3, 1944, North American *Mitchell* B-25 medium bombers flew out of their 10th Air Force Base in Burma to raid targets in Japanese-occupied China. While attacking bridge approaches at Hsenwi, Namhkai, and Kawnghka, the B-25s were set upon by an undetermined number of "glittering" objects that buzzed and circled all nine aircraft, which experienced complete instrument failure and progressive loss of power to the engines. The foo fighters maneuvered so erratically at such high speeds that gunners were unable to track them, much less get off a single shot at them. Only after the objects broke off the action were the bombers' electrical systems and full engine rpms restored.[11]

Some of the most compelling armed-forces encounters with off-world craft during the Pacific campaign were experienced by officers and men aboard vessels of the U.S. Navy. An extraordinary instance occurred early in the conflict, as an invasion fleet assembled among the Solomon Islands, east of Papua New Guinea, for America's first counter-offensive of the war, scheduled to begin on August 7, 1942. Two days before, at 10:00 a.m., as the men aboard USS *Helm* were readying their destroyer for Operation Watchtower, lookouts sounded the alert to an unidentified aircraft rapidly approaching between three thousand and four thousand feet in a clear, cloudless sky.

The craft was spotted through a pair of 750-power field binoculars by a security detail observer, who determined that the ninety-foot-wide bogey was a silvery cigar-shape, topped by a "round dome." (*Bogey* was a term commonly used for UFOs in military reports.)

"Both the captain and the executive officer had a good look," Keith Chester writes, "and they confirmed it had the appearance of a 'streamlined cigar,'" with "portholes around the dome." When it approached within three thousand yards, the *Helm*'s antiaircraft gunners commenced firing—to no effect. When three nearby cruisers and seven destroyers joined in the shooting, the object "executed a sharp turn, increased its speed, and proceeded to circle once around the entire fleet."[12]

With this, every gun in the task force opened up on the object. A veteran of the encounter recalled how "directional control released all guns, and said for the gun captains to go local control [fire free]. Although the [fire-control] director could keep up with him [the bogey], they [the gunners] weren't able to take enough lead out of their machines [machine guns] to allow us to swing far enough ahead to hit him. So, we just swung wild and just started throwing shells in and

Figure 4.3. USS *Helm*.

firing with the .50s and whatever else available to try and get at least one hit. With so many explosions near, we couldn't tell where we were shooting, or anybody else, so there was just no way really of getting a crack at him." The director of control insisted that the lone intruder "had reached speeds of one thousand miles per hour."[13]

The craft passed undamaged through the massive concentration of firepower spewed skyward by the whole invasion armada, then vanished in an incredible display of speed. Because of its thousands of eyewitness participants, the August 5, 1942 incident was perhaps the best-attested UFO sighting of World War II.

Where an entire task force failed, carrier planes of USS *Wasp* fared no better. During the early afternoon of February 7, 1945, while the warship cruised off the Ulithi atoll of Alethea in the Caroline Islands, Commander Norman P. Stark was informed of a rapidly incoming radar contact at thirty thousand feet, ten miles west. He immediately launched five Grumman F6F *Hellcats,* but the fighters' top speed of 391 mph was inadequate to intercept the supersonic bogey. Another similar event occurred at Ulithi four months later. Lookouts aboard the SS *Calvin Victory,* cruising sixteen knots on a westerly course from Eniwetok, an atoll in the Marshall Islands, pointed out "a silver object directly overhead" at around 2:00 p.m.[14]

On the bridge at the time was Captain Wesley Brown Jr., who, after observing through 50×7 binoculars that the contact was "bright silver, circular in shape," ordered the freighter's bow-mounted, .50-caliber machine gun and eight 20-millimeter cannons to open fire. By then, gun crews had visually sighted in on the target at an estimated altitude of four thousand feet. Although the craft held position directly above the vessel and took no evasive action, the crew fired eight to ten shots, with no observable impact. Because of the ineffectiveness of his gunners, as well as the object's apparent lack of interest in carrying out an attack, Brown commanded them to cease firing. Meanwhile, as recorded in his ship's log, the craft kept pace high above the *Calvin Victory* for the remainder of the afternoon, disappearing only with nightfall. After the war, Brown became the head of the police science and administration department at Northern Arizona University, and wrote of his South Pacific encounter to the renowned ufologist J. Allen Hynek in 1974.

The first documented sightings of USOs (unidentified submersible objects) were made by American service personnel during World War II. During the night of October 12, 1943, Seaman Matthew Mangle was keeping watch aboard a U.S. Navy supply vessel in the Persian Gulf when he observed a "huge disc beneath the surface of water glowing with soft green light," as it "paced the ship at twelve knots, before speeding up, moving out of sight."[15]

From January 26 to 31, 1945, as the USS *McCracken* cruised between the Solomon Islands, Louis Graci and four other sailors watched as their troopship almost passed directly over a submerged, round object lying still at shallow depths. "Sharply outlined," it was the size of a gun turret, about twenty feet across, with a dull, silvery finish. Graci and his mates refrained from reporting their sighting at the time, dismissing it as a monster sea turtle.

The Second World War's outstanding USO experience took place in mid-1945. A U.S. Army attack transport ship was wallowing through

Figure 4.4. USS *McCracken*.

ten-degree rolls amid heavy seas and strong winds in the open ocean past the Aleutian island of Adak, on a return voyage to Seattle. The overburdened USS *Delarof* had been hauling munitions and supplies during early summer from Washington state to Alaska. Near dusk one early-summer evening, several crewmen yelled out suddenly at the sight of a strange, large vehicle shooting into the air from underwater.

Private Robert S. Crawford was then on port side, near the communications room, where he was one of the radio operators, when he heard the commotion. He saw a large, peculiar vehicle ascending roughly vertically upwards, one-quarter to two miles away, in the west. It stood out dark and round against the setting sun, rising to an angular elevation of five degrees before arcing into a level, circular path. Crawford could clearly see that the featureless disk, without insignia or portholes, was one hundred fifty to two hundred feet in diameter as it silently circled the transport at about the speed of a small airplane, perhaps one hundred miles per hour, no more than five hundred feet above the rough sea. Low speed and altitude afforded a clear view of the craft as it flew in a leisurely circular pattern overhead, presenting itself an easy target for the ship's gunners. Although they were ready to pull triggers at the merest suggestion of attack, they held their fire and their breath. Completing a third leisurely circuit of the *Delarof,* the object departed towards south-southwest.

Following its disappearance in that direction after sundown, some crew members saw "three flashes of light from the area where it had vanished."[16] Back in Seattle, fourteen of them signed a written statement affirming the accuracy of their observations. Among the eyewitnesses, Robert Crawford went on to become a consulting geologist with the Indiana Soil Testing Laboratory in Griffith, Indiana. While a graduate student at the University of North Dakota, he shared his wartime sighting with his teacher, geology professor N. N. Kohanowski, who was then a science adviser to the National Investigations Committee on Aerial Phenomena, an organization for studying unidentified flying and submersible objects from the 1950s to the 1980s.

Perhaps the most disturbing account of its kind was related

five years after the war by Edward W. Ludwig. During the last week of June 1944, he was the executive officer of a small Coast Guard–manned cargo vessel approaching the tiny island of Palmyra, about eight hundred miles southeast of Hawaii. Ludwig received a radio message appealing for his assistance in searching for a Navy patrol plane believed lost at sea. Despite prolonged and extensive scouring of the area by Ludwig's ship in company with dozens of other rescue vessels and aircraft, "we found nothing," he said. "Not even a scrap of floating debris or spot of oil to indicate where the plane had crashed." This was highly unusual, because aircraft downed at sea invariably scatter the surface with abundant wreckage.

Twenty-four hours later, Ludwig was on watch on the bridge of his ship when a bright light suddenly appeared in the midnight sky. He reported that he "soon saw that the object in the sky was neither plane nor star. It was definitely round, a sphere, hovering above me, motionless and silent, and at least five times as bright as the most brilliant star. The sphere began to move with almost imperceptible slowness. Then it stopped . . . For half an hour the light continued its slow, purposeful maneuvers, until it covered an area of approximately 90 degrees. At last, it headed northward, away from the island and in the direction where the plane had been lost."

He made official inquiries about the lighted sphere, wondering to himself if "the two incidents—the sphere and the lost plane—might be related. The Naval lieutenant in charge told me that absolutely no aircraft had been aloft that night, and that no Japanese could possibly be within 1,000 miles. He was extremely puzzled by the problem of the missing plane. Its radio direction finder, he believed, had somehow malfunctioned, resulting in a reversal of directions. But this theory, of course, would not explain why two experienced pilots, familiar with the area, would fly directly into the setting sun, away from the island, instead of in the opposite and correct direction. I will never forget the lieutenant's final words. 'Perhaps,' he suggested, 'the inhabitants of the strange sphere wanted specimens.'"[17]

5

Close Encounters of the Axis Kind

With a hundred billion stars in our galaxy alone, what would make us think that we are the only life form?

WERNHER VON BRAUN[1]

Wernher von Braun's question was answered definitively on February 3, 1942, when aviatrix Hanna Reitsch, Germany's famous female test pilot, took off in the world's first operational rocket-powered fighter plane. While the still-experimental Messerschmitt 163A V4 *Komet* was climbing at 525 feet per second to seven and a half miles above the earth, almost straight up into the sky, a silvery, luminous disk shot past her as though the *Komet* were standing still. It went to sixty thousand feet, twenty-six hundred feet higher than the Messerschmitt's maximum ceiling. The object, without insignia, vanished almost as quickly as it had appeared.[2] Perhaps someone aboard the wingless intruder wanted to show that mankind's latest aircraft wasn't so hot by comparison.

Had U.S. flight crews witnessed Reitsch's close encounter, they would have undoubtedly recognized what she saw as a typical foo fighter. Assuming that such nimble enigmas were Nazi secret weapons of some unknown type, the Americans were surprised to learn after the war that German flyers had no less frequently witnessed the same phenomenon, which they similarly attributed to the technology of their enemies.

Bundesarchiv, Bild 183-W-0901-512
Foto: Becke, Heinrich von der I 27. August 1938

Figure 5.1. Hanna Reitsch after one of her several record-breaking flights.
Photo courtesy of German Federal Archive. Photograph by Heinrich von der Becke.

According to Henry Stevens, author of *Hitler's Flying Saucers,* "rumors of these objects circulated in [Luftwaffe] pilot circles since the summer of 1944," the same year they were first glimpsed in significant numbers by Allied airmen.[3] When their aircraft and several RAF bombers had been buzzed by a foo fighter after dark on January 1, 1945, pilot Lieutenant Jack Green and his navigator, Lieutenant Warren Barber, were told by an ex–intelligence officer that "the German pilots that were up that night reported identically the same thing as the British and us . . . they [the Luftwaffe flyers] could never figure out what it really was."[4]

A typical German encounter confirmed, rather unusually, by both visual and ground radar contacts at the same moment, took place on March 14, 1942, at 5:35 p.m. As the pilot of a Messerschmitt 109 F-4/Z (specially designed for high-altitude performance) was flying patrol 39,370 feet over Norway's Banak peninsula, he was approached by a featureless, cigar-shaped object 50 feet in diameter and 330 feet long. It kept pace with him for a moment, then "shot straight up at impossible speed."[5]

Foo fighters were even seen by civilian ground observers in Germany. In late June 1944, Martha Fritsch, wife of physics professor Alois Fritsch, "saw the outline of a perfectly elliptical flying object in the twilight," writes Stevens, "which appeared to her to be operating by some other means of flight that was normally the case, because of its sudden, directional changes. Her reaction was that it was an enemy flying object, and it scared her."[6]

Another ground sighting was made about the same time by Heinz Heller, commanding officer of a German Army truck company, in Couville, France, after the British, Canadians, and Americans had landed at Normandy. The convoy was concealed under an overhanging orchard, where he and most of his men were asleep at 3:00 a.m., when the sharp report of a gunshot abruptly brought them to their feet. It had been fired by the sentry, who had observed "a round shaped thing looking like a discus of about twenty meters [sixty-five feet] diameter, very slightly luminescent," moving about twenty miles per hour, some thirty feet above the ground, and "then accelerated vertically at an incredible speed, shining stronger, and making a swooshing sound." He had fired his rifle not at the "thing," but to awaken his comrades. In recounting this sighting, author Keith Chester relates how, the following morning, "the orchard's owner was questioned, and said his grandfather once had seen a similar 'apparition' over the same field."[7]

The crew in the German submarine U-629 experienced a remarkable close encounter out at sea in the North Atlantic Ocean, during their vessel's tenth patrol. One clear, calm evening, between March 10 and 14, 1944, the Type VIIC boat was surfaced in the Bay of Biscay, when the radar operator reported an airborne contact approaching at exceptionally high speed. Before *Oberleutnant zur See* (equivalent to lieutenant junior grade in the U.S. Navy) Hans-Helmuth Bugs (pronounced "Books"), who was keeping his lookouts company in the conning tower, could sound the alarm, the sub was "approached abeam by a flying

Figure 5.2.
Lieutenant Hans-Helmuth Bugs.

disk that winked white, yellow and red" at the Germans, but made no threatening moves. Whatever message the anomalous vehicle may have been attempting to send them they could not guess, and refrained from responding with their signal light. The otherwise motionless disk hovered as though nailed in place, perhaps forty feet above the sea, for less than five minutes, as though waiting for an answer to its tricolor display, then disappeared vertically into the night sky at an impossible speed. In a reaction typical for the times, Lieutenant Bugs "surmised that the Allies were cunningly using some sort of strange new aircraft."[8]

On June 7, 1944, during the U-629's next cruise, an RAF B-24 *Liberator* long-range heavy bomber of 53rd Squadron attacked with depth charges in the English Channel as the crew was about to intercept Allied naval forces supporting Operation Overlord's invasion of France. U-629 was sunk with the loss of all hands.

As Germany's chief source of oil, Romania was often targeted by U.S. bombers. Immediately following one such raid on August 1, 1943, engineer George Zmeuranu was standing near Ploiesti's Vage oil refinery, where one of its petroleum tanks was still burning, when he "noticed a pointed object coming from the north, . . . It was yellow . . . but with a whitish tail, which, when it met the clouds of smoke, seemed to shorten and vibrate in a strange way. (The object) traveled at a high rate of speed. Over the burning refinery it turned, stopped momentarily, then zigzagged toward the north and disappeared."[9]

Three years earlier, in the south of Hungary, Romania's next-door neighbor and Axis partner, *Altábornagy* (lieutenant-general) Vilmos Nagy was overseeing midsummer maneuvers of the Hungarian 1st Army, when his troops were astounded to see something he described as an immense "fiery cartwheel" slowly ascend from a hilltop near the village of Báta, before it suddenly shot away vertically at tremendous speed, without a sound, vanishing into the early-afternoon sky.[10] Nagy informed Miklós Horthy, Hungary's regent, that the object was doubt-less a secret Soviet spy device of some kind.

Although not officially one of the Axis partners, Spain sent 45,482 volunteers to fight on the Eastern Front in Germany's 250th *Infanterie-Division,* otherwise known as the *División Azul,* or "Blue Division," which derived its name from blue-shirted Falangist victors in the Spanish Civil War. At the Battle of Krasny Bor, where the Spaniards defeated a Soviet attempt to relieve the Wehrmacht siege of Leningrad between February 10 and 13, 1943, hundreds of them reported seeing a

Figure 5.3. Spanish Blue Division volunteers near Leningrad.

"washtub-shaped" vehicle of great size noiselessly suspended about three hundred feet over the fighting for perhaps five minutes before moving off faster than any aircraft with which they were familiar.[11]

"A German test pilot was trying out a new Messerschmitt Me 262 *Schwalbe* ["Swallow"] jet fighter," on September 29, 1944, according to Yves Naud, "when his attention was suddenly caught by two, luminous points situated on his right. He shot at full speed in their direction, and found himself face-to-face with a cylindrical object, more than 300-feet long, with some openings along its side, and fitted with long antennae placed in front up to about halfway along its length. Having approached within about 1,500 feet of the craft, the pilot was amazed to see that it was moving at a speed of more than 1,200 mph," twice the speed of his jet, at that time, the world's fastest operational warplane.[12]

Five years later, ground personnel observed something remarkably similar silently hovering over Davis Monthan Air Force Base for about ten seconds, "fluttering as it disappeared" in Arizona's cloudless spring sky. Materializing around 5:00 p.m., May 5, 1949, the object they described was "black, round and flat in shape, similar to a wash-tub."[13] The following year, on the late afternoon of September 20, the object, or something like it, appeared over a small city in southeastern Missouri. "Many residents of Poplar Bluff described the UFO as a 'translucent washtub,'" writes author Bryce Baker.[14]

SIGHTINGS IN AND NEAR JAPAN

Japanese airmen were photographing unidentified flying spheres and disks five years before the Yanks encountered identical foo fighters over Europe. After carrier-based Nakajima B5N torpedo bombers spear-headed the attack on Pearl Harbor, crew members aboard the formidable aircraft were joined by extraterrestrial escorts all the way back to their ship.

For most of World War II, Japanese encounters with foo fighters were nonviolent. That would change, however, on April 24, 1945, at the Imperial Japanese Navy's Genzan Air Group Base in Wonsan, a

Figure 5.4. Imperial Japan's most commonly reproduced wartime foo-fighter photograph, taken above the Sea of Japan sometime in 1942. The Japanese aircraft appearing in the shot are invariably misidentified as Mitsubishi Ki-21 medium bombers, but they are actually Kawasaki Ki-48 light bombers.

port city located on the eastern side of the Korean peninsula, facing the Sea of Japan. Around 3:00 p.m., ground observers sounded their alarm at the approach of unidentifiable aircraft approaching at one thousand feet. A trio of Mitsubishi A6M2b *Zero* fighters was scrambled and soon after closed with two unmarked silver disks, each an estimated one hundred feet in diameter.

With their twin wing-mounted cannons, the Japanese pilots immediately commenced firing on the strange vehicles, one of which was repeatedly struck by 20-millimeter rounds but remained airborne, though it was apparently somewhat damaged. Its companion then shone a bright beam of light on the nearest *Zero,* which spun out of control into the sea. With this parting shot, the intruders rapidly ascended beyond the capabilities of their piston-driven pursuers and disappeared at high altitude.[15]

Ufologists contend that, for reasons unknown, some multiple sightings of such phenomena seem to cluster around specific geographic areas. Less than seven years later, the Americans made their own sighting in the same area of Korea. Around midnight, January 29, 1952, crew members aboard a Boeing *Superfortress* observed "'flying discs' moving parallel to their plane at a high altitude," a United Press International wire story reported in Washington, D.C.'s *Daily News* for February 19. "The objects remained with the B-29 over Wonsan for five minutes and with the B-29 over Sunchon for one minute," according to an Air Force spokesman. "He indicated that several were sighted, but did not give the number." At the same time, another B-29 from a different squadron over Sunchon, about ninety miles northwest, also encountered unknown craft, "described by four eyewitnesses as globe-shaped, bright orange in color, and emitting an occasional flash of bluish light. . . . While officials declined to elaborate on the bare announcement that a full investigation is underway, the open-minded Air Force attitude toward the new reports contrasted with the blunt skepticism it has voiced about previous sightings of mysterious objects in the skies."[16]

Ufologists assert that some multiple sightings of such phenomena were made during the last two years of the Pacific war, and that foo fighters were encountered almost as often by B-29 flight crews high above Japan as by their comrades in B-17s over Europe. The Japanese people themselves were not unacquainted with these *soratobu enban,* as they were called. On May 23, 1945, and again two days later, after the Americans fire-bombed the capital city, a Tokyo businessman "observed from his air-raid shelter, two, odd-shaped, blue-grey aircraft . . . shaped like discs. As they slowly passed overhead, he described them as 'round-ish objects, like hot cakes, about twenty yards [in diameter].'" They then moved off "without making a sound."[17]

Japan's final brush with otherworldly vehicles came just after she agreed to lay down her arms. During the early morning of August 28, 1945, members of the first postwar U.S. peace delegation boarded a twin-engine Curtiss C-46 *Commando* transport plane at Iejima, a small island not far from Okinawa. They were scheduled for a fuel stop at Iwo Jima before flying on to Atsugi airfield near Yokohama for the discussion of surrender terms with Japanese government officials. At ten thousand feet, between Iejima and Iwo Jima, Sergeant Leonard Stringfield had been casually gazing out the airplane's starboard side window when his attention was suddenly riveted by the abrupt appearance of "three, teardrop-shaped objects. They were brilliant white, like burning magnesium. Flying in a tight formation, the objects were traveling in a straight line through drifts of clouds, seemingly parallel to the C-46 and equal to its speed. . . . They seemed to be intelligently controlled. . . . Stringfield saw no wings or fuselage."[18]

At that same moment "the magnetic navigation instrument needles in the cockpit went wild," as the left engine sputtered oil and began to lose power. The transport faltered and lost altitude, dropping some fifty feet by its port wing in a matter of seconds. Its alarmed copilot suddenly appeared in the cabin to announce the obvious—"We're in trouble!"—and shoved a pair of binoculars at Stringfield, desperately ordering him to find some spot of dry land in the vast stretch of ocean below for them to land. The plane was going off course. After less than a minute of terror aboard the hapless *Commando,* "the three objects disappeared into a cloud bank. When they pulled away, the C-46's engine revved up and returned to normal again. The plane immediately began to gain altitude" and was "able to safely arrive at Iwo Jima without further incident."[19]

Stringfield's harrowing encounter had been preceded by another daylight sighting made 5,255 miles away by USAAF crews in the process of bombing Marseille on April 25, 1944, during which they too saw groups of tear-shaped craft apparently monitoring the slaughter of more than two thousand French residents in the burning city below.[20]

The Axis experience with off-world vehicles was fundamentally similar to those confronted by the Allies, which lends these shared incidents some measure of credibility.

PART TWO

Confrontations at the Edge of the Earth

6
The Battle of Antarctica

We deal now, not with things of this world alone, but with the illimitable distances and as yet unfathomed mysteries of the universe. We are reaching out for a new and boundless frontier . . . of spaceships to the moon; of the primary target in war, no longer limited to the armed forces of an enemy, but instead to include his civil populations; of ultimate conflict between a united human race and the sinister forces of some other planetary galaxy; of such dreams and fantasies as to make life the most exciting of all times.

GENERAL DOUGLAS MACARTHUR

With the momentous words "These proceedings are closed," General Douglas MacArthur, representing the victorious Allies, accepted Imperial Japan's surrender aboard the battleship USS *Missouri* on September 2, 1945, thereby officially concluding World War II.[1] Peace prevailed around the world for the first time in six years, as nations everywhere drastically scaled down their armed forces. But less than one year after General MacArthur officially closed the book on mankind's bloodiest conflict, a huge armada departed U.S. waters on August 26, 1946, toward the Antarctic for Operation Highjump.

Its flagship was the USS *Philippine Sea*, Captain Delbert S. Cornwell commanding her 3,448 officers and enlisted men. At 27,100 tons, she was among the largest aircraft carriers ever built, powered by eight boilers and four Westinghouse geared-steam turbines for a combined 150,000 horsepower and a range of 20,000 nautical miles. In addition to the *Philippine Sea*'s one hundred fighters, dive-bombers, and torpedo bombers, she bristled with arrays of 5-inch artillery and 40-millimeter Bofor antiaircraft guns. Four-inch, 2.5-inch, and 1.5-inch steel armor protected the 888-foot-long hull, hanger deck, and conning tower.

The heavily armed and armored aircraft carrier was screened by destroyers USS *Brownson* and USS *Henderson* as well as the submarine USS *Sennet,* with ten officers and seventy-one enlisted men aboard. All warships were supported by the tankers USS *Canisteo* and USS *Cacapon,* plus the supply ships USS *Merrick* and USS *Yancey.* Their passage through Antarctic waters was cleared by the icebreakers USS *Burton Island* and USCGC *Northwind.* Two seaplane tenders, USS *Pine Island* and USS *Currituck,* were also part of the fleet.

The Martin PBM *Mariner* and another half dozen examples of the Sikorsky H-5 helicopter (referred to in the Navy as the HO3S *Dragonfly*) flitted between USS *Philippine Sea* and the seaplane tenders.

The number of ships and aircraft necessitated their division into an Eastern Group commanded by Captain George J. Dufek, a Western Group headed by Captain Charles A. Bond, a Central Group, Rear Admiral Richard H. Cruzen commanding, and a Carrier Group with none other than Richard E. Byrd Jr. in overall command. This is the same Admiral Byrd that was world-renowned for his epic polar explorations during the 1920s and '30s. He was usually to be found aboard the USS *Mount Olympus* (Captain R. R. Moore commanding), an amphibious-force command ship with advanced communications equipment and extensive combat information spaces for large-scale landing operations.

Collectively the four groups were known as Task Force 68. Their assignment, referred to officially, if rather vaguely, in an initial report as "The United States Navy Antarctic Developments Program," was to establish Little America IV, a research base in the Antarctic; to train personnel and test equipment in frigid conditions; to determine

Figure 6.1. Sikorsky R-4 helicopter landing on icebreaker USCGC *Northwind* followed by the Operation Highjump task force.

the feasibility of establishing, maintaining, and utilizing bases in the Antarctic; to investigate possible additional base sites; to develop techniques for establishing, maintaining, and utilizing air bases on ice; and to increase knowledge of hydrographic, geographic, geological, meteorological, and electromagnetic propagation conditions in the area.

The report also mentioned that the expedition aimed at consolidating and extending United States sovereignty over the largest practicable area of the Antarctic continent, a goal previously and emphatically denied in repeated public pronouncements issued by the U.S. government, even before Operation Highjump's inexplicably premature end. In any case, its officially modest and entirely peaceful agenda was dwarfed and contradicted by the prodigious firepower and armed might assembled by Task Force 68, which was clearly nothing less than a massively armed invasion for conquest of "the largest practicable area of the Antarctic continent."[2]

In fact, few research scientists and very little investigative equipment were included. Moreover, most of its stated objectives were never attempted, much less achieved. No personnel training or equipment testing took place. No effort was made to explore possibilities for other base sites involving aircraft or ships. No practice maneuvers or exercises of any kind were undertaken. And whatever was learned, if anything, about Antarctica's hydrographic, geographic, geological, meteorological, or electromagnetic propagation conditions was never disclosed. While Operation Highjump's declared goals represented hardly more than an academic exercise, it was in reality an entirely military affair. Just before departing for Antarctica, Byrd declared to representatives of the American press, "My expedition has a military character."[3]

Professional physicist and historian Joseph Farrell tells how "Byrd was returned to Washington, D.C., debriefed, and his personal and operational logs from the mission were seized and remain classified to this day."[4]

Thirteen warships, supported by a flotilla of supply vessels, plus 112 aircraft and 4,700 servicemen organized by U.S. Navy commanders and rear admirals far outstrips the requirements of some scientific investigation, no matter how ambitious. This unlikely armada entered the Ross Sea ice pack on December 31, 1946, finally landing at the Bay of Whales by January 15 the following year. Work commenced at once on building a headquarters, Little America IV, one of the few previously announced expedition goals actually attained.

Just forty days later, the Central Group cast off to join the rest of Task Force 68's units already withdrawing toward South America for repairs, thus prematurely terminating their massive, costly mission, which had been originally scheduled from half a year to eight months. Even so, in only eight weeks, its aircraft logged 220 hours flying time over 22,700 miles—an area half the size of the United States—taking some 70,000 reconnaissance photographs, only a select few of which were subsequently released to the public by the Navy. To this day, the remainder, if they still exist, are still classified. The aerial survey also recorded ten new mountain ranges.

Immediately after arriving in several Chilean ports for repairs as unusual as they were extensive, word of the apparently aborted expedition's high strangeness and the disasters that plagued it began spreading like wildfire from loose-lipped Operation Highjump sailors, even though they were under orders to discuss events of the previous several weeks with no one outside the task force.

Admiral Byrd himself contributed to the dire speculation. The mainstream press in Chile quoted some of his men to the effect that his task force had "run into trouble" and suffered "many fatalities"[5]—hardly what one would have expected to hear from the leader of a purely scientific enterprise. Van Atta published the results of his startling interview, headlined "Aboard the USS *Philippine Sea,* Mount Olympus on the High Seas," in the March 5, 1947, edition of *El Mercurio,* a conservative newspaper and Chile's largest, "considered the country's paper-of-record," whose "Valparaiso edition is the oldest daily in the Spanish language currently in circulation," having been first published in 1827.[6] Van Atta wrote:

> Admiral Richard E. Byrd warned today that it was imperative for the United States to initiate immediate defense measures against hostile forces threatening from the Arctic or Antarctic. The Admiral explained that he was not trying to unduly alarm anyone, but the cruel reality is that, in case of a new war, the United States could be attacked by flying objects which could move from pole to pole at incredible speeds.[7]

During the 1947 interview with *El Mercurio,* Admiral Byrd stressed that his statement was made as part of a recapitulation of his own polar experience. Talking about the recently completed expedition, Byrd said that the most important result of his discoveries was the effect they could have on the security of the United States. He repeated the above points of view, resulting from his personal knowledge gathered both at the North and South poles. The fantastic speed at which the world is shrinking, recalled the admiral, was one of the most important lessons he learned during his recent Antarctic exploration.

"'I have to warn my compatriots,' Byrd said, 'that the time has ended when we were able to take refuge in our isolation and rely on the certainty

Figure 6.2. Admiral Byrd said as much as he dared about "flying objects which could move from pole to pole at incredible speeds."

that the distances, the oceans, and the poles were a guarantee of safety."[8]

On his return to Washington, D.C., after Byrd's interrogation by Security Services officers, he never uttered another word about Operation Highjump, which was simultaneously classified, thereby legally preventing any of its veterans from ever discussing the mission. Shortly thereafter, the U.S. Navy published a brief and rather evasive summary of the Antarctic expedition's "achievements," which nonetheless stated that some losses had been incurred.

Although these were glossed over and minimized, the anonymous report nonetheless admitted that fully *half* of Byrd's seaplane and helicopter forces had been lost, and that he himself was nearly brought down in the aircraft he was flying, avoiding a crash only because he jettisoned everything on board in order to stay aloft, save the barest essentials and the reconnaissance films he had just taken. During that perilous flight, he had gone missing for more than three hours in an episode of lost time that was officially blamed on failed radio communications. (He was in excess of three hours overdue, but his plane did not run out of fuel?) The summary further admits that Task Force 68 did indeed suffer some human casualties, but all were supposedly due to accidental causes.

On December 30, 1946, three men flying *George 1,* their Martin flying boat, died when it crashed, allegedly during a blizzard. Six surviving crew members were rescued thirteen days later. Another man supposedly died in a construction accident, totaling the number of American fatalities at four. The official summary concludes by explaining that the mission was terminated because of the early approach of winter and worsening weather conditions, which were supposedly just what the Americans had specifically come for and required to test themselves and their equipment.[9]

A brief film about Operation Highjump, ironically entitled, "The Secret Land," was released in 1948. Although it was more of a chest-pounding propaganda piece for the U.S. Navy than a real documentary, it gives viewers some feeling, however incomplete, for the expedition.[10] The short went otherwise unnoticed by the general public, and, beginning with the onset of the Korean War two years later, soon fell into virtual obscurity over the next forty years. After the collapse of the Soviet Union in 1991, however, millions of the defunct regime's secret papers were suddenly declassified, among them, surprisingly, a 1947 description of Task Force 68's mission to Antarctica.

SOVIET KNOWLEDGE

That Joseph Stalin should have known far more about the expedition than the American people is not surprising. America's close alliance with Stalin during World War II allowed his spies to infiltrate all levels of the U.S. government, including its armed forces. This espionage peaked, but did not end, with the 1953 conviction of Julius and Ethel Rosenberg for their betrayal of America's atomic-bomb research to their Communist handlers. As early as the 1930s, through the Second World War and into the so-called Cold War, U.S. congressman Samuel Dickstein of New York was a Democratic party confidant of President Franklin Roosevelt, all the while serving as a paid agent of the NKVD, the forerunner of the Russian secret police later called the KGB.[11] There were many others like him, and, because of the high positions they often attained, they had access to classified accounts of undertakings such as Operation Highjump.

Details of the expedition, hidden from the U.S. public and the rest of the outside world, were transmitted by a Soviet operative to the

Kremlin, where they languished until their rediscovery before the turn of the twenty-first century. Shortly thereafter, a Moscow Television documentary featured a spokesman from the Russian Army (Dimitri Filippovitch, lieutenant adjutant) and Vladimir Wasilev, a physicist with the prestigious Russian Academy of Sciences. They finally disclosed the Stalin-era report about Task Force 68's covert experiences in Antarctica.

Quoted in the report is radioman John P. Szelwach, who served aboard the USS *Brownson*. Around 7:00 a.m., in the early-morning darkness of January 17, 1947, just two days after Admiral Byrd's Central Group made landfall at the Bay of Whales, Szelwach said, "We observed the following: On the horizon, a bright, colorless light. We thought it was another ship. We were below the Antarctic Circle in unchartered waters [off Charcot Island, in the Weddell Sea]. Our radar was activated to no avail. I and my shipmates in the pilothouse port side observed for several minutes the bright lights that ascended about forty-five degrees into the sky very quickly. We couldn't i.d. the lights, because our radar was limited to two hundred fifty miles in a straight line. Our quartermaster, John Driscoll, recorded this in our log."[12]

Nearly three hours later, the lights (five of them) reappeared in the same area of the Weddell Sea, and began to rapidly close on the destroyer. Commander H. M. S. Gimber ordered the ship's 40-millimeter Bofors antiaircraft guns and 20-millimeter Oerlikon cannons to commence firing on the objects, which flew over the *Brownson* at high speed and low altitude (about two hundred feet), without achieving any hits.

Figure 6.3. The USS *Brownson*.

According to the Soviet espionage report, this encounter opened a series of brief but fierce skirmishes that lasted over the next several weeks between Task Force 68 and the lights, resulting in "dozens" of officers and men killed or wounded.

The most casualties were suffered by Admiral Byrd's Central Group, which, as even the sanitized postexpedition U.S. Navy version of the report admitted, had to be evacuated by the Burton Island icebreaker from the Bay of Whales on February 22, 1947. A variety of silvery, strangely configured craft then executed noiseless, menacing passes at the naval units, which fired their ordnance at the triangular and boomerang-like vehicles. No casualties were sustained on either side during these first, fleeting near misses, and the unidentifiable vessels did not return fire before quickly vanishing into the morning sky.

A few hours later, in the early afternoon, an enormous, cigar-shaped object floated silently, like some gargantuan dirigible, low above the surface of the sea, toward the task force. When the unmarked intruder unintentionally drifted within range of the USS *Sennet,* Commander Joseph B. Icenhower ordered the submarine's deck guns to commence firing. A direct hit with a five-inch shell amidships caused the huge craft to veer wildly out of control, then crash nose-down into the water. It was Task Force 68's only kill.

After four days of encounters, in a kind of parting shot, the spherical lights executed a dramatic attack witnessed by Lieutenant John Sayerson, a flying-boat pilot aboard one of the seaplane tenders. Sayerson reported:

> The thing shot vertically out of the water at tremendous velocity, as though pursued by the devil, and flew between the masts [of the ship] at such a high speed that the radio antenna oscillated back and forth in its turbulence.
>
> An aircraft [a Martin flying boat] from the *Currituck* that took off just a few moments later was struck with an unknown type of ray from the object, and almost instantly crashed into the sea near our vessel. I could hardly believe what I saw. The thing flew without

making any sound, as it passed close over our ships and harmlessly though their lethal antiaircraft fire. Having personally witnessed this attack by the object that flew out of the sea, all I can say is, it was frightening.

About ten miles away, the torpedo-boat *Maddox* burst into flames and began to sink. Despite the danger, rescue boats went to her aid before she sank, twenty minutes later.[13]

The NKVD report refers to Sayerson's ship as the "Casablanca," probably because the Russian spy had trouble pronouncing its real name, *Currituck*. The Soviet agent also stated that an American vessel set afire and destroyed was the USS *Maddox,* either a torpedo boat or torpedo-carrying destroyer. Official records list only the *Henderson* and *Brownson* as part of Task Force 68, which possessed no torpedo boats. Both destroyers survived the mission and are accounted for. A USS *Maddox* was indeed sunk by enemy action, but five years earlier by a German dive-bomber during the Allied invasion of Sicily.

Actually, there were at least three American destroyers known by the name USS *Maddox* (DD-168, DD-622, and DD-731), all of them contemporaneous. The U.S. Navy has long been notorious for falsifying

Figure 6.4. A U.S. Navy PBM Martin *Mariner* flying boat hoisted aboard a seaplane tender.

the identity of its ships and rewriting their histories if they somehow run counter to or embarrass official policy.

Cases in point include 1944's Battle of Slapton Sands before the Normandy invasion, in which a number of vessels were sunk and many servicemen were killed by Kriegsmarine torpedo boats—an event that went unacknowledged for the next half century. Reports of another American massacre, off the Italian coast near Bari in 1943, were censored when numerous Allied units, illegally carrying nerve gas, were sunk by the Luftwaffe. The largest loss of U.S. troops at sea (1,015 fatalities) in a single incident occurred when the British troopship HMS *Rohna* was sunk by a German guided missile in the Mediterranean on November 26, 1943. Only after aged veterans won a lengthy and costly lawsuit against the U.S. Navy fifty-seven years later did they receive official recognition for their role in the disaster. So too the *"Maddox"* cited by Soviet espionage was similarly consigned to an official memory hole.

The February 26 engagement was the last experienced by Task Force 68, which by then was already in headlong retreat from Antarctica. Although identity of the invincible "lights" escaped Lieutenant Sayerson, he wondered if they were perhaps German "wonder weapons" operated by survivors of the recently defeated Third Reich flying out of a secret Antarctic base. His speculation is still shared by some investigators today, not without cause.

Figure 6.5. A *Maddox*-class destroyer of the type sunk by extraterrestrials in Antarctica.

7

The German Connection

It is as impossible to confirm UFOs in the present, as it will be to deny them in the future.

WERNHER VON BRAUN[1]

Nine years before the mighty forces of Operation Highjump had been routed from the South Polar region, the *Schwarzwald,* a freighter built during 1924, was refitted in Hamburg shipyards for Germany's most ambitious Antarctic expedition at a cost of about one million reichsmarks, almost a third of the entire mission's budget.

Renamed the *Schwabenland* after the Swabian region in southern Germany, the vessel was mounted with steam catapults for a pair of Dornier Do J II *Wal* ("Whale") seaplanes. Dornier's reliable, rugged, seaworthy aircraft had established its suitability for polar operations as early as 1925, when famed Norwegian explorer Roald Amundsen flew two of them into the Arctic. Now, thirteen years later, they were being loaded with specially designed Zeiss RMK 38'33 Reihenhaus *bildkameras* and miles of film.

By late 1938, the German Society of Polar Research was ready to undertake its assignment: locating an area in Antarctica for establishment of a whaling station as a means of augmenting their country's production of fat. At the time whale oil was the most important raw material for the production of margarine and soap in Germany. It

Figure 7.1. The *Schwarzwald,* later known as *Schwabenland,* was involved in Germany's expeditions to Antarctica.

Figure 7.2. Logo for Germany's 1938–9 polar expedition.

was also something of a Scandinavian monopoly: Germany was the second-largest purchaser of Norwegian whale oil, importing some 200,000 metric tons annually. To avoid this dependency on foreign imports, the Reich needed to find alternative sources outside the Arctic.

The mission, which was not secret, was headed by Alfred Ritscher (1879–1963), a veteran Arctic explorer and captain in the Kriegsmarine. He and thirty-three other members of the German Society of Polar Research, together with the *Schwabenland*'s twenty-four officers and crew,

Figure 7.3. Captain Alfred Ritscher. Photograph from the Austrian National Library.

were addressed in Berlin by none other than Admiral Richard E. Byrd Jr., who, in the next decade, would be heading his own expedition in the same direction. Thus the first connection between Task Force 68 and the Third Reich appears early on as a prelude to Operation Highjump. Byrd evinced sincere enthusiasm for the Germans' undertaking, wishing them good fortune, but regretfully turned down Ritscher's invitation to join, because of deteriorating relations between their two nations.

On December 17, 1938, the New Swabia Expedition left the port of Hamburg, arriving one month and two days later at the Princess Martha Coast of Antarctica. After dropping anchor at 4°30' W and 69°14' S, Ritscher and company spent three weeks at Queen Maud Land, the same area later invaded by America's Task Force 68. They flew their seaplanes, nicknamed *Passat* and *Boreas,* in fifteen missions across some 370,000 square miles of the continent, taking tens of thousands of photographs and making a color film of their finds.

These included a mountain still known as Ritscher Peak, Schirmacher Oasis (named after its discoverer, *Boreas* pilot Richard Heinrich Schirmacher), and an ice-free region, some 300 square miles in extent, embracing a trio of large lakes, plus several smaller lakes filled with relatively warm, brackish water of green, blue, and red algae and separated by barren, reddish brown rocks. Although the Germans reconnoitered nearly a fifth of Antarctica—most of it unexplored—they left no permanent structures, save for a few hundred small aluminum stakes flying swastika pennants dumped by the Dornier Whales on snow-covered ground between 20° E and 10° W.

In honor of his ship, Ritscher christened this area Neuschwabenland, or "New Swabia," a purely cartographic designation, never intended as a territorial claim. The name still appears on many maps of Queen Maud Land, from which the Germans departed on February 6, 1939. Their successful expedition had been exclusively an economic and scientific affair, contrary to postwar foolishness about "Nazi grasping at the South Pole." It was the precise opposite of the Americans' massive attempt at a military invasion with Operation Highjump. Soon after the expedition arrived back in Hamburg on April 11, plans were laid for a return to Queen Maud Land, but these were forever canceled by the outbreak of war in September.

Over the next six years of international conflict, no U-boat put in at New Swabia or anywhere else along the Antarctic coast, contrary to postwar speculation, if only because the Kriegsmarine's submarine force was taxed to its limits and beyond by the exigencies of transoceanic combat. All its U-boats have been satisfactorily accounted for since, and absolutely no evidence exists to even suggest that a temporary or permanent Wehrmacht installation of any kind was based in Neuschwabenland.

The Germans did establish a secret wartime base in the Arctic, as proved by the October 2016 discovery of its remains on Alexandra Land, an island more than 620 miles from the North Pole. Constructed in 1942, *Schatzgräber* (Treasure Hunter) was an important tactical weather station for the reports it transmitted to Berlin concerning Allied supply convoys heading for Murmansk in the Soviet Union. Russian archaeologists retrieved more than five hundred artifacts from *Schatzgräber,* including a cache of seventy-five-year-old documents (well preserved by the low temperatures) that describe the immense hardships of survival above the Arctic Circle and the abandonment of the facility in 1944, when supplies could no longer get through. If the Germans could not maintain an outpost there, they would have been far less capable of doing so in the South Polar regions, where sufficient outside support to sustain even a few dozen personnel was impossible.

Nor did Hitler's aeronautical engineers ever develop the kind of overpowering spherical "lights" that attacked Task Force 68. At the time of Admiral Byrd's early 1947 interview with *El Mercurio,* no one, not even German scientists, had built "flying objects which could move from pole to pole at incredible speeds."

Although Captain Ritscher's South Polar quest had been an entirely academic enterprise, it was not above certain suspicions. Antarctica's 300-square-mile anomaly discovered by the Dornier *Wal* pilot (scouted years later by Lieutenant Commander David Bunger flying his Martin *Mariner* for Task Force 68) was, as Admiral Byrd stated, "a land of blue and green lakes and brown hills in an otherwise limitless expanse of ice"—an idyllic location for an installation, if not for U-boats, then for something else.[2]

And why was Ritscher's full-length feature film documenting the 1938–39 expedition—shot in expensive color footage—withdrawn from German movie houses after only one week, never to be seen again, save in brief outtakes? And even that version was highly edited and truncated. Furthermore, like the mostly lost photographic record of Operation Highjump, only a handful from the many stills taken over New Swabia by the specially designed Zeiss cameras have ever been made public. Although the German Society of Polar Research took more than sixteen thousand aerial photographs of Antarctica in 1939, Ritscher allowed publication of only a chosen few rather unenlightening examples, primarily showing the *Schwabenland* and its Dornier seaplanes or Ritscher's men standing amid small swastika pennants. The rest have never been seen by outsiders.

Soon after the *Schwabenland* returned to Hamburg, speculation began circulating, even among professional scientists, that the unusually taciturn spokesmen of the Deutsche Antarktische Expedition were participating in a cover-up of some kind to conceal the sensitive nature of some undisclosed find. The controversy naturally fed rumors of secret Wehrmacht military bases in the South Polar region. When these conjectured emplacements proved nonexistent, a few ufologists wondered if Luftwaffe technology in the form of postwar *fliegende Untertassen* was at the hidden heart of Neuschwabenland. "Flying saucers" there may have been in Antarctica, but they were not made in Germany.

His vehicles' confrontations during Operation Highjump clarify Admiral Byrd's otherwise inscrutable comments to the Chilean press soon after the battering his naval units took in the South Polar Sea. He remarked that "the most important result of his observations and discoveries is the potential effect that they have in relation to the security of the United States"—this at a time when America was the world's sole, undisputed superpower, all other militaries having been more or less reduced. Only with the defeat of Task Force 68 still fresh in his mind was he able to tell how "the United States could be attacked by *flying objects,* which could move from pole to pole at incredible speeds."[3]

Sixty years later, aerospace engineer Professor Valeri Burdakov and astrophysicist Yuri Bondarenko, in a Moscow Television documentary about Operation Highjump, told how electromagnetically operated extraterrestrial vehicles would naturally base themselves at Antarctica and the Arctic in order to take advantage of magnetic energy streaming from the Earth's South to North poles. Our planet, they explained, is like a large bar magnet, which continuously repels these lines of force at one end and attracts them at the other. An electromagnetic-propulsion technology might be able to ride such magnetic flows much as a ship rides the currents of the sea.[4]

As noted earlier, the U.S. Navy's published report about Operation Highjump declared that one of its primary goals was to study the South Polar region's "electromagnetic propagation conditions."[5] To carry this out, each seaplane was equipped with a magnetometer, a device that registers anomalies in the earth's magnetism, thereby determining hollow spaces under the surface ice or ground.

From the foregoing facts, however incomplete, the most credible possible reconstruction of events, at least in general outline, begins in 1938 or 1939 with the accidental find by German Antarctic Expedition members of a base near the coast of New Swabia built and occupied by beings from another world who possessed highly advanced flight technology. Returning with this disclosure to Hamburg, Ritscher began organizing a return trip until its cancellation by the advent of war. One year following its conclusion, the former Kriegsmarine captain arrived in Washington, D.C., to share the Deutsche Antarktische Expedition's discovery with his prewar American colleague, Richard Byrd.

Photographic evidence documenting an extraterrestrial installation was excerpted from the German Polar Society's more than sixteen thousand otherwise censored prints and miles of largely classified motion-picture film. Many of these images had been captured by the seaplanes *Passat* and *Boreas* as they reconnoitered the anomalously ice-free region with its warm water, the likely location of the alien base. Presented with such disturbing evidence, Byrd shared it at once with an old friend, the secretary of the navy. For James V. Forrestal, the German visuals represented nothing less than a revelation as soon as military photo analysts determined that they were unquestionably authentic. For the previous eleven months, he had been driven to distraction by the most serious breach in American national security since Pearl Harbor.

NUCLEAR CONCERN

It began a few days after January 20, 1945, when Washington State's Hanford Engineering Works Plant in Richland began processing plutonium for the manufacture of nuclear weapons. The large production facility had been built near the Columbia River, which cooled the site's reactor piles. These were necessary for building the two atomic bombs that were eventually dropped on Hiroshima and Nagasaki. As such, it was the most top secret, best-guarded location in North America, its vicinity strictly off-limits to all aircraft. Thus radar operators stationed

Figure 7.4. The Hanford site's B Reactor during construction, late 1944.

just across the river were alarmed when a blip appeared on their instrument screens, which indicated the bogey's position directly over the factory.

The operators alerted Pasco Naval Air Station, about sixty miles away, where two night fighters were immediately scrambled to intercept the intruder. These were Grumman F6F *Hellcats* capable of climbing 3,500 feet per minute to a service ceiling of 37,300 feet and a maximum speed of 391 mph. Impressive as their performance may have been in 1945, it fell far short of closing within firing range of the target. Nevertheless, Lieutenant Commander Richard Brown was able to make it out visually as a blinding red ball of fire before it flew off at an unapproachably fast speed in the direction of Seattle and vanished off the air base's radar.

Over the next four and a half months, Hanford was similarly reconnoitered on three additional occasions. During a second intrusion, the object disappeared before the *Hellcats* could get airborne. But during the next attempted intercept, Lieutenant Junior Grade Clarence R. "Bud" Clem, a U.S. Naval Reserves pilot, got a good look at the brilliant fireball, which evaded him in a straight-line ascent. These encounters reported by the Air Group 50 officers were confirmed sixty-nine years later, when Robert Hastings, a retired laboratory analyst at Philips Semiconductors in Albuquerque, New Mexico, received pertinent Headquarters 4th Air Force records from UFO historian Jan Aldrich.

"One of them," Hastings writes, "dated January 23, 1945, and directed to the Commanding General of the Army Air Forces and the Assistant Chief of Air Staff, Training," told how, in the original document's own words, "the 13th Naval District has made arrangements for Naval Air Station, Pasco, to employ both radar and fighter aircraft in attempting interception of these unidentified aircraft," including a "battery of searchlights."[6] A follow-up record, dated within the next forty-eight hours, likewise referred to the Hanford intrusion.

Five months later, in mid-July, America's second nuclear facility had just been activated in Oak Ridge, Tennessee, when several unknown disks flew over it. "They appeared to have a bright, aluminum finish," recalled eyewitness Charlie T. Hamlet, superintendent of the *Times News,* in nearby Kingsport, "and traveled at tremendous speeds."[7]

A few days later, yet another radar contact was made directly above Hanford's restricted area around noon. Six U.S. Navy pilots pushed their *Hellcats* beyond the warplanes' certified performance limitations to approach, but they could not intercept the high-flying vehicle. It was described by Ensign Roland D. Powell from about four and a third miles away "as the size of three aircraft carriers side by side,* oval shaped, very streamlined, like a stretched-out egg, and pinkish in color . . . some kind of vapor was being emitted around the outside edges from portholes or vents. The object was observed at noon in a clear sky at an estimated altitude of sixty-five thousand feet."[8]

---

*Powell's comparison of the size of the vessel was based on his recent service aboard the aircraft carrier USS *Cowpens.*

Because the warplanes could not interdict the immense intruder at such a high altitude, it circled at leisure over the plutonium-processing plant. Twenty minutes later, it disappeared from tracking radar by shooting straight up at an incomprehensibly high rate of speed. Forrestal naturally assumed that the "fireballs" and the colossal oval were Japanese secret weapons, probably sent to them on U-boats from Germany, where similar foo fighters were observed by Allied airmen. He believed that the appearance of these objects over Hanford and Oak Ridge indicated that the enemy was aware of America's nuclear facilities. The secretary of the navy feared that such invulnerable reconnaissance was a prelude to a no less unstoppable attack.

One month following Ensign Powell's encounter, World War II ended. U.S. government research teams meticulously sifted through the ruins of imperial Japan, searching for clues to the strange aircraft that had deftly defied the *Hellcat* interceptors, but they found nothing even remotely suggesting such advanced designs. The aircraft were chalked up as unsolved mysteries of some kind, and were generally forgotten in the fleeting period of postwar peace that preceded the Cold War. It was therefore with no little shock and dismay that, less than a year after the destruction of the Axis powers, Forrestal learned that the wonder weapons he assumed were Japanese or German reappeared in American skies.

On July 24, 1946, lieutenants Jack E. Puckett and Henry F. Glass, pilot and copilot, respectively, of a C-47 Skytrain cargo plane flying from Langley Field, Virginia, saw a cylindrical-shaped craft to their southeast, twenty-six thousand feet over the Atlantic Ocean. Around 9:00 p.m., as Puckett and Glass were about to descend toward Florida's McDill Field, in Tampa, the object, "approximately twice the size of a B-29, with luminous portholes," suddenly flew on a collision course with them. Coming to within a thousand yards of their flight path at an estimated two thousand miles per hour, it emitted "a stream of fire that trailed about half a length behind it, until it disappeared over the horizon."[9]

The next day, half a world away, in the Marshall Islands, at the Bikini atoll, the United States conducted the last of two atomic bomb tests collectively known as Operation Crossroads. Detonated ninety feet under water, "Baker" produced a characteristic mushroom cloud, rising several thousand feet above the western Pacific Ocean. Uncharacteristic, however, were three disk-shaped objects filmed skirting the neutron flash where no known aircraft could have survived, while a fourth was seen moving away from the explosion at a lower altitude.[10] Ten days later, another trio of "silver disks" was observed flying in a triangular formation over Lake Michigan at the Great Lakes Naval Training Center, near North Chicago, Illinois.[11]

Forrestal was beside himself with uncertainty and dread, as national security seemed at the mercy of these anonymous violators of American airspace. It was then, in the midst of his consternation, that Richard Byrd providentially approached the bemused secretary of the navy with Ritscher's still-photography and motion-picture proof of Antarctica's UFO base. Forrestal resolved at once to crush it with an armada strike force, with Admiral Byrd in command. Although the operation's chief aim was neutralizing the South Polar nest, hardly less important would be capturing specimens for analysis and reproduction of the high technology that gave the disks their speed. Forrestal became so alarmed that he prioritized the armed invasion of Antarctica in order to extirpate its extraterrestrial occupiers.

Task Force 68 was indeed thrown together with a frantic haste, as though America were on the brink of war, Byrd later stressed in his *El Mercurio* interview. The new icebreaker the *Burton Island,* for example, had only recently been commissioned, and was still undergoing sea trials off the California coast when she was drafted for Operation Highjump. Pulling a freshly commissioned ship off its sea trials certainly points to the mission's sense of urgency, which was still echoed months later, even after conclusion of the expedition, when Byrd could only talk about potential attacks coming from over the polar regions. The very name of the operation's code designation—Highjump—hinted that it was conceived from the beginning as an attack on enemies operating at extreme altitude. As massive and foredoomed as it was well-documented, 1947's engagement became the first pitched battle in our planet's War of the Worlds.

As a disquieting footnote to this early confrontation, long after Task Force 68's South Polar conflict, its largest warship was again on active duty. By late January 1952, USS *Philippine Sea* began patrolling the east coast of the Korean peninsula for her second deployment in the "police action" there. During the early afternoon of February 2, her radar operators picked up an anomalous contact approaching at fifty-two thousand feet, which was visually confirmed moments later by three lookouts on deck through long-range field glasses. When the unidentified vehicle came within twenty miles of the aircraft carrier, general quarters were sounded. But as her crew rushed to battle stations, the object was seen to instantly and impossibly reverse course in an opposite direction, flying away at a speed that radar operators rated at 1,800 mph, far beyond the capabilities of any Korean War aircraft. The entire encounter was documented in a report filed by the commander of naval operations, Far East, with the U.S. chief of naval operations.[12]

Had the *Philippine Sea* been monitored for the previous five years by her extraterrestrial opponents from Operation Highjump? In fact, a connection had already been made.

Figure 7.5. The USS *Philippine Sea* with the American battleship *Wisconsin*. Each vessel experienced serious encounters with extraterrestrial intruders.

8

Seeing Is Believing

Unidentified flying objects are entering our atmosphere at very high speeds and obviously under intelligent control. We must solve this riddle without delay.

REAR ADMIRAL DELMAR FAHRNEY,
U.S. NAVAL RESERVE[1]

America's earliest major military clash with off-world forces had taken place in Antarctica during January 1947. Although it is the stuff of which science fiction is made, the encounter was amply if not completely documented, and is undeniably part of the mid-twentieth-century historical record. Human and extraterrestrial warriors, as described in the previous chapters, did indeed engage in a firefight near the South Pole shortly following World War II.

Only after all its officers died off, mostly from old age, did additional information pertinent to Highjump become available in the form of several old photographs released publicly for the first time by a French publication in 2015. At the same time several other old photographs were also made publicly available. They were supposedly taken through the periscope of a U.S. Navy submarine cruising near the Arctic Circle between Iceland and Norway's Jan Mayen Island during early 1971. They document large unconventional craft in flight not far from the camera, and no more than one hundred feet or so above the surface of the sea.

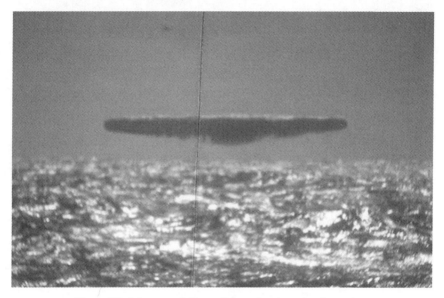

Figure 8.1. A large metallic craft hovering low over the water.

In these days of Photoshop, evidence of this kind no longer means what it *used* to mean. Acceptance of what these images suggest is not a matter of seeing what one wants to see. It is a matter of refusing to dismiss the obvious just because such things are not supposed to exist within the parameters of conventional wisdom. If the universe is infinite, so are its possibilities.

One of the more startling photos shows sunlight glinting on the surface of a choppy sea reflecting identically off the upper surface of the featured UFO (figure 8.1). In this specimen, as in the others, all details of the objects and their natural environment are harmonious within each shot's depth of field. In other words, nothing suggests that images of the unusual craft were separately grafted onto an otherwise normal photograph of the ocean.

In another shot appears a delta-shaped vehicle—remarkably, because triangular UFOs were reported only infrequently before the late twentieth century (figure 8.2.). Now they are among the most commonly observed unidentified flying objects around the world.

Photographs of a cigar-shaped object may be the most revealing of

Figure 8.2. A delta-shaped
UFO above the ocean surface.

the set, because arranging them in order reveals an apparent sequence of events. They show an elongated, cylindrical craft of large size (in view of its apparent relationship to the sea). The next shot shows the same vehicle in serious distress, as it violently emits great clouds from at least two breaches in its hull and another from one end, as the object appears to lurch out of control (figure 8.3, on page 98).

In the next photograph of the set (not seen here) a bright orange dot appears left of center amidships—suggesting an artillery shell at the moment of impact detonation. The final photograph shows the same craft falling end first into the sea, from which walls of rising water spurt dynamically upward along the flanks of the object (figure 8.4, on page 98). In a final shot, it remains afloat, one end up, settled more peacefully into the ocean.

Thus arranged, these images appear to represent a large flying vehicle fired upon and downed by conventional artillery operated by a surfaced submarine. At least two of them carry original captions. One reads, "Official Photograph. Not to be Released. CT." The other reads, "Unauthorized Disclosure Subject. Security Certificate SSN 674. Criminal Section." "SSN 674" was the U.S. Navy's designation for

Figure 8.3. An unidentified flying object in serious distress.

Figure 8.4. The cigar-shaped vehicle crashes into the sea.

USS *Trepang,* an American submarine that did, in fact, undertake experimental operations in the Arctic Ocean during March 1971. Contacted by telephone in July 2015, "Admiral Dean R. Sackett [USN (ret.)] said, 'I only saw ice,'" and "denied [having] seen anything unusual while on board the *Trepang.*" He was its chief officer for this cruise.[2]

Earlier undersea operations in the area included USS *Skate,* during July 1958, and, the following month, USS *Nautilus,* the world's premier nuclear-powered submarine and the first vessel to complete a submerged transit at the North Pole. None of these ships was equipped with surface artillery, which had been phased out years before they were commissioned. Yet the impact blast on the side of the cigar-shaped UFO clearly shown in one of the photos is consistent with the explosion of a 5-inch shell fired from a 127-millimeter deck gun belonging to USS *Sennet.* The diesel-electric submarine, also armed with single Bofors 40-millimeter and Oerlikon 20-millimeter cannons, participated in Operation Highjump.

Figure 8.5. USS *Sennet* participating in Operation Highjump.

All of the photographs in question were made from above sea level, indicating that they were shot through a periscope at a time when the *Sennet* was operating on the surface of the South Polar Sea, consistent with the deployment of her deck-mounted guns. The prints themselves are a washed-out color, almost black-and-white, characteristic of the late Second World War era, unlike the bolder, sharper hues more typical of photography during the mid-1950s, and certainly inferior to the kind available by the early 1970s. In short, the photographs of an elongated craft in the process of being shot down by the deck weapons of a surfaced submarine could not have been made through the periscope of USS *Trepang* in the Arctic.

They were taken instead by—or on the orders of—Commander Joseph B. Icenhower, chief officer aboard USS *Sennet,* part of Operation Highjump's Central Group between January 17, 1947, when U.S. Navy warships first engaged in combat with UFOs, and February 26, as the fleeing Americans suffered their final losses in Antarctica (an aircraft and one destroyer). Associating these photographs with the 1971 submarine is almost certainly a result of deliberate disinformation. U.S. Navy historians have been notorious for manipulating ship identification since World War II, when such falsification was used in the interests of military security.

Figure 8.6. Commander Icenhower aboard USS *Sennet* during Operation Highjump.

Researcher Alex Mistretta cites John Greenewald, who postulates that the UFOs in the old photos may not be extraterrestrial in origin, but were actually balloons used for target practice in the past.[3] If so, the photographs of such unmanned craft could only have been taken between 1849 and 1915, when "balloon carriers" were indeed operated by the navies of Great Britain, France, Germany, Italy, Russia, and Sweden, but color photography as used in the UFO shots was not available to any of them. Moreover, these balloons provided aerial reconnaissance before the advent of seaplanes and were never used for target practice. They were invariably tethered, contrary to the photographed craft, which shows no indications of tethering.

In any case, the delta-shaped object is certainly unlike any balloon ever known. Surviving designs of nineteenth and early-twentieth-century balloon carriers match none of those appearing in the controversial photos. All periscope images of the unusual craft suggest the objects were metallic, yet no historical balloon carriers were covered in aluminum. More decisively, the cigar-shaped object cannot have been a flimsy, hollow bag of laminated canvas stretched over thin frameworks of light wood or holed aluminum, because, as is shown in its photograph, great masses of water burst into the air on either side of and high above the craft as it sank. It must have been a weightier affair to generate such dynamic results.

All photos were released in early 2015 by the French magazine *Top Secret,* whose editor received them from an anonymous source. Perhaps it was an aging veteran of Operation Highjump, still loyal to his security oath of more than seventy years before, but nonetheless determined to unburden his conscience before he died of old age by releasing at least part of the truth.[4] In any event, the photographs show that the extraterrestrial craft may have been superior to human weapons technology in the mid-twentieth century, but they were not impenetrable to accurate Navy gunfire. And although destroying an intergalactic contrivance from outer space with a Second World War–era submarine designed for inner space may seem absurd, it is less so than a similar kill made during World War I by a mere 7.92-millimeter machine gun fired from Baron von Richthofen's 93 mph biplane.

Icenhower did not deliberately pursue the cigar-shaped contact, but had been inadvertently holding a position relative to it when the target randomly came within range of his deck gun, enabling him to fire with accuracy. The *Sennet* had apparently gone unrecognized by the alien pilot, who took no evasive maneuvers and neglected to shield his vehicle, which was downed by a chance encounter with the surfaced Navy vessel.

When he saw that the downed cigar-shaped monstrosity was still afloat, although half down by the bow, Commander Icenhower ordered a boarding party. Arriving at the disabled craft, the *Sennet's* crew members broke into it and hurriedly removed whatever they could lay their hands on. How they reacted to the vehicle's occupants, if any survived the crash, is not known. Like all boarders, they were doubtless heavily armed and probably disinclined to take enemy prisoners alive while ransacking their sinking vessel. In any case, the Navy men salvaged whatever they were able to tear out of the craft's interior as quickly as possible and carried it off on away-boats to the waiting *Sennet,* which rejoined the other units of Task Force 68 in their retreat from Antarctica.

Figure 8.7. A kind of flying wing, unlike anything known on Earth at the time, banks over the Antarctic sea.

PART THREE

Silent Pursuit

9
Payback at Roswell

The intelligence office of the 509th Bombardment group at Roswell Army Air Field announced at noon today, that the field has come into possession of a flying saucer.

ROSWELL DAILY RECORD,
TUESDAY, JULY 8, 1947.[1]

Back in the States, the materials retrieved by the *Sennet* were closely examined by government scientists. All they could deduce from such unfathomably bizarre technology was that it had not been produced by any power on Earth, Nazi or Soviet, and they left the secretary of the navy to draw his own conclusions. The incredibly high speeds, dazzling maneuverability, and invisible shielding the lights displayed in the Antarctic made them invincible against Operation Highjump's conventional weapons, save for the *Sennet's* lucky shot.

Forrestal could not count on a repeat of such good fortune, so he decided upon an alternate strategy. He wasted no time in setting up a trap for the extraterrestrial bogeys by installing additional radar in New Mexico at the approaches to the USAAF Alamogordo Bombing and Gunnery Range, which later became part of White Sands Missile Range. It was here that the United States conducted the Trinity operation, its first detonation of an atomic bomb, on July 16, 1945. A more immediate draw for the nosy aliens was the 509th Operations Group, the only squadron authorized to carry nuclear bombs, stationed at Roswell.

Investigator Scott Ramsey writes, "Roswell Army Air Field was the repository of our arsenal of nuclear weapons and bombers that could be delivered anywhere in the world . . . early, powerful radar was being installed in the state to protect military and research installations." In the 1990s, he was able to determine that at least one of these early radar stations was operating by summer 1947, at El Vado Lake, 300 miles northwest of Roswell. "The locals say the installation was a complex radar site."[2]

THE TRAP

Forrestal's plan was to lure the off-world intruders into the short range of powerful radar arrays he and the Atomic Energy Commission had posted around Los Alamos, together with related research and Air Force sites throughout New Mexico, as early as 1946. When the anticipated alien craft descended low and slowly enough for radar operators to track their position, high-intensity radar energy would be focused on the off-world disks, baking their interiors at four-hundred-degree-plus temperatures and turning them into flying microwave ovens. The scheme was not as fantastic as it may have seemed to mainstream generals, since the application of radar as a weapon of sorts was already known by then.[3]

Ramsey tells of Lee Crane, who resided a few miles from the El Vado radar installation, just three years after Forrestal's trap was set: "Lee said that Air Force personnel often came down to eat [at a local diner] and sometimes even brought freshly killed ducks that had been knocked out of the air by the powerful micro-wave radar being used at their facility. Lee remembered that the airmen would actually ask the owner to finish cooking the birds after the ducks flew into the powerful radar waves of the facility and dropped half-cooked to the ground."[4] Forrestal (who had been named secretary of defense in the meantime) hoped to similarly drop at least one half-cooked alien somewhere in the Land of Enchantment.

Ramsey goes on to quote an anonymous physicist he believes was probably the University of Minnesota's John Torrence, who was in charge of operations research at the U.S. government's Office of Scientific Research and Development during the late 1940s: "In the laboratories and also at Alamogordo and Los Alamos and at different parts of the country we have *tenescope* observers [a tenescope is a range-finding optical instrument], who spend twenty-four hours a day watching for evidence of objects or ships flying in the sky. Everything that comes within the range of these *tenescope*s is noted. If it is unfamiliar and lands, the Air Force is aware of it almost immediately."[5] Since the extraterrestrial intruders seemed chiefly interested in America's nuclear facilities, Forrestal hoped they would scent the combined radioactive bait of Trinity's lingering residue and the Air Force's latest atom bombers at Roswell long enough for his observers to get a fix on them.

Sure enough, less than two weeks short of the Trinity blast's second anniversary, and just four months after Operation Highjump had been aborted, a pair of silvery disks appeared over the prepared bombing range. Their position was forwarded to radar operators, who focused intense microwave transmissions from their multiple instrumentation on the targets, which immediately careened out of control. One ricocheted off a six-thousand-foot ridge north of Capitan Peak in the Capitan Mountains east of White Sands, then crashed southeast of Corona, thirty miles north of Roswell. Its companion hit the desert no less catastrophically west of Socorro, in an area known as the Plains of San Agustin. The narrowing of concentrated radar beams on the vehicles had indeed turned them into flying microwave ovens, in which the occupants were instantly cooked.

The Roswell mortician who examined the alien corpses, observed that "the skin was black, perhaps due to exposure in the sun [or radar burns]."[6] Patricia D. Netzley, author of *Alien Encounters,* tells of "the poor condition of their bodies (due to physical impact, possible burning)."[7] According to researcher Anthony Bragalia:

Skeptic and amateur astronomer, Timothy Printy, reports that on June 26, 1956, a plane filled with fuel crashed a few miles south of the base and its crew burned to death. He says autopsies had to be performed on the deceased to determine each one's identity, and that "the descriptions of the bodies in the autopsy reports closely match" descriptions of the condition of the aliens' bodies.[8]

GRISLY EVIDENCE

Only eight months following the incident, another UFO wreck took place in New Mexico, 375 miles northwest of Roswell near the small town of Aztec. Authors Scott Ramsey, Suzanne Ramsey, and Frank Thayer, Ph.D., not only establish the certainty of its occurrence, but may also provide a revealing connection to the earlier crash. In their book, eyewitness Doug Noland explains that the skin of the lifeless extraterrestrial bodies appeared to be charred, perhaps from exposure to heat, even though the interior of the craft had not been burned. Preacher Solon Brown, who had been called to the scene, also noted the burned appearance of the alien corpses.[9]

Similar skin burns had not been found at the earlier Cape Girardeau wreck, where the corpses were, according to investigator Paul Blake Smith, "not even burned. An eyewitness at the scene claimed he did not recall seeing a single scorch mark or fire damage . . . on the diminutive ET bodies themselves."[10] This was because the crash was a mishap brought about by southeastern Missouri's gusty wind conditions on April 12, 1941, unlike the New Mexico UFOs, which were deliberately brought down by ground weapons. Charred bodies at Roswell and Aztec suggest that both events resulted from the concentration of high-intensity microwave energy deliberately beamed at specific targets by Air Force radar operators lying in wait for the low-flying off-world vehicles.

In a personal email, prominent ufologist Stanton Friedman writes, "I have said that there might have been a midair collision between a UFO pilot and his wingman, because of their flying through a radar tracking (not search) beam, producing a temporary glitch in guidance or propulsion system. . . . We know a tracking beam was on, because a rocket launch was due from White Sands."[11] It is less likely that the two craft blundered into a tracking beam than that they were victims of a planned attack, like the unfortunates at Aztec who were to follow them eight months later. The crashes of three UFOs in the same state, less than one year apart, were not accidents.

Wreckage from the Roswell crashes was recovered by personnel of the decoyed 509th Operations Group. It was then flown to the Carswell Army Air Force Base in Fort Worth, Texas, before removal under armed guard to Dayton, Ohio's Wright Field for examination. Not three years later, a Federal Bureau of Information file addressed to director J. Edgar Hoover, on March 22, 1950, read that both downed craft "were described as circular, approximately fifty feet in diameter. Each one was occupied by three bodies of human shape, but only three feet tall, dressed in metallic cloth of a very fine texture. Each body was bandaged in a manner similar to the blackout suits used by speed flyers and test pilots . . . no further evaluation was attempted."[12]

Hoover shot back, "We must insist upon full access to discs recovered! For instance, in the L.A. case, the Army grabbed it, and would not let us have it for cursory examination."[13] He was referring to a UFO shot down during 1942's Battle of Los Angeles and subsequently retrieved by the Americans, as described by General George C. Marshall.

Although millions of people around the world are familiar with the so-called Roswell incident of July 3, 1947, few realize that it was the eventual outcome of a Third Reich South Polar expedition and Operation Highjump's defeat in Antarctic waters. Fewer realize what became of James Vincent Forrestal as a result. Two months and two weeks after Roswell, he was elevated from his position as secretary of the navy to secretary of defense, and later awarded the Medal of Honor by President Harry S. Truman himself. All in heartfelt if unspoken gratitude for his alien takedown at Roswell?

TOP SECRET

On September 23, as Forrestal arrived at his new offices in the Pentagon, a newly completed report entitled "Air Material Command Opinion

Concerning Flying Discs" was dated by General Nathan Twining. "This 17-page document," writes author Tony Brunt, "was prepared by a panel of sixteen military and civilian appointees in the wake of the Roswell recoveries. It recommended an operation called Majestic 12, as a 'fully funded and operational Top Secret Research and Development intelligence gathering agency' dealing with the UFO issue. This recommendation was approved at the meeting in the Oval Office," with "Truman instructing Forrestal to begin funding and organizing the MJ12 initiative."[14] The covert committee of scientists, military leaders, and government officials had been formed by presidential order to facilitate recovery and investigation of alien spacecraft, and to determine how the United States should engage extraterrestrial life in the future.

General Twining set the tone of the investigation: "This 'flying saucer' situation is not at all imaginary or seeing too much in some natural phenomena. Something is really flying around. The phenomenon is something real and not visionary or fictitious."[15] Roswell disabused the Americans of their assumption that all UFOs were enemy secret weapons—first German, then Japanese, and finally Russian or Russo-German—and were instead operated by intelligent creatures from outer space. Now, at least, Twining and others knew they were not confronted by fellow humans.

From the beginning of Majestic 12, Forrestal opposed the continued suppression of information concerning extraterrestrial violation of U.S. airspace, and urged gradual disclosure. For this he was rigorously criticized by his colleagues, who argued that common knowledge of technologically and militarily superior nonhumans from another world would utterly unhinge society, diminish faith in religion, undermine trust in the armed forces, and lead to a collapse in the international economy. This was the majority opinion, and it was so adamantine that Forrestal not only quit Majestic 12 but resigned as secretary of defense on March 28, 1949.

Forrestal was now free to approach the dilemma without restrictions imposed upon him by government censors. Among his few friends, Admiral Byrd shared his determination to acquaint the public

Figure 9.1.
Secretary of Defense
James V. Forrestal.

with "this 'flying saucer' situation," as General Twining had character-ized it. Together Forrestal and Byrd endeavored to find proper channels for disseminating MJ12's suppressed information by extending tentative feelers to prominent editors, columnists, and reporters. These moves were no sooner made than they were monitored by President Truman's agents, who were increasingly alarmed at a perceived breach in national security.

On May 22, 1949, Forrestal fell to his death from the sixteenth floor of the National Naval Medical Center in Bethesda, Maryland, where he had been supposedly recovering from severe depression. An offi-cial Navy review board described him as a suicide victim. This version almost immediately came under suspicion, which grew throughout subsequent decades, until the late 1980s, when photocopies of original U.S. government briefing papers describing "Operation Majestic 12" were published. Related photocopies appeared in after years. Paragraph 11 was chilling: "The untimely death of Secretary Forrestal was deemed necessary and regrettable."[16]

The MJ12 documents are still dismissed as fake by many ufologists, but internal evidence establishes their authenticity, if only because the language is couched in late 1940s U.S. military vernacular, which would have required the unlikely skills of a hoaxer fluent in period speech. For example, the White House memoranda quoted in chapters 3 and 4 could only have been written by FDR himself or someone skilled in consistently and flawlessly mimicking his personal phraseology, as anyone familiar with his personal writing style may easily recognize. Although investigators are still divided over MJ12's trustworthiness, its authenticity was competently established following years of painstaking research undertaken by ufologist Stanton Friedman, formerly a nuclear physicist for such companies as General Electric, General Motors, Westinghouse, and McDonnell Douglas. His *Top Secret/Majic: Operation Majestic-12 and the United States Government's UFO Cover-up,* effectively establishes the controversial documents' government provenance.[17]

INCREASED CONFLICT IN THE SKIES

While military spokesmen announced in the press that wreckage from a weather balloon had been mistaken for a crashed "flying saucer" at Roswell, they and the rest of their colleagues were secretly gearing up to confront an expected extraterrestrial counterattack for their killing of half a dozen aliens. As the sun arose on July 6, 1947, Army, Navy, and National Guard aircraft began patrolling the Pacific Northwest, despite low fuel reserves, which gives some indication of the urgency attached to their alert status at the time. California-based North American P-51 fighters were on station at 35,000 feet over Manhattan Beach and Van Nuys, while additional *Mustangs* from the Oregon National Guard and twin-engine Douglas A-26 *Invader* light bombers carrying long-range cameras equipped with telescopic lenses cruised above Oregon's Cascade Mountains and the city of Portland. General Irving O. Schaeffer, in charge of Colorado's National Guard, stated "that he had his fighter planes on standby, ready to make an intercept at a moment's notice."[18]

They did not have long to wait. The very next day, Vernon Baird, piloting a P-38 Lockheed *Lightning* for the Fairchild Photogrammetric Company, was mapping territory between Helena, Montana, and Wyoming's Yellowstone National Park for the U.S. Bureau of

Reclamation when a pearl-gray disk topped with an opaque canopy or dome aggressively chased him at 32,400 feet. As the 15-foot-wide, 4-foot-thick vehicle began rapidly gaining on Baird's photoreconaissance plane, traveling at 360 miles per hour, he executed a tight, evasive right turn that his mysterious pursuer appeared to have difficulty following. Violently buffeted by prop wash (an air current created by the rotating action of a propeller) from the combined 3,200 horsepower of the *Lightning's* twin Allison piston-driven engines, the closing UFO suddenly split into two clamshell-like pieces that fluttered down into the remote Tobacco Root Mountains of Montana.[19]

On July 7, a yellowish-white spherical object traveling at 200–225 miles per hour at 10,000 feet passed over Major J. C. Wise as he was completing final flight checks for his XP-84—a secret version of Republic's *Thunderjet*—prior to takeoff from California's Muroc Air Base.[20] The next day, at 11:50 a.m., a white-aluminum-colored oval sprouting two oscillating projections from its upper surface suddenly dropped out of the clear sky from almost 20,000 feet to hover briefly over an Air Force testing strip at Rogers Dry Lake before slowly disappearing at treetop level toward Mount Wilson.[21]

That afternoon, at 3:50, a *Mustang* pilot spotted a wingless, tailless, silvery object 40 miles south of Muroc at 20,000 feet. He gave chase, but the target instantly accelerated far beyond his firing range.[22] At that same moment, no less than one hundred Navy servicemen saw the same craft fly over Pearl Harbor, Honolulu. Yeoman First Class Douglas Kacherle reported, "It moved extremely fast for a short period, seemed to slow down, then disappeared high in the air."[23]

Encounters continued after nightfall. Around 10:20 p.m., an undetermined number of illuminated spheres assembled over Muroc at 8,000 feet, but vanished before interceptors could be scrambled. A similar formation was observed that same evening on the other side of the continent by Lieutenant Commander L. D. Patterson at the Naval Air Station in Norfolk, Virginia. A quartet of "egg-shaped, phosphorus-colored discs" passed in formation over the 1380th Army Air Force Base in Fort Pepperell, Newfoundland, on the night of July 9, around 11:30, followed ten minutes later by a single, similar object. Newfoundland was again visited the following day by a silver disk approximately 100 feet in diameter at 5:50 p.m. as it passed over the 1388th Army Air Force Base at Harmon Field. During the previous seventy-two hours, military eyewitnesses had made eight UFO sightings.[24]

The clear skies over California were quiet again until 3:50 p.m. on July 29, when Lieutenant Ward L. Stewart was alerted by Captain William H. Ryherd to a shiny, white disk, about twenty-five feet across, keeping pace with a Lockheed P-80 *Shooting Star* directly above the jet fighter's approach to Hamilton Field. A second identical though somewhat smaller object was seen flying a right-to-left, protective maneuver over the first craft at about 6,000 feet, as both made a beeline for Oakland, proceeding out over the Pacific Ocean, where they were lost to view. A B-29 veteran pilot and experienced aviator, Lieutenant Stewart told intelligence officers that the objects he and Captain Ryherd saw were "unlike any conventional type of aircraft he had ever seen."[25]

The Roswell crash had ignited a spate of UFO sightings and encounters seldom matched before or since, making 1947 a banner year of its kind. No earthling had been hurt, and the extraterrestrial counterattack for which Armed Forces commanders had braced themselves did not occur. Instead, the off-world intruders confined their reaction (if that is what it was) to the Roswell incident by flying reconnaissance of the military's restricted areas. But their apparently peaceful posture would change radically shortly after the New Year.

10

Crashes—Ours and Theirs

One must consider the fact that misidentification of these space craft for an intercontinental missile in a re-entry phase of flight could lead to accidental nuclear war with horrible consequences.

J. ROBERT OPPENHEIMER AND
ALBERT EINSTEIN IN A JOINT MEMO, JUNE 1947.[1]

Around 1:45 p.m., on January 7, 1948, Sergeant Quinton Blackwell, the tower operator at Godman Army Airfield near Louisville, Kentucky, received a telephone call from security police alerting him to an unidentified aircraft hovering directly overhead. After notifying tower commander Colonel Guy F. Hix, Blackwell rushed outside with Captain Gary Carter, who spotted the high-altitude object using a pair of 6 × 50 field glasses, through which it appeared as a white sphere. They were joined by other officers and men, who likened it to a "parachute with the bright sun shining on top of the silk." Private First Class Stanley Oliver said it resembled "an ice-cream cone topped with red."[2]

These sightings were identically confirmed by Colonel Hix, who dispatched a radio message to an incoming flight of warplanes on a return ferry mission from Dobbins Air Reserve Base in Marietta, Georgia, ordering them to close with and identify the stationary object. One of the fighters was low on fuel, so dropped out, while the

Figure 10.1.
Captain Thomas F. Mantell Jr.

remaining three followed Kentucky Air National Guard pilot Captain Thomas F. Mantell Jr. toward the target. They were flying shiny specimens of the new F-51 *Stallion,* 1947's souped-up version of the better-known *Mustang.* Captain Mantell's F-51 could climb to just under 42,000 feet, but it did not carry oxygen tanks, limiting its service ceiling to 15,000 feet. Above that altitude, human consciousness is progressively compromised until one blacks out.

At 10,000 feet, Mantell radioed that the assigned target was "in sight above and [a]head of me, and it appears to be moving at about half my speed, or approximately 180 miles per hour." Still below the 15,000-foot barrier, he got a better visual of the craft: "It appears to be a metallic object, or possibly a reflection of sun from a metallic object, and it is a tremendous size." Nearing 20,000 feet, he told his wingmen, "Look, there it is out there at twelve o'clock!"[3]

But both of the wingmen, unused to the increasingly thin oxygen, were falling behind and urged him to break off the intercept. Mantell responded that he would climb only another 2,500 feet after the intruder and abandon further pursuit if he could get not get an improved sighting after ten minutes. At 3:15, he informed Godman Tower, "I'm still climbing [at 3,200 feet per minute]. The object is above and ahead of me, moving at about my speed [around 385 mph] or faster. It appears to be a metallic object, tremendous in size, directly ahead and slightly above. I am trying to close for a better look."[4]

Just three minutes later, Mantell's plane spun out of the sky to crash on a Kentucky farm outside Franklin, a mere 750 feet from the owner's home. No one on the ground was injured, but "Mantell's body was partially decapitated, yet still inside the aircraft," writes encyclopedist Michael David Hall. "It was not burned, radioactive, nor riddled with bullets, as later, sensationalized accounts claimed."[5]

Official Air Force comments stated simply that the pilot had mistaken the planet Venus for an unidentified flying object, climbed too high in pursuit of this heavenly illusion, run out of oxygen, fainted, and crashed to his death. Military spokesmen continued to uphold their celestial explanation even after their own chief UFO-debunking astronomer, J. Allen Hynek, pointed out to them that Venus had been invisible during the Saturday afternoon in question.[6]

Captain Edward J. Ruppelt, assigned by the Air Force to study "flying saucers," believed Mantell had been deceived by *Skyhook*, a U.S. Navy research balloon released that very morning from the Clinton Air Force Base in Ohio. Stiff wind currents at that time blowing from the north may have pushed *Skyhook* over Louisville. But in fact this balloon was sighted by two men separated by hundreds of miles; one in Kentucky, the other in Tennessee. They clearly and correctly identified the same object through their telescopes as a large balloon. If it traveled in a straight line between both observers, *Skyhook's* flight path would have taken it nowhere near Louisville on January 7. Additionally, no balloon could stop in midair and hold its position directly over Godman Field for more than two hours, especially given the strong winds blowing there at the time.

To be sure, officers and men on the ground saw something entirely different through their powerful field binoculars. They were, moreover, intimately familiar with weather and research balloons and quite capable of readily distinguishing them from everything else in the sky. Captain Mantell's in-flight description bore no resemblance to that of a balloon. He said, for example, that the object he followed was "of tremendous size." *Skyhook* was more than forty feet shorter than the wingspan of B-29 *Superfortress* heavy bombers with which he had been acquainted for four years. Mantell also said that the contact appeared "to be a metallic object, or possibly a reflection of sun from a metallic object." *Skyhook* balloons were translucently white and unable to accelerate from a stationary position to speeds between 180 and 385 mph within a few minutes, as he reported, even in the grip of the most powerful jet stream. It was not without cause that Air Force officials never used a misidentified research balloon as an excuse for Captain Mantell's crash. A World War II veteran of the Normandy invasion, he was known as "a very cautious pilot," with 2,867 hours of flight time, with 67 of them in the F-51.[7] Yet this careful, experienced airman was said to have hallucinated and passed out for lack of oxygen when he foolishly exceeded the 15,000-foot-altitude upper limits of human consciousness.

As long before as World War I, aviators routinely climbed 5,000 feet higher, for short duration periods with little or no side effects. Typically, a skilled flyer can function reasonably well at that altitude for up to ten minutes. British ace James McCudden, awarded the Victoria Cross for his fifty-seven aerial victories in World War I, often flew solo missions above 15,000 feet and up to 20,000 feet in his Royal Aircraft Factory S.E.5, a pursuit plane, without oxygen. He once recalled that after two hours' patrol at 18,000–20,000 feet, his only complaint was a 24-hour headache. Imperial Germany's Rumpler C.VI *Rubild* was a photoreconaissance biplane with an oxygen supply so unreliable its two-man crew was only able to suck sips of it at a time. Yet they flew the *Rubild* to just below 24,000 feet on a regular basis throughout 1918.

Mantell's radioed promise limiting his stay at 25,000 feet to ten minutes was within the operational purview of a pilot more experienced than his two wingmen, who, increasingly oxygen-deprived, lagged far behind. One of them, First Lieutenant Albert Clements, was at least able to "discern a bright-appearing object . . . slightly lower and to the left of the sun," before peeling away and returning to Godman Field.[8]

Why then, did Captain Mantell fatally lose control of his aircraft? His last transmission was recorded at 3:15. Recovered from the wreckage, his perfectly preserved wristwatch had unaccountably stopped just three minutes later, at least five minutes before the F-51 struck the ground. What happened at 3:18? If the captain had blacked out, he only nodded off for a second or two, because crash investigators determined that Mantell had tried to regain control of his airplane by throttling back the engine, adjusting the fuel mixture, and altering propeller pitch. The time he took to follow these standard emergency procedures suggests that he was not unconscious, but fully conscious for all or virtually all of his descent. Instead of passing out, had his aircraft been disabled by a UFO's electromagnetic surge, as others had been from World War II hence?

Ruppelt stated "that many at TID [Technical Intelligence Division, USAF] had adopted the 'interplanetary' option by the end of the investigation [into Mantell's crash], because all others were exhausted."[9] Indeed an extraterrestrial cause was the most logical explanation. Scott Ramsey tells how an anonymous physicist (almost certainly, John Torrance Tate) drew a conclusion concerning the form of weaponry operated by these vehicles, on the basis of at least four alien wrecks recovered by the U.S. Navy and Army from 1941 to 1948: "The craft had a way of demagnetizing any object that came in contact with it, hostile or otherwise. He speculated that the demagnetizing, or degaussing, would destroy or disintegrate any object in the path of the craft."[10]

His supposition was borne out in numerous Second World War reports of sudden power outages, electrical failures, avionic anomalies, inoperable instruments, whirling compasses, radio communication breakdowns, and a variety of dangerous electromagnetic disturbances experienced by aircrews of every combatant nation whenever their warplanes were approached by the foo fighters. Something of the kind happened to Mantell's F-51 (as can be inferred from his stopped wristwatch), because Air Force investigators were never able to find anything among the fighter's remains they could identify as having caused the crash. It was as though the aircraft had inexplicably ceased to function in midair, and nothing he could do would save it from breaking up between 20,000 and 10,000 feet while disintegrating in its helpless plunge.

The alien intruder Mantell had been ordered to intercept stood fixed in the sky over Godman Airfield for another thirty minutes after his death before it was lost to view by 3:50. It was not the only such craft seen that day, an observation that underscored the extraterrestrial character of the captain's lethal encounter.

A full ninety minutes prior to Mantell's visual contact with the object—half an hour before it was even first spotted by Sergeant Quinton Blackwell—Kentucky state police received multiple reports of a large, unidentified vehicle flying over Maysville, just eighty miles east of Louisville. It was sighted again twenty minutes later at 1:35, this time west of Louisville and Godman Tower. Civilian eyewitnesses described a silver disk without insignia, 250–300 feet in diameter, moving silently and slowly at no more than 1,000 feet above the towns of Owensboro and Irvington. Their sighting complemented Captain Mantell's radioed comment that the object he saw was "of tremendous size."

Four hours after Mantell crashed, officers at Ohio's Clinton County Air Force Base, outside Wilmington reported seeing a bright light in the night sky "dancing" up and down, while changing color from red to green, before shooting off into the southwest at beyond supersonic speed, trailing exhaust.[11] In addition, a red light on the object hovering high over Louisville had been noted by some of the Godman Field observers the previous afternoon. Shortly following the Clinton County sighting, around 7:35, Lockbourne Air Force Base, in Columbus, Ohio, was being speedily circled by a luminous sphere that fell from the heavens, likewise trailing an exhaust, this one amber-colored. Having completed three circuits of the entire base at approximately 1,000 feet, the object streaked straight up at terrific velocity, coming to a dead stop just beneath low cloud cover. It hung motionless there for about a minute, then plummeted back down to earth, poised a few yards above the ground. After another ten seconds, the sphere rose swiftly, returning momentarily to its previous position below the overcast sky from which it vanished away in the blink of an eye toward the northwest.[12]

These remarkable daylight and after-dark sightings made by his fellow Air Force officers bracketed Captain Mantell's crash. In doing so, they indicated that it had been brought about by close proximity to an off-world craft. Whether the craft had deliberately downed his airplane or he had inadvertently strayed within the alien vessel's overpowering electromagnetic field, his death was avenged eleven weeks later, when Secretary Forrestal's weaponized radar claimed another extraterrestrial kill, 375 miles northwest of the earlier intercept at Roswell.

Before day dawned on March 25, New Mexico police officer Manuel Sandoval looked up into the dark sky to see a large circular or oval object moving slowly and silently about 100 feet above the ground toward the Four Corners area, where the states of Arizona, Colorado, New Mexico, and Utah meet. The large vehicle seemed to be in trouble, almost out of control, "wobbling as it flew," according to another eyewitness, Telesforo Archuleta, who saw sparks jump from the vehicle's rim as it scraped the side of a mesa.[13] The object coasted to a stop on the broad summit of another flat plateau above Hart Canyon Road, not far from the small town of Aztec. A few ranchers and men from the El Paso Oil Company had observed something gradually coming down in the remote tableland and told their friends, who converged on the mesa shortly before sunrise.

The inert wreck they beheld was a metallic, lens-shaped, one-hundred-foot-wide disk, "with no noticeable seams, rivets, bolts, or weld marks," according to Doug Noland, one of the oil-field workers. "It looked as though it was molded," and comprised "a very thin cross section, only about eighteen to twenty feet high, but very thin at the outer edges," including "gold-color rings—three, if I remember correctly—that ran around the entire outer edge of the disc. . . . I could see no damage to the craft at all. It was lying at an angle, as though it was lying on the ground with no support, but it had a bubble or reverse dome on the bottom that was giving it support."[14]

"It sort of reminded me," stated another witness, Ken Farley, "of two pie pans with a bubble for a top and bottom. The top bubble was larger than the bottom. The craft was lying at an angle, maybe twelve degrees or so."[15]

Noland and his companions not only touched the object, but climbed on it. "The craft was brushed aluminum, looking to be very smooth, but not highly polished aluminum, like you see on an airplane. . . . The windows or portholes looked like mirrors until you would look closer; then you could see through them." He and the others peered through to see two small bodies "slumped over what appeared to be a control panel of sorts." Fourteen more diminutive corpses were found on another level deeper inside the vessel. Each of them was identical: about four feet tall, with spindly arms and legs extending from an unathletic torso topped with a bulbous head featuring impenetrably dark, oversized eyes.[16]

Moments after his sighting, Archuleta had notified Kirtland Air Force Base in Albuquerque, 180 miles to the southeast, of the incident by telephone. So the eventual appearance of military personnel at the Hart Canyon site was no surprise, at least to him. Flying in on Sikorsky H-5 and Bell H-13 *Sioux* helicopters, they commanded the spectators to leave at once after harshly ordering them never to discuss the crash with anyone. As far as everyone was supposed to be concerned, it never happened. Noland remembered, "We were threatened with our lives if we ever spoke of this."[17]

The authorities did more than terrorize a few local residents into submission. They engaged in a disinformation campaign commensurate with the magnitude of discovery at Aztec. Never before or since had such a detailed, up-close, firsthand description of an off-world vehicle come down to us. Never before or since have so many physical remains of its alien occupants been retrieved from a single location. Accordingly, such evidence was so thoroughly misrepresented to the general public at large that most ufologists, professional and amateur alike, dismissed the Hart Canyon controversy as a self-evident hoax, until it was virtually forgotten. Even Hall, in his encyclopedic *UFOs: A Century of*

Sightings, never once mentions Aztec. Not until sixty-eight years after the event were the results of its most exhaustive investigation published by Scott Ramsey, a specialist in magnetic fields (appropriately enough) and electrical wire, together with his wife, Suzanne, a radio-show hostess, and Frank Thayer, Ph.D., professor emeritus at New Mexico State University.

> Our research is a compilation of work gathered for almost twenty-nine years. In that time, we have traveled to more than twenty-eight states; personally spent $500,000; and archived fifty-five thousand documents from sources including the United States Army, United States Air Force, FBI and CIA, and directly from the desk of J. Edgar Hoover.[18]

The Aztec UFO Incident not only confirms beyond question that it actually took place, but explains what occurred thereafter. "We are certain from all reports we have examined," write the authors, "that both the U.S. Army and U.S. Air Force were involved in the Aztec recovery. The separation between the two services was still very new, so a joint effort made perfect sense."[19] They quote a physicist involved who spoke anonymously about the craft's transference to Los Alamos, where his colleagues and aeronautical engineers found it had been originally constructed of segments "fitted in grooves, and were pinned together around the base." As for the deceased "little people" aboard, "some of them had been dissected and studied by the medical divisions of the Air Force."[20]

The abundance of information presented by the authors indicates the cause of the Hart Canyon crash: "This object had been reported as flying over the top secret Los Alamos National Laboratory, northeast of Cuba [a New Mexico town not far from Aztec], and around the Los Alamos radar facility near El Vado, as well. This craft was something the military, as well as the Atomic Energy Commission, would have to take very seriously, and would have been as much a threat as a Soviet spy plane or bomber; yet the saucer's fantastic performance characteristics made it very difficult to bring it down."[21] That is, until Secretary Forrestal weaponized New Mexico's radar arrays.

"Two *tenescopes* caught this unidentified ship," according to the unnamed physicist, "as it came into our atmosphere. They watched its position and estimated where it would land." Then, when it slowed within range of America's chief nuclear facility, the vessel was blasted with lethal beams of high-intensity microwave energy. Police officer Sandoval described the disk during its last moments of flight as "wobbly and seemed to be fluttering as a leaf," before it crashed on the Hart Canyon mesa. His eyewitness report suggests the piloting skills of its occupants, dying of their radioactive burns, were rapidly deteriorating. Noland later remarked, on seeing their corpses, that they were "charred a dark brown. I mean, they did not appear to be of dark skin—just seemed to have been exposed to heat."[22]

Noland also observed how "the interior of the craft was not burned," comparing conditions with the baking chamber of a microwave oven, which cooks food placed in it without affecting its wall surfaces. They "seemed to be charred a very dark, chocolate color," the nameless physicist confirmed, "their bodies had been burned. . . . The simple fact was that there they were dead from either burns or the bends." Another area resident on the scene, Baptist preacher Solon Brown, recalled that "the little bodies had passed on, as they seemed to have been burned."[23]

The Ramseys and Thayer wonder if the disk outside Aztec "crashed or was shot down," just as Roswell's two extraterrestrial spacecraft were "possible shoot-downs."[24] The condition of the alien bodies—which accorded with radioactive poisoning—at both sites in proximity to Forrestal's microwave artillery at El Vado and associated radar stations indicated a deliberate, successful attack against otherworldly vehicles in the ongoing conflict between earthly armed forces and otherworldly intruders. Americans have long been accustomed to waging covert wars, and this one was no different, at least in terms of secrecy. Until now, our enemies were always mortal men, and strategists could anticipate human nature. But how does one prepare against a nonhuman foe?

11

Cat-and-Mouse Encounters

We only have to look at ourselves to see how intelligent life
might develop into something we would not want to meet.
STEPHEN HAWKING[1]

The Hart Canyon crash triggered an intense spate of UFO sightings by civilians and military personnel around the world. Six days after that incident, USAAF first lieutenant Robert W. Meyers was flying a Republic P-47 *Thunderbolt* in clear daylight with unlimited visibility 1,500 feet over the central Philippines during a routine training mission with three other *Thunderbolt* pilots from the 67th Fighter Group. At 9:55 a.m., Meyers noticed a kind of flying wing with a "turtle back" traveling beneath them at about 200 miles per hour, just 500 feet over the surface of the Pacific Ocean. He tried to alert his students to the 30-foot-wide "half-moon," but his radio had suddenly become inoperable. Theirs had ceased to function at the same time, so everyone communicated by sign language and wing waggling.

Hand-gesturing to his charges to maintain their position, Meyers broke formation with a rapidly descending 240-degree left turn in pursuit of the strange craft. His itchy trigger finger was on the control-stick button, which could instantly unleash a volley of .50-caliber rounds from eight M2 Browning machine guns mounted in the leading edge of the P-47's wings. The silvery boomerang, topped only by a small dorsal fin, evidenced no power units, exhaust trails, cockpit, or landing gear. Abruptly accelerating, the unidentified vehicle was out of visual range within the next five seconds.

After Meyers reported his encounter, an Air Force intelligence officer described him as a "reliable, non-excitable individual, who appeared quite positive about his statements."[2]

Three days following Meyers's April 1 experience, a golden-hued, white sphere, "slightly concave on top," passed high over New Mexico's Holloman Air Force Base at "tremendous speed" for about thirty seconds after executing "at least one vertical loop."[3]

Otherwise quick to explain away such things as wayward weather balloons caught in strong winds, Air Force public relations could not dismiss this sighting so handily because it had been made by three men professionally trained as balloon spotters at Holloman's own Geophysics Laboratory Section. They observed that the object's violent maneuvers far surpassed the stress limitations of any known aircraft, let alone a balloon, which was additionally incapable of flying against the wind, as the spheroid had done. Its only similarity to a balloon was a complete absence of sound, as confirmed by highly sensitive 400-meter atmospheric noise receivers at the base.

Six days later, another soundless craft, as reported by USAAF first lieutenant Aytch M. Johnson Jr., appeared in clear skies with unrestricted visibility over Fairbanks, Alaska, on the early afternoon of April 18, 1948. He stated that an "oscillating, round and flat object" approached the 375th VLR Weather Squadron out of the northwest, traveling 250 to 300 miles per hour at around 2,000 feet, at 1:06 p.m., twice jumping 500 feet in one or two seconds, before vanishing into the southwest.[4]

During the early morning of July 24, crew chief Walter Massey witnessed a brightly self-illuminated, "cylindrical shaped object with a long stream of fire coming out of its tail end" as it traversed the dark sky over Robins Air Force Base in Macon, Georgia, at 1:45 a.m.[5] One hour earlier, an identically reported craft flew on a collision course with Eastern Airlines flight 576, twenty miles southwest of Montgomery,

Alabama. Approaching at 5,000 feet and approximately 800 miles per hour, it missed the twin-engine DC-3's right wing by about 700 feet. Much nearer the object than Massey, Captain Clarence S. Chiles and First Officer John B. Whitted could see how its underside was lit with a "deep blue glow," while the midsection featured "two rows of windows from which bright lights glowed," and a "fifty-foot trail of orange-red flame" shot out the back of the vehicle. Their close-quarter observation disqualified the object as a missile, as some skeptics believed it must have been.[6]

Sightings such as these persisted into fall 1948, when an encounter second only in curiosity to that year's Aztec crash involved a North Dakota Air National Guard pilot as he attempted an after-dark landing at the Fargo airport. As George F. Gorman was making final approach around 9:00 p.m. on October 1, a "blinking light" making "remarkable revolutions" veered within 3,000 feet of his F-51. He canceled his landing and gunned the Stallion's 1,720-horsepower Packard engine in pursuit of the luminous orb. It did not try to escape, but flipped around, then charged at him. Gorman yanked the control stick to narrowly avoid colliding, followed by the tightest turn an F-51 could make, rounding on the object. It bounced out of his gun sights to get on his tail, and he dove away. For twenty-seven minutes the two vehicles jousted in the night skies of North Dakota, neither able to secure a firing advantage over the other.

"Each time Gorman tried to turn around and pursue," writes Hall, "he found it necessary to make an extensive series of turns, only to end up repeating the same scenario all over again."[7]

The nimble orb was also faster than Gorman's 437-mile-per-hour fighter. Their inconclusive duel was observed by a pair of pilots in a Piper J-3 *Cub* light aircraft circling below the action, and by the chief of Fargo's control tower, watching through binoculars. What became known to ufologists as the Gorman Dogfight ended in a draw, when the "blinking light" shot away vertically at an impossible speed to disappear among the stars in a matter of two or three seconds. Upon landing, four different Geiger counters revealed that the metal skin of his F-51

Figure 11.1. An F-51 similar to the *Stallion* flown in the Gorman Dogfight.

had been exposed to higher than normal levels of radioactivity, although Gorman himself suffered no ill effects.

Other Air Force pilots continued to file reports of sightings and sometimes of similar dogfights from around the world, including the first exclusively radar-visual contact made by the three-man crew of a Northrop P-61 *Black Widow* night fighter, the first American aircraft specifically designed to use such a tracking system. Flying out of the USAF 68th Squadron based in Japan during the night of October 15, 1948, the *Black Widow* closed on an unidentified contact traveling approximately 220 miles per hour, 2,305 feet over the city of Fukuoka, in clear, moonlit conditions. At 11:05 p.m., the object accelerated instantly to an incredible 1,200 mph—almost three times faster than the 366 mph airplane—while impossibly executing a split-S maneuver in a 180-degree turn that took it directly beneath the *Black Widow.*

The object then virtually jumped nine miles away, where it held a stationary position. When the lumbering fighter-bomber finally caught up with it, the craft literally shot another nine miles ahead, waiting again for the pursuing airmen in their P-61 to catch up. Three times more "the same scenario took place," writes Hall, "as if the strange machine was playing a game with them."[8] Apparently bored with this amusement, it eventually rose at terrific speed to vanish off their radar screen within seconds.

Perhaps the ufonauts wanted to demonstrate their astronomically huge technological edge over earthbound aircraft. Or perhaps they just wanted to play tag with the *Black Widow,* as its crew members believed.

If so, something of that alien whimsy recurred March 17, 1949, over the Killeen Base of Camp Hood, Texas, located halfway between Austin and Waco. It was here that Air Force authorities, under a gathering storm of political pressure to either definitively disclose or debunk the extraterrestrial *cause célèbre,* instructed Captain Horace McCulloch to replicate a typical UFO sighting with flares, which observers sometimes compared with off-world craft. If he could put on a convincing show of military pyrotechnics the persistent and troublesome controversy might be finally and conclusively put to rest.

As assistant G-2 (secret intelligence) of the 2nd Armored Division, McCulloch was skilled in deception, and he was confident that the test he designed would be sufficiently persuasive for staging repeated demonstrations on behalf of America's public-information services. The national press, newsreels, and television were expected to offer these fiery displays as visual proof that Americans were mistaking common signal rockets for flying saucers. At 7:52 p.m., as the captain and his squad were finalizing the first group of standard-ordnance flares for test-firing, "he and his men themselves saw aerial phenomena" descending from the night sky in the form of "large green, red, and white flare-like objects flying in generally straight lines." The things were seen in "seven separate sightings by trained artillery observers in different locations."⁹

That the flare-like UFOs stole McCulloch's thunder implies that their alien operators had telepathically learned of his test in advance. Preempting him as they did demonstrated an ironic sense of humor.

The UFOs returned to Killeen later that same month, on the thirty-first. During early-morning hours, telephone communications went down after a reddish-white spheroid appeared over Camp Hood's nuclear materials depot. The fastest object of its kind recorded to date was clocked by Professor Charles Moore in the company of his scientific colleagues, U.S. Navy commander R. R. McLaughlin and J. Gordon Vaeth, general supervisor of the Office of Naval Research at White Sands Proving Grounds.

On April 24, at 10:20 a.m., they had just released a small weather balloon when Moore noticed something resembling a tiny white dot hovering high above it at about 5.6 miles altitude. He looked through an ML-47 theodolite, a surveying instrument with a rotating, 25-power telescope for measuring horizontal and vertical angles while taking elevation and azimuth readings. Focusing in on the object floating high over New Mexico, he saw a flat, silver disk 40 feet in diameter and 100 feet long. After a minute or so of observation, the oval object dropped without a sound in front of a mountain range, then just as quickly swung upward into the bright sky and out of sight. Its speed, recorded by the theodolite, was 7 miles per second, or 25,200 miles per hour.¹⁰

A bizarre sighting was made by U.S. Army personnel at Fort Bliss, in El Paso, Texas, during the late morning of May 5. At 11:40, two majors, a captain, and several hundred field artillerymen were in training at the Waco Number 4 desert practice range with concentrated groups of 150-millimeter howitzers when an oblong white disk suddenly swooped down from the sky and dove directly into their field of fire. It passed amid the intense hail of bursting shells for 30 to 50 seconds before emerging unscathed to fly away at phenomenal speed in the company of another disk.

Like the *Black Widow* fighter-bomber's encounter the previous

Figure 11.2. A *Twin Mustang*.

October, the aliens may have wanted to impress the Army with their technological superiority. One of them nonetheless fled from a North American F-82 *Twin Mustang,* the last piston-driven fighter ordered into production by the USAF. The plane had been dispatched on the afternoon of May 21 from Moses Lake Army Air Force Base in Washington State, to intercept a silver disc "visually sighted by crew and personnel from the Hanford radar station and confirmed on radar . . . hovering in restricted airspace over the Hanford Atomic Plant at an altitude of seventeen thousand to twenty thousand feet."[11] America's first nuclear factory was still under extraterrestrial surveillance.

Even more harassed by off-world machines was Camp Hood, where base commanders were determined to put a stop to the intruders. For three minutes after 6:05 p.m. on June 6, civilian observers "tracked a hovering orange object about thirty to seventy feet in diameter . . . one mile above ground, three miles south of the observation post." The alien spacecraft began slowly "moving in level flight, then exploded in a shower of particles."[12]

Although eyewitnesses were too far from the action to see what sort of weapon had been fired at the obliterated target, its effectiveness was beyond doubt. Why the intruder had been so quickly and thoroughly destroyed by ground forces was perplexingly contrasted with the death-defying gauntlet of detonating howitzer shells run with impunity by an alien disk the month before. Perhaps, some ufologists speculated, the unsuspecting alien captain of the Camp Hood kill had let his guard down by failing to lower the same kind of impenetrable shields the May 5 spacecraft apparently activated at Fort Bliss.

A prominent scientist at the time who sighted an off-world craft was Clyde W. Tombaugh, discoverer of the dwarf planet Pluto in 1930. Nineteen years later, six or eight rectangular, blue-green lights swiftly but noiselessly flew in a geometrically-spaced formation over the back-yard of Tombaugh's home in Las Cruces, New Mexico, around 9:45,

Figure 11.3.
Clyde W. Tombaugh
(1906–1997).

on August 20. "I have done thousands of hours of night sky-watching," Tombaugh stated, "but never saw a sight so strange as this."[13] Judging from his description of the "geometrically-spaced" lights, they may not have been individual objects flying in a fixed pattern, but fixtures in the underside of a single large vehicle. In any case, growing numbers of sightings such as his were making Air Force officials increasingly nervous. Nor were alien spacecraft invariably the benign apparitions Tombaugh witnessed.

On the night of January 22, 1950, U.S. Navy lieutenant Ronald Smith was piloting a routine security flight near the Bering Sea, at Kodiak, Alaska. At 4:40 a.m., a blip on his radarscope traveled so fast it left a trail across the screen. He alerted crew members, who immediately sighted the target close a 5-mile gap in 10 seconds at 1,800 miles per hour. It then executed a 180-degree turn to aim directly at the patrol plane. Smith "considered this to be a highly threatening gesture," and switched off his aircraft lights as the luminous object, narrowly missing a head-on collision, vanished into the night.[14]

Near misses such as this one contributed to increasing anxiety throughout the Air Force. Midmorning, March 8, 1950, saw America's most important military installation go on full alert, sirens screaming, when radar operators confirmed a contact—as solid as it was unidentified—on a determined heading for Ohio's Wright-Patterson Air Force Base. F-51 interceptors were scrambled, including two from the Air National Guard. Not long after takeoff, their pilots made visual contact with the intruder, which they described as spherical, "huge and metallic." It chose not to engage them, however, and escaped into the clouds at high speed.[15]

Later that month, a gigantic B-36 became the target of harassment by a much smaller alien vehicle while flying over Texas Naval Air Station, in Dallas. The largest mass-produced piston-engine aircraft in aviation history, with the longest wingspan of any combat warplane ever built (230 feet), Convair's 131-ton *Peacemaker* contrasted with the diminutive, 40-foot-wide spacecraft that repeatedly buzzed it shortly before noon on August 16.

Figure 11.4. A B-36 (right) in scale with a B-29 and airfield personnel.

Gunners defending the B-36 were ordered to withhold fire, even when the pestiferous silver disk came up threateningly under the belly of the behemoth before breaking off its shadowboxing and flying away within two or three seconds. The monstrous *Peacemaker's* confrontation with the unknown was the last of these cat-and-mouse encounters between fast-flying aliens and the United States Air Force, whose commanders were then gearing up for their own terrestrial conflict.[16]

PART FOUR

Mid-Twentieth-Century Encounters

12

The Korean War Era

During the Korean War, both American and Korean pilots reported encounters with flying saucers.
BURKE JOSSLIN, *KOREA HERALD* STAFF REPORTER[1]

"This event that I am about to relate to you is the truth," Francis P. Wall told John Timmerman, an associate of the J. Allen Hynek Center for UFO Studies in Chicago, "so help me God."[2]

Following their January 1987 interview, noted UFO researcher Richard F. Haines checked U.S. Army records, which listed Wall as a private first class Korean War veteran assigned to the unit he described. It belonged to the 25th Infantry Division, 27th Regiment, 2nd Battalion, "Easy" Company, stationed in North Korea's Ch'ŏrwŏn County, Kangwŏn province, known as the Iron Triangle for the heavy artillery barrages it suffered. During the night of April 18, 1951, Wall and his comrades were in position on the slopes of a mountain overlooking a small village that had recently been abandoned prior to its bombardment by American guns. As shelling commenced, Wall stated:

> We suddenly noticed, on our right-hand side, what appeared to be a jack-o-lantern come wafting down across the mountain. And at first no one thought anything about it. So we noticed that this thing

continued on down to the village to where, indeed, the artillery air bursts were exploding. It had an orange glow in the beginning. We further noticed that this object was [so] quick that it could get into the center of an airburst of artillery, and yet remain unharmed.

The infantrymen observed the strange performances for almost an hour.

But then this object approached us. And it turned a blue-green brilliant light. It's hard to distinguish the size of it; there's no way to compare it. The light was pulsating. This object approached us.

I asked for and received permission from Lt. Evans, our company commander at that time, to fire upon this object, which I did with an M-1 rifle, with armor-piercing bullets. And I did hit it. It must have been metallic, because you could hear when the projectile slammed into it.

Now why would that bullet damage this craft if the artillery rounds didn't? I don't know, unless they [the occupants of the "jack-o'-lantern"] had dropped their protective field around them, or whatever. But the object went wild, and the light was going on and off. It went off completely once, briefly. And it was moving erratically from side to side as though it might crash to the ground. Then, a sound—we had heard no sound previous to this—the sound of, like, diesel locomotives revving up. That's the way this thing sounded.

And then, we were attacked. We were swept by some form of a ray that was emitted in pulses, in waves that you could visually see only when it was aiming directly at you. That is to say, like a searchlight sweeps around and . . . you would see it coming at you. Now you would feel a burning, tingling sensation all over your body, as though something were penetrating you.

So the company commander, Lt. Evans, hauled us into our bunkers. We didn't know what was going to happen. We were scared. These are underground dugouts where you have peep holes to look out to fire at the enemy. So, I'm in my bunker with another man.

We're peeping out at this thing. It hovered over us for a while, lit up the whole area with its light, and then I saw it shoot off at a 45 degree angle, that quick, just there and gone. That quick. And it was as though that was the end of it.

But, three days later the entire company of men had to be evacuated by ambulance. They had to cut roads in there and haul them out. They were too weak to walk. They had dysentery. Then subsequently, when the doctors did see them, they had an extremely high white blood cell count, which the doctors could not account for.

Wall and his comrades decided not to report the incident to their superior officers, "because," he said, "they'd lock every one of us up and think we were crazy." [3]

As Wall's experience shows, UFO experiences during the Korean War era differed from World War II encounters in that the enigmatic objects interacted with military personnel on the ground as well as in the air over Asia and America.

On the late afternoon of September 19, 1950, not three months after President Truman ordered U.S. air and sea forces to defend the South Korean regime against Communist invasion from the north, police stations and newspaper offices across five counties in southeast Missouri were deluged with telephone calls and telegrams reporting "a translucent silver sphere" or an object having "a bright gold center with lavender edges," hovering over Poplar Bluff, a small city of fifteen thousand residents. [4]

The nearest Air Force base, located outside Memphis, Tennessee, about 145 miles due south, was notified and immediately dispatched an F-51 fighter flown by Lieutenant Claude Haverty to investigate the sighting. He soon made visual contact of his own. The object, he reported, was "like a big silver marble" that moved off at his approach to the town of Malden, 30 miles to the southeast, then proceeded at an altitude between 60,000 and 80,000 feet over the New Madrid area, at the Illinois border. "Its behavior was reported as hovering stationary to moving at a terrific rate of speed after it turned its lights on," writes reporter Bryce Baker. "The object also made no sound and left no exhaust trail."[5]

Running low on fuel, Haverty broke off pursuit, but only after confirming that the metallic contact moving under its own power was not a weather balloon, as his superior officers initially suspected and afterward announced. They ordered his replacement, another F-51, into the air at once. By the time Lieutenant Donald Soefker arrived over New Madrid, the object had gradually descended to 40,000 feet. He got a good, long look at the "spherical and elliptical shape" before it took off vertically at an astounding velocity, vanishing almost instantaneously into the bright, clear afternoon sky. Looking up after its disappearance, Soefker saw a small but indefinite number of "white and green lights above him . . . [they] appeared to move in bursts of extremely high speed northward," according to a report in the *Southeast Missourian*.[6] Less than twenty-four hours later, a passenger plane flying over Poplar Bluff toward Memphis was narrowly missed by a speeding object in the same airspace where lieutenants Haverty and Soefker had encountered the silvery sphere the previous afternoon. "I was flying at eighteen thousand feet," reported American Airlines captain Garman, "and it looked as though it just came across our nose. I tell you, I never saw such a brilliant flash of light before. No, it wasn't a clear light. It seemed to be burning with an orange, yellow, and blue flame. I tell you, it lit up the whole sky."[7]

At that same moment, 1:35 a.m., a terrific explosion in the night sky was heard by many thousands of persons on the ground across southeastern Missouri and southwestern Illinois, into Kentucky and parts of Tennessee. Later that same morning, at 10:19, a specimen of the latest Air Force jet fighter slammed into a hillside near Piedmont, Missouri, forty miles northwest of Poplar Bluff. Although the F-89 was totally destroyed, pilot Lieutenant Logan MacMillan ejected in time and was able to walk to the nearest post office, where he telephoned his superior officers back at their Memphis-area base. They restricted all public information about the crash to a terse press release explaining that no one was injured and no property damaged.

Figure 12.1. A Northrop F-89 *Scorpion*.

Northrop's *Scorpion* was an all-weather interceptor, the first jet fighter designed as such. More interesting to alien intelligence, perhaps, it was also the first combat aircraft armed with air-to-air nuclear weapons, the unguided *Genie* rocket. While Air Force spokesmen dismissed Poplar Bluff's "big silver marble" as a wayward weather balloon, and determined that Lieutenant Soefker's sighting of white and green lights at high altitude did not merit comment, astronomers told how Captain Garman and tens of thousands of persons over a four-state area experienced a falling "meteor," and the crashed F-89 was given short shrift in the local press.

But no officials could explain how all these events could have been centered in southeastern Missouri within the same eighteen-hour period. The Northrop *Scorpion* appears to have been downed by either the big silver marble or its escorting white and green lights, probably, as many previous accounts indicate, through disabling the jet fighter's avionics. This supposition is underscored by the craft's nuclear-weapons capabilities—an apparent sore point with extra-terrestrial sensitivities. If this is the case, then it was the first such attack of the Korean Conflict era.

That epoch's war in the air with off-world vehicles was mostly char-acterized by near misses aggressively initiated by UFOs seemingly bent on collision courses. The first such confrontation took place during the evening of November 7, 1950, a little more than four months after hostilities began, not over Korea, but east of Lakehurst, New Jersey. U.S. Navy lieutenant junior grade Robert Haven was piloting a Douglas AD-4Q *Skyraider* ground-attack bomber at 3,500 feet, when, at 7:15 p.m., he noticed a steady white light to his right, about 500 feet higher and some 5 miles away, heading toward the southeast. As he made a slight climbing turn to the left to get on the tail of the object, it abruptly came around in a 100 degree sweep, diving directly at him from 4,000 feet—too fast for Haven to execute an evasive maneuver.

Bracing for impact, he watched helplessly as the luminous spher-oid flashed over his cockpit canopy at 200 feet. Uniquely for so close a pass at such high velocity, neither wash nor slipstream trailed the object, which traveled at almost 900 mph, then slowed to less than half that speed. Undaunted, Haven pulled the *Skyraider* over in the tightest right turn it could make in order to pursue the unidentifiable craft. It sud-denly climbed to 2,000 feet per minute, looped around and came back yet again at the AD-4Q, which narrowly maneuvered out of harm's way. Thrice more, Lieutenant Haven and his otherworldly opponent banked and charged, though his target assiduously avoided drifting within fir-ing range of the *Skyraider's* four 20-millimeter AN/M3 auto-cannons. During their wild skirmish, it seemed clear to him that the spher-oid's pilot was determined to collide, and only disengaged at around 11,500 feet with the approach of USAF interceptors. In a matter of sec-onds, the object shot vertically to 25,000 feet, where it disappeared.[8]

A similar "fireball" dove on and nearly struck a North American F-86D *Sabrejet* over Hungnam, in the Hamyong-Namdo province, during the first such tangle over North Korea, in the midafternoon of October 12, 1952. Shots had been fired the previous summer, after radar at a secret USAF installation detected an unidentified aircraft approaching from the northeast at Mach 1, about 70 mph faster than the world's fastest fighter. But unlike that episode, this time, the UFO

Figure 12.2. North American F-86D *Sabrejet* fighters.

instantaneously dropped its speed from 770 mph to a mere 100 mph as it neared the airfield, where a pair of *Sabrejets* was scrambled.

As the jets climbed to 40,000 feet, the intruder slipped from radar screens, perhaps in an evasive descent. Tower operators ordered one of the pilots to maintain altitude at 20,000 feet, while the other dove to 5,000 feet; it was hoped that between the two of them, they might make visual contact with the target. Sure enough, the F-86 assigned to the lower altitude began converging on a silver-metallic object that looked "like a doughnut with no hole in the middle."[9]

It gradually picked up speed, but as the *Sabrejet* continued to gain on the UFO, the pilot's efforts to alert first his higher-flying wingman and then the base failed after his radio inexplicably died. Pushing his aircraft to its performance limits, he was only 1,500 feet behind the speeding "doughnut," just within firing range of his six machine guns. Realizing he could not hold that distance much longer, the pilot unloosed a stream of .50-caliber rounds at the intruder, which escaped vertically into the sky at an incalculably high rate of speed.

Back in the United States, the following December 4, a glowing object rapidly ascended toward USAF lieutenant Robert Arnold's North American T-28 *Trojan,* approximately 6,000 feet over Laredo, Texas. He caught sight of the bright, bluish-white light at 8:46 p.m., and put the *Trojan* trainer in a tight left turn to get a better look at it. As he did so, the object leapt in seconds to 3,000 feet above him, then dropped down to his altitude, flying eastward to a point in the evening sky where it paused as though it had been nailed among the stars. Two seconds later, it suddenly flew at him head-on at high speed, "wavering slightly at about three hundred feet, as if determining which side to pass the aircraft."[10]

The mysterious light missed Arnold's left wing by no more than 150 feet in a blurred, reddish-bluish haze somewhat shorter than the 33-foot length of his T-28. Fearing renewed attack, he turned off the *Trojan's* running lights while spiraling down to 1,500 feet. The object came about and dove on him once more, but after a few seconds inexplicably broke off pursuit, pulled up, and climbed out of sight at 9:53. Lieutenant Arnold's ordeal had lasted a full seven minutes.

Hanford, Washington's much-reconnoitered nuclear power plant was again the focus of alien scrutiny on December 10. Over the facility, at about 7:15 p.m., between 26,000 and 27,000 feet, hovered a large white sphere with reddish light behind two apparent portholes. The airborne ARC-33 radar of a dispatched Lockheed F-94 *Starfire*—America's first day-or-night, all-weather jet fighter—locked on the contact, which was visually confirmed by both crew members multiple times. Seemingly annoyed by such persistent scanning, the object abruptly rushed at the *Starfire,* which banked at the last moment to avoid a collision. The off-world craft proceeded on its way, disappearing around 7:30 p.m.[11]

Also on December 10, yet another near collision occurred over Hungnam, North Korea, when a U.S. Navy pilot's Grumman F9F *Panther Jet* was almost grazed by an orange fireball. The previous May 31, before sunrise, another *Starfire* pilot had himself initiated two separate head-on attacks against "a round, brilliant, bluish-white light" sighted earlier by ground observers. In his own words, he "descended in a port turn to intercept an unidentified object 6,000 feet below [his position], on a 90-degree turn course and an altitude of eight thousand feet."[12]

As he did so, the light began a port climb to intercept his descending F-94, thereby silhouetting the Lockheed jet against the dawn light. To extricate himself from this vulnerable position, the *Starfire* pilot hit its afterburner. During the ensuing dogfight, neither opponent was able to get astern of the other. After several more inconclusive passes, the off-world craft disengaged by increasing its speed, departing on a 45-degree heading.

These Korean War–era confrontations were in marked contrast to the foo-fighter encounters of World War II, which were mostly benign. Something had changed. In the first half of the twentieth century, most sightings included relatively small alien craft 100 feet or less in length or diameter. Very few were described as "huge," as Captain Mantell did. That perception too was to change.

U.S. Marine Corps naval aviator Major Donald E. Keyhoe told of an escort carrier (possibly the USS *Rendova*, CVE-114) cruising under an overcast sky off the Korean coast in concert with fourteen other warships. On an undisclosed night in early 1951, the vessel's combat information center (CIC) picked up a bogey that began circling the entire task force under 20,000 feet. The alarm was sounded, and every man rushed to his post at general quarters. Minutes later, Grumman F9Fs were launched through pitch-black conditions into the lightless sky, then were guided

Figure 12.3.
Major Donald E. Keyhoe, USMC.

toward the intruder by radar operators. They were especially perplexed by the *Panther Jet* pilots' inability to find it after almost two hours' flight time, because their scopes indicated that the unidentified contact was larger than the aircraft carrier itself!

Instruments were checked and rechecked again and again; they functioned perfectly, while the colossal target "was tracked by radar operators on all fourteen ships." It continued to leisurely and invisibly circle high overhead, lost to view in the impenetrable darkness, but "neither an attack nor message to bring enemy bombers" was forthcoming. The first wave of interceptors returned to the flight deck, to be replaced in the night air by another squadron, nearly seven hours after the alert had been given.

Flying blind, entirely by instruments, the lead pilot suddenly yelled over his radio, "Target joining up on wingman!" The gargantuan UFO had stopped circling the task force to suddenly swing around behind one of the jets. "Close in for visual on target!" the CIC operator commanded in preparation for orders to commence firing with the *Panther's* four 20-millimeter cannons. Just as the pilot began his turn, the object increased speed, "leaving the plane behind. In less than ten minutes, the radarscopes showed it was two hundred miles away."[13]

Another atypical but relevant encounter occurred in broad daylight far from Korea. During the early afternoon of March 29, 1952, "two, fiery discs" appeared over the uranium mines in the Belgian Congo. After hovering at low altitude for several minutes, the objects zigzagged away toward the northeast. Among their witnesses on the ground was Commander Pierre, local chief officer of the Luchtcomponent, the air arm of the Belgian armed forces, who rushed to the nearby Elizabethville Airport (today's Lubumbashi International Airport). There he took off in a new Dassault M.D.450 *Ouragan* fighter. Ascending at 7,480 feet per minute, he made visual contact with one of the luminous vehicles, describing it as a bright sphere that seemed to irregularly reconfigure itself into "plates, ovals and lines," then back again, before both accelerated away together into the sky.[14]

The presence of these craft over an important source of uranium underscored the aliens' apparent interest in human development of atomic weapons, including numerous UFO encounters over America's nuclear research and production plants, such as Washington state's Hanford facility.

On June 29, E. T. Scoyen, superintendent of Sequoia and Kings National Parks in California, reported a 1,000-foot-wide disk race past the granite-dome formation of Moro Rock to illuminate a nearby canyon with brilliant yellow light. The craft was observed by other park authorities over three days and nights. At that time USAF fighters were stationed in California's southern Sierra Nevada Mountains to intercept the intruder "with extreme prejudice."[15] They had no difficulty visually confirming the immense vehicle flying only a few hundred miles per hour at low altitude, an apparently easy target. The F-51s dove on it, but were afforded no opportunity to fire their .50-caliber machine guns, because the disk instantaneously increased speed far beyond the performance envelope of any earthbound airplane, playfully outmaneuvered its piston-driven pursuers in a kind of mock dogfight, then left them far behind as it streaked away into the sky.

Smaller versions of the gigantic Moro Rock intruder would appear in greater numbers the next month over the nation's capital amid one of the most outstanding sightings ever witnessed. Beginning at 11:40 p.m., on the night of July 19, 1952, air-traffic controllers at Washington, D.C.'s National Airport picked up seven unidentified contacts moving across their radarscopes and heading for the city center. Minutes later, an operator at Tower Central "could see one of the objects from his control tower window." It resembled a "huge, fiery-orange sphere," according to another tower operator. "At one point," writes Hall, "as many as twelve UFOs were simultaneously seen by radars and described as having solid returns."[16] At the same time, communications began going down. Washington, D.C., television station WTOP "experienced interference with its signals," and commercial radio reception was disrupted. As the orange fireballs "were nearing the restricted airspace above the Capitol Building and the White House," fighter jets were scrambled at Delaware's Newcastle Air Force Base.[17]

Lieutenant William Patterson's Lockheed *Starfire* was vectored by ground radar toward a group of intruders. Approaching them, "he saw four, white 'glows,' and closed in for the long-awaited intercept . . . the orb-like lights came right at Patterson and clustered around his aircraft. Desperate for a course of action, Patterson radioed ARTC [Air Route Traffic Control] for assistance. He wanted to know what to do. . . . [There was] a stunned silence among the tower personnel at that moment. No one could say a word. Fortunately, the orbs then pulled away from Patterson's aircraft."[18]

Next day, across the country morning newspapers headlined, "Interceptors Chase Flying Saucers over Washington, DC —Air Force Won't Talk." USAF public-relations officers were in fact speechless, unable to dream up any prosaic explanation for the previous night's events—save the obvious, and they could never admit to that.

Less than two months following one of the single greatest mass sightings of UFOs ever made, a related series of events—different but no less momentous—occurred on the opposite side of the Atlantic. It was set in the largest naval operation since World War II, with the participation of nine countries, fielding two hundred vessels and a thousand aircraft serviced by more than eighty thousand men. This vast array of international armed forces was staged to discourage the Soviet Union from any designs its leaders might have on Western Europe. Although they would be closely monitoring the Allied maneuvers, the Russians were not the only covert observers of Exercise Mainbrace.

Just hours before it began, the Danish coastal destroyer *Willimoes* was patrolling a southeasterly heading ten nautical miles north of the Baltic island of Bornholm, east of Denmark, during the night of September 13, 1952. On watch at the bridge was the ship's second-in-command, Lieutenant Commander George Smidt-Jensen, who was joined by another officer, a journalist covering the maneuvers, and newspaper photographer Mogens Holmberg. At 10:20 p.m. the moonless sky was clear and the sea calm, when all four men simultaneously observed an object approaching at high speed from the southwest.

Passing almost directly overhead at approximately 2,000 feet, the flying triangle was illuminated by three greenish-blue lights, one at each corner, while emitting a softly whistling sound, as it sped in the direction of the naval forces assembled for action at dawn the next day. Smidt-Jensen estimated the delta-shaped craft's speed at 1,500 kilometers per hour (960 mph).[19] Holmberg attempted to photograph the peculiar vehicle, but in his hurried excitement, before he could take a shot he accidentally smashed his camera against a steel bulkhead protruding unseen in the darkness.

Fleet operations began without incident before sunrise and uneventfully fulfilled their objectives over the next week. But on the morning of September 20, sonar operators aboard four American destroyers reported that their warships were being paced by a large, unidentified target less than 100 feet beneath the surface. It was cruising at an incredible 35 knots, or 40 mph—more than twice the underwater speed of any known submarine. In the blink of an eye, the contact vanished from their sonar screens, breaking into the air from the depths of the North Sea before the eyes of startled crew members on deck.

It was a dull-silver metallic disk, "one quarter of a mile wide," remembered Navy veteran Harry Jordan, *one quarter of a mile wide! And it came up out of the water, and it dinged one of the ships, and that was later reported as a collision between two destroyers."[20] The immense craft gained high altitude within one or two seconds, then made a beeline toward the USS *Franklin Delano Roosevelt,* on station about forty miles to the north.

Jordan told how the aircraft carrier, on which he served as a radio operator, "attracted UFOs, because of all the technologies and all the armaments that she had, and all the nuclear weapons."[21]

In fact, the "Roosy," as she was called by her crew, the first warship equipped with atomic capabilities, would be dogged at least twice more by UFOs over the next eleven years. She was under way sometime between 8:00 and 9:00 p.m. in September 1958 when a large cigar-shaped vehicle aglow with a bright, reddish-orange luminescence, rose suddenly from the waters near Guantanamo Bay, Cuba, to drift about forty feet above the surface on an opposite heading parallel with the *FDR,* not far from her starboard side. Among the twenty-five eye-witnesses to this apparition was Chet Grusinski, a metalwork engineer and fireman, who observed that the silently moving craft featured "a row of windows with figures inside, and it got close enough to feel the heat on my face. And those figures looking at us through those win-dows, and the impression that I got [was] that those figures looking at us were not human beings."[22] The forty-five-second encounter con-cluded with the object's abrupt disappearance into the starry sky.

In addition, on the night of October 2, 1963, while the *Roosevelt* was cruising off the Mediterranean island of Sardinia, an object descended toward her from 80,000 feet at 4,000 mph in sharp, right-angle turns resembling a zigzag pattern that would have reduced any human occu-pants aboard to jelly. It then hovered briefly at low altitude directly over the carrier in full view of numerous crew members before ascending out of sight in a matter of seconds.[23]

Figure 12.4. The USS *Franklin Delano Roosevelt.*

But the *Roosevelt*'s first close encounter was during Exercise Mainbrace in 1952, with the quarter-mile-wide unidentified submerged object that went airborne after it "dinged" a destroyer while exiting the North Sea. The enormous incoming vehicle, now at approximately 10,000 feet, was visually confirmed around 11:00 a.m. by hundreds of service personnel on the carrier's flight deck and aboard nearby escort vessels. Among observers at the *FDR*'s combat direction center was Associated Press cameraman Wallace Litwin, who snapped two photographs of the object; both would appear in newspapers around the world.[24]

Later that same day, three Danish Navy officers saw a much smaller USO jump suddenly from the Baltic Sea, swiftly attain altitude, then proceed at an incomprehensively high speed toward the *Roosevelt*'s position. In less than twenty-four hours, six British pilots reported seeing another USO rise abruptly from the North Atlantic, not far from the coast of Scotland, and fly toward the same warship. A final encounter occurred around 7:30 p.m., on September 25, the last day of the exercise, when four Royal Danish Air Force officers and sixteen radar personnel beheld a large, metallic ball poised at approximately 21,000 feet above Denmark's Karup Air Base. As reported by Lieutenant Colonel Kurt Abildskov, the motionless globe appeared to have been continuously and rapidly encircled by four smaller spheroids before all the objects flew off together toward the distant *Roosevelt*.[25]

According to Pia Knudsen, a Danish researcher who conducted an in-depth investigation of Mainbrace, the eleven-day naval exercise was beset with seven or eight UFO and USO sightings made by many hundreds or, more likely, a thousand or more American, British, and Danish eyewitnesses as well as those of other nationalities. Along with the Washington, D.C., sightings of the previous July, it was the greatest mass observation of extraterrestrial craft in history.[26]

Despite the many occasions on which the intruders were seen during Mainbrace, no injuries or serious damages were incurred, although the *Willimoes,* the destroyer from which the first such sighting was made, suffered an unusually high number of electrical malfunctions that prevented her from further participating in the maneuvers. More extraordinarily, her crew was plagued throughout the operation by numerous instances of mental fatigue and indiscipline very uncommon in the Danish Navy. While no cause-and-effect relationship can be proved to connect these electronic and personnel problems with Smidt-Jensen's September 13 sighting, they must at least give us pause for consideration in view of electromagnetic interference with man-made instruments and human thought processes reported by observers of UFOs before and since.

Nine weeks before Mainbrace and just days after the flight of the UFO formation over Washington, D.C., a United Press International dispatch carried by the *Los Angeles Times* for July 30, 1952, told how "Robert L. Farnsworth, president of the United States Rocket Society, urged the nation's top defense officials today to restrain the armed forces from shooting at 'flying saucers.'" As long ago as 1945, this Chicago office manager of the Pennsylvania Oil Company was perhaps the first American who envisioned the application of atomic energy in rocket-propulsion systems for deep-space travel. "Farnsworth said hostile action might alienate mankind from 'beings of far superior powers.' He said there were unconfirmed rumors that the armed forces had been ordered to shoot at any unidentified objects in the sky." In a telegram to President Truman, Farnsworth "said that should these objects 'be extraterrestrial, such action might result in the gravest consequences.'"[27] They were not long in coming.

On July 12, 1953, Transocean Air Lines flight 512 departed the Pacific island of Guam at 12:04 a.m., with forty-nine passengers and eight crew members on a flight to Oakland, California, the location of the airline's corporate headquarters. At 5:39, the Douglas DC-6A made a scheduled landing on Wake Island to board another passenger, top off its fuel tanks, and check advance weather conditions. A storm front was moving across the eastern Pacific, but it was not serious enough to warrant canceling further flight. The four-engine airliner departed Wake at 6:58 for an estimated nine-hour flight to Honolulu, a final stopover before Oakland. The captain punctually radioed his 100-nautical-mile position report at 7:29, and another scheduled position report precisely 1 hour later. He gave his cruising altitude as 15,000 feet, but said nothing further. Both transmissions were entirely routine.

When, however, the captain missed his next scheduled position report, an alert was issued by Wake Island. The U.S. Navy immediately dispatched a dozen Lockheed PV-2 *Neptune* maritime patrol planes, each with a range of 2,157 miles, plus nineteen ships from Pearl Harbor, including the destroyers *Epperson* and *Walker,* together with the troopship *Barrett*. On July 13, the *Barrett* reported finding first debris, then fourteen corpses. Additional rescue support was summoned to the area, where eleven additional bodies were spotted but could not be recovered because of rough seas and the presence of numerous sharks. The search ended two days later.

Investigators with the Civil Aeronautics Board determined that flight 512 had crashed into the Pacific Ocean roughly 340 miles east of Wake Island. Although all fifty-eight passengers and crew members were killed, the *Barrett* retrieved an empty, inflated life raft identified with the missing airliner, suggesting that a few persons had temporarily survived. CAB investigators found no evidence of an onboard fire based on the condition of the dead and the debris, nor was there anything to suggest that the aircraft had broken up in midair.

Instead the plane had hit the surface of the sea with terrific force. Sabotage was considered but ruled out. The Transocean captain was an experienced veteran pilot with a perfect career record. Another commercial airplane, approximately 30 miles north of flight 512's scheduled

Figure 12.5. A Lockheed P-2V *Neptune.*

route reported "an extensive thunderstorm area accompanied by heavy turbulence," but these conditions were not deemed especially hazardous, certainly nothing beyond the performance capabilities of the rugged DC-6.[28] It had received regular maintenance and servicing, with no service complaints concerning mechanical difficulties of any kind. Maintenance and inspection records were unremarkable.

"The plane had just been inspected," writes Keyhoe, "and was in perfect shape."[29] Precise sequences for fuel loading were established by Douglas, so as not to exceed design limitations or place excessive stress on the airframe, but investigators learned that flight 512's fuel had been properly loaded in Guam. They were especially perplexed by several details in the case. Shortly before 8:41 hours, when the crash occurred, "Wake Island radio picked up some very strange messages on the international distress frequency," according to Keyhoe. "They could not make heads or tail of them."[30]

More puzzling was a green "flare" seen in the general vicinity of flight 512's final moments by the first officer and his copilot of another aircraft *en route* from Honolulu. Distress flares for civilian as well as military use were invariably red. Green flares, seen less frequently, signaled, "I'm returning to base," a wholly inappropriate message in these circumstances. Moreover, commercial airliners were not even equipped with green flares. Even as Navy rescue efforts were still under way, Keyhoe told how "several plane crews and search vessels reported seeing green lights or fireballs," origins unknown.[31] Almost certainly they were not flares, but more reminiscent of Private Wall's account at the beginning of this chapter of an orange UFO that "turned a blue-green brilliant light" when it attacked his company. This was the same "bluish-green" kind of object Smidt-Jensen observed from the bridge of his Danish destroyer just before the commencement of Exercise Mainbrace.

The Korean "police action," which claimed 62,046 U.S. casualties, came to an end on July 27, 1953. That same day, CAB investigators terminated their formal inquiry into the crash of flight 512 with the words "probable cause unknown."[32]

13
Cold War, Hot Saucers

I must say that if listeners could see for themselves the mass of reports coming in from the airborne gendarmerie, from the mobile gendarmerie, and from the gendarmerie charged with the job of conducting investigations, all of which reports are forwarded by us to the National Center for Space Studies, then they would see that it is all pretty disturbing.

M. ROBERT GALLEY,
FRENCH MINISTER OF DEFENSE[1]

Robert Farnsworth's concern about "unconfirmed rumors that the armed forces had been ordered to shoot at any unidentified objects in the sky" had been prompted the day before, on July 29, 1952, by a *Los Angeles Times* article by Darrell Garwood, previously published with the Fall River, Massachusetts, *Herald News*. The headline read, "Jets Told to Shoot Down Flying Discs. Air Force Puzzled but No Longer Skeptical." The Washington, D.C., reporter interviewed a USAF major, who said that his orders to fire on unidentified flying objects were not "rumors." Garwood told how "jet pilots are operating on twenty-four-hour, nationwide alert to chase the mysterious objects and 'to shoot them down' if they ignore orders to land. . . . Several pilots, according to the Air Force, have tried to shoot down the mysterious discs, but the 'steady bright lights' in the sky have out-flown the pilots."[2]

Similar reports appeared that same day in other dailies across the country, from the *Washington Post,* in a story by John G. Norris, to Seattle's *Post-Intelligencer,* under the heading, "Air Force Orders Pilots to Shoot Down Flying Saucers if They Refuse to Land." The page 1 article explained, "In Air Force parlance, that means that if a 'flying saucer' refuses to obey an order to land, jet planes are authorized to shoot them to earth, if they can get close enough to do so."[3]

As Major Keyhoe stated, "there were standing orders [in the USAF] to pursue all UFOs."[4] This policy was in place in 1952 when an unidentifiable contact, holding position high above Fort Knox, was tracked by radar operators. They vectored a P-51 fighter pilot on an intercept heading with the intruder, who approached it within visual range and soon began "describing [over his radio] what he had seen, and then disappeared. They never found him. . . . I don't recall that they ever found pieces of the aircraft."[5] It and its pilot had been either vaporized or captured in toto.

The following year, on the night of May 20, 1953, USAF lieutenant Milton Torres and another pilot received urgent orders to scramble their F-86D *Super Sabrejets.* Both men had been on standby for almost an hour at an RAF base at Manston, in Kent, England, where ground

Figure 13.1. Lieutenant Milton Torres in 1957.

radar operators continued to track a UFO with "very unusual flight patterns" over East Anglia.[6]

Torres and his wingman climbed through the visually impenetrable overcast at 12,150 feet a minute and soon picked up the contact on their AN/APG-36 all-weather radar fitted in a radome (an aerodynamic shield), in the nose above the intake. The object, clearly defined on the scopes of either interceptor, was about 185 feet in diameter and traveling somewhat beneath 700 mph. Pushing their performance envelope at Mach .93, the *Sabrejets* could barely keep up with the unknown intruder when Torres was radioed by ground control to fire on it immediately with his twenty-four Mk4 air-to-air, unguided rockets. He retracted the underfuselage tray, loaded with two dozen 70-millimeter *Mighty Mouse* folding-fin aerial rockets, and locked his radar on the target. As his finger was about to squeeze the trigger, the object accelerated instantly to Mach 10, 7,000 mph faster than its previous speed and ten times the speed of sound. Radar screens in the air and back at Manston went blank. Torres was sworn to secrecy concerning the failed intercept, but went public with it in the early twenty-first century.

Six months and one day later, on October 21, an RAF pilot flying a Gloster *Meteor* over Warwickshire, England, was similarly vectored by ground radar operators at 9:18 p.m. to a UFO circling the Graydon atomic-energy facility. As he approached the large silvery disk, it shot out six smaller orbs of light that scurried erratically in various directions throughout the night sky. One of them made straight for his jet fighter, almost colliding with the plane before the pilot could make an evasive maneuver. Thereafter all the objects vanished in the blink of an eye. The British pilot felt lucky to be alive, because the luminous spheroid had virtually grazed his starboard wing.[7]

Soviet airmen the previous summer had been far less fortunate. On August 7, a pair of Mig-15 jets was ordered, as Torres had been, to destroy an undetermined number of UFOs over Ishimbay, a town in southern Russia. But all air-to-air missiles launched by the Soviet Air Forces pilots were successfully parried from their targets to crash and detonate harmlessly below on the taiga, a swampy, coniferous forest, some of which caught fire and burned with the exploding warheads. Immediately following this deflected attack, all radar and radio operations went silent within a 120-mile radius of Ishimbay. When they were restored after twenty minutes, all contact with the Mig pilots had been lost. Neither wreckage nor human remains were ever found, despite weeks of extensive search-and-rescue efforts undertaken throughout the taiga. An unofficial consensus of military opinion held that the two aircraft with their four men had either been abducted whole or totally atomized.[8] In either case, the Ishimbay incident is among the most numerically significant disappearances of its kind in the annals of ufology. It was not, however, the only one.

That same year, in early autumn, secret flight testing of the latest Soviet warplane was under way at remote Kunashir, southernmost island of the Kuril Islands north of Japan. Also known to Ainu natives as Black Island for its age-old demonic reputation, Kunashir "experienced many UFO sightings," according to Stonehill, "but none as dramatic as this." Circling out over the Pacific Ocean on its return to the military airfield on Kunashir, the aircraft "mysteriously vanished as observers looked at it; first visually, then on radar screens."[9]

Instruments were checked and rechecked, but they operated perfectly, and would have followed the warplane's precipitous descent had it crashed into the sea. Instead it simply dematerialized at altitude. Recovery vessels and spotter aircraft intensely investigated the area of possible splashdown, but found no trace of man or machine.

Yet another midair disappearance of the extraterrestrial kind took place during 1953, this one in the United States near the Canadian border. On December 23, northern Michigan's Air Defense Command radar detected an unidentified contact clocked at 500 mph, 8,000 feet over Lake Superior, with no known point of origin. Pilot Felix Moncla Jr. and radar operator Robert R. Wilson hopped into their Northrop F-89C on an intercept mission off Sault Ste. Marie's Soo Locks.

One hundred sixty miles northwest of them, and seventy miles near Keweenaw Point, ground control guided Lieutenant Wilson toward

Figure 13.2. First Lieutenant Felix Moncla Jr.

the intruder, which he had already picked up on his own scope. As the aircraft approached its target around 2:00 p.m., ADC radar operators watched the returns from both the F-89 and the UFO merge. Suddenly, however, the returns faded from the screen altogether. No blips of any kind followed.[10] Returns on the *Scorpion* indicated it had not fallen from altitude, but, like the contact it pursued, impossibly vanished into midair. No distress calls were received, as all radio communication with the aircraft had fallen silent.

A task force of helicopters, ambulance planes, flying boats, and Michigan Coast Guard vessels sprang into action, scouring Lake Superior for three weeks, but detected no oil slick or any scrap of debris. Persons aboard ships and planes in the broad search area reported no falling aircraft, no crash, and nothing unusual, even though the event occurred during broad daylight, in clear conditions, during midafternoon. Ignoring the total lack of eyewitness testimony and physical evidence, U.S. Air

Force officials at first claimed that Lieutenant Moncla had mistakenly attempted to intercept a Royal Canadian Air Force C-47 transport plane, causing the planes to collide and crash into Lake Superior.

When skeptics pointed out that the alleged cargo plane's top speed of 224 mph was 276 mph slower than the radar-tracked UFO, Air Force spokesmen changed their explanation, insisting the Canadian aircraft in question was actually a jet fighter. Canadian government representatives responded by citing RCAF logbook records showing that none of their aircraft went missing on December 23. USAF officials threw up their hands, declaring the entire incident was an insoluble mystery. Later they yet again changed their version of events, chalking them up to pilot error and vertigo, without evidence of any kind whatsoever.

Official denial and foolishness to the contrary, the merging and simultaneous disappearance of radar blips for the interceptor and the unidentified contact, plus the total absence of debris, suggest that both Moncla and Wilson, together with their 18½-ton aircraft flying at 600 mph, were captured by a UFO, which carried them off to God knows where. In a series of incidents between August and December 1953 without precedent and not since repeated, seven airmen in two different countries appear to have been abducted in midair.

Fifty days after the *Scorpion's* disappearance, Second Lieutenant Lamar Barlow flew out of McChord Air Force Base in Tacoma, Washington, piloting a *Sabrejet* fully armed with twenty-four air-to-air missiles—a weapons array not normally carried on routine instrument

Figure 13.3. Memorial to Lieutenant Moncla at Moreauville, Louisiana's Sacred Heart Cemetery. Photograph by Gordheath.

training flights, such as the mission to which he had been allegedly assigned. One and a half hours after taking off at 10:25 that morning, Barlow began repeatedly radioing "May Day 2" over the airmen's international distress frequency, explaining that his magnetic compass had ceased to function, getting him lost in rainy, overcast conditions. His dilemma was further compounded by dwindling fuel reserves, enabling him to stay aloft for only another thirty minutes. Radar operators located his position sixty miles north of Vancouver and vectored him toward the Sea Island Airport for an emergency landing, as he had reported total instrument failure in his last transmission.

Before 1:00 p.m. on February 12, 1954, the F-86 slammed into 2,700-foot-high Grouse Mountain, located above North Vancouver, in British Columbia, at a velocity exceeding 760 miles per hour. Lieutenant Barlow was found dead, still strapped into his seat. Military police roped off the extensive wreckage site until their search for the fighter's remaining missiles could be retrieved. USAF spokesmen explained that a "phantom radar echo" had misled McChord operators in providing the pilot inaccurate directions that led to the crash. Investigator Gord Heath's in-depth examination of the incident provoked some disturbing questions, however:

> Why was the jet armed with twenty-four rockets on an instrument training mission? The fact that the jet was armed implies to me that it was either on an air defense mission or a weapons training mission of some sort. One intriguing detail in the [contemporaneous] news reports was that most of the twenty-four rockets were recovered, but that a few were still missing.[11]

Had Barlow fired them at a UFO? "This would explain why the aircraft was armed," said Heath. "This might also explain why the aircraft penetrated far into Canadian airspace during a pursuit. This might also explain multiple instrument failures possibly caused by proximity of the aircraft to a strong electromagnetic field. It is of some peculiarity that the plane experienced first a compass failure [unusual to the point of

Figure 13.4.
Second Lieutenant Lamar Barlow.

impossibility, given its simplicity], followed later by total instrument failure"—also highly anomalous because, of the 9,860 *Sabrejets* built from 1948 to 1994, none of them save Barlow's experienced across-the-board instrument failure.

"Encounters between UFOs and aircraft often lead to instrument malfunctions and failures," Heath continues. "It is also a quite peculiar coincidence that a phantom 'radar echo' was sited [*sic*] as a contributing cause to the crash. At this time [1954], UFOs were often explained [away] as 'phantom radar echoes' by the U.S. Air Force. . . . One mystery is that the real F86's radar return should have been showing an IFF [identification, friend or foe] code. This should make it easy for the radar operator to distinguish the F-86 from a real ghost echo or UFO, unless the IFF signal transmission had also malfunctioned. Similarly, it is conceivable that radar operators lost contact with the pilot due to temporary radio malfunctions although no such malfunctions were mentioned." In fact, Barlow reported universal instrument failure in his last transmission, which was not received immediately prior to the crash, but at least ten minutes before. Heath also asks:

Why was the jet flying at the speed of sound [unless in pursuit on a fast intruder], when all logic suggests it should have been flying at a low speed for its emergency landing approach? Which makes more sense: The radar operators ignored the jet flying off into Canadian airspace until the pilot suddenly realizes he has only 30 minutes of fuel and has no clue about his position or the radar operators guided the pilot in pursuit of a UFO into Canadian airspace?[12]

Answers came to light on the early evening of July 1, as reports of a "gleaming, disk-shaped apparatus," in the words of Major Keyhoe, began to pile up in newspaper offices and police stations across the Empire State's southern border with Pennsylvania. Word of the UFO was passed on to Griffiss Air Force Base in Rome, New York. "The officer in charge said he believed it to be a partially deflated balloon," according to the records of the Condon committee (a group funded by the U.S. Air Force at the University of Colorado to study unidentified flying objects under the direction of physicist Edward Condon), "and if it were still there the next day, he would have it investigated."

Local sightings persisted and multiplied into the following morning, when a Lockheed F-94C jet fighter attached to the 27th Fighter Interceptor Squadron was diverted from "a routine training mission" by ground control "to intercept an unknown aircraft at ten thousand feet."[13]

Piloted by Lieutenant William E. Atkins, with Lieutenant Henry F. Coudon as radar observer, number 51-13559 was one of two *Starfires* ordered to pursue the object in an "active Air Defense mission," signifying "imminent enemy attack," a high-level alert that contradicted official Air Force characterization of the incident as routine. A Pentagon spokesman later stated that the "unidentified plane [*sic*] was about seventy-five miles northeast of Rome, on the edge of the Griffiss' patrol zone, when the jets intercepted it" in clear weather conditions.

Keyhoe tells how "the pilot could actually see the unknown— a strange, gleaming object moving swiftly above. Pulling into a tight climbing turn, he started to close the gap. At the same time, his radar observer started to contact the unknown. But there was no response. Suddenly, as the plane streaked toward the UFO, a wave of heat mysteriously filled the cockpit. It was like the blast of a furnace; the stifling heat was increasing with each second. Frantically he looked around. The radar officer's face was a blur in the waves of heat. At any moment, it seemed that the whole plane might burst into flames."[14]

James H. Douglas, undersecretary of the Air Force, said that "preliminary reports indicate that a fire developed in the forward section of the aircraft in flight and that the heat in the cockpit became so intense that the pilot and radar observer were forced to leave the aircraft at an altitude of seven thousand or eight thousand feet."[15]

Earlier, Atkins's subordinate officers claimed there had been no fire on board 51-13559, instead, lieutenants Atkins and Coudon supposedly ejected because a faulty control panel emergency light indicated the aircraft's higher than normal internal temperatures. Although any airplane is potentially flammable, the F-94 had a good safety record, with no reports of accidental fires on any of its other 855 examples produced from 1950 to 1959. Contemporaneous newspapers reported that "an Air Force officer had said there 'must have been an explosion.' . . . A Friffiss' [sic for Griffis] spokesman . . . said fire broke out in the cockpit of the ill-fated craft. . . . The air base said the pilot and radar observer stuck to the plane 'until the last minute.' . . . A spokesman quoted Atkins as reporting that he ordered Coudon to bail out, then jumped himself from about seven thousand feet."[16]

Such coverage implies that the Lockheed jet was experiencing trouble serious enough to convince both officers that they must hastily abandon it, even over a civilian population center, rather than taking a few minutes to find less inhabited terrain. This is standard procedure when one's aircraft is not experiencing an immediately life-threatening condition, which hardly defines a stuck emergency light. Had that been the case—a common enough occurrence—Atkins would not have precipitously hit the ejection-seat button, but simply nursed his *Starfire* back to the Griffiss Air Base, which was not far away. Clearly something far more urgent compelled him and Coudon to jump, such as the blast of a weapon fired at them by the UFO they pursued.

"The crew told Intelligence that it was so fast that they didn't have time to think," said USAF Captain Edward Stone. "You're a pilot, Don. You know that you'd never bail out over a town like that if you could possibly stick it out."

"Unless the ship was on fire," Keyhoe interjected.

"Even then," said Stone, "pilots have stuck long enough to get away from cities. And some poor devils have even ridden them down. But these guys were hit so suddenly that they were almost out of their minds. One second everything was normal; then, suddenly, it was like an inferno. Whatever hit them must have come from that saucer."

"You think it was some kind of heat beam?"

"It must have been that. But why? That's what scares me."

Keyhoe put his finger on the crux of the matter: "Until that moment, the *Starfire's* jet engine had been working perfectly. Half-dazed, the pilot and radar officer bailed out."[17]

As they drifted safely to Earth, their pilotless jet careened out of control over New York about 12:30 p.m. before it stalled, then plummeted and began breaking up in large pieces falling toward the town of Walesville, eleven miles southwest of Utica. Alvia Sancher was inside his home when he heard a noise that "sounded like a rocket or a siren."[18] His neighbor, Mrs. Doris Monroe, was preparing lunch while her children played outside and her husband, Lloyd, was at work in a foundry, when the body of the falling plane plunged through the roof of her one-story home, instantly incinerating it.

"Griffiss said that fuel in the burning plane apparently exploded when the jet crashed," reported the *Troy Record,* a local newspaper. "I ran to the window," said Sancher, "and heard the crash. Then I saw the plane or part of it, as it hit the house across the street. Something smashed through a window near the porch of the house."[19] The oldest Monroe child, Kenneth, said he was playing in the yard with the other children when "all of a sudden, there was smoke and fire, and I heard my mother screaming."[20]

At that same moment, "a section of the burning craft, probably a wing, struck the car carrying the Phillips family home, presumably from the Rome State School, where both husband and wife were employed as occupational instructors. Their sedan burst into flames, ploughed into the home of Mrs. Mary Peck, 79, and set the colonial frame structure afire. Mrs. Peck fled to safety."[21]

The victims were Stanley Phillips; his wife, Florence; and their eleven-year-old son, Gary. Other townspeople were struck and injured, mostly burned, by aircraft debris scattered all over the community. Heat from the F-94's disembodied engine was so intense that it melted the macadam road on which it had fallen. Altogether, four persons died, with two houses and an automobile destroyed, plus property damage throughout the small town. Although USAF spokesmen made no further mention of the UFO that had prompted the doomed *Starfire* to undertake an "active Air Defense mission," the incident was written up in Project Blue Book files as "Walesville, NY, July 2," under July 1954 "Sightings."[22] (Project Blue Book was a series of systematic studies of unidentified flying objects conducted by the United States Air Force from 1952 to 1969.)

In fact, the July 2 disaster's extraterrestrial nature was underscored by other UFO reports that "began to jam switchboards in Utica, Rome, and Frankfort, New York" immediately thereafter, according to Keyhoe.[23]

Atkins's plane was not, however, the only American jet fighter apparently downed in 1954 by an off-world vehicle. On the early morning of August 14, an unidentified USAF interceptor fell into Chesapeake Bay, not far from Washington, D.C. Within the hour, the captain of a rescue boat dispatched to find and retrieve the pilot's body radioed that a large silver disk was hovering directly overhead, as though monitoring the vessel's progress. Just minutes later, an F-51 pilot involved in the search bailed out after transmitting a distress call, in which he reported a collision with some unknown object that put his aircraft into an irreversible tailspin.[24]

Within three days, the Russians experienced their own extraterrestrial confrontation. At 8:12 a.m. on August 17, writes Stonehill, someone was jamming the radar receivers of "an antiaircraft unit guarding a missile battalion very close to the Chinese border. . . . A few moments later, an object resembling a rocket was observed, but it had no stabilizers, and moved horizontally at low speed. Its movement resembled that of a dirigible. Three missiles were fired at it. They exploded before reaching the target. The object rapidly ascended and soon disappeared. A commission from the Ministry of Defense arrived the next day to investigate. Because its members found no objective reasons for missiles having been fired under the circumstances, the commanding officer of the missile battalion was removed from his position."

Stonehill goes on to tell how "various [USSR] air force orders, prior to 1977, absolutely forbade any contacts with UFOs. . . . The subsequent military order regarding these objects could be summed up as follows: There must be no reaction to *letayuschiye tarelki* (Russian 'flying saucers')."[25] This admonition was affirmed by Randle: "There was an order issued to the pilots that told them not to fire on the UFO. According to the General of the Army, Ivan Tretyak, the order was issued because 'such an object may possess formidable capabilities for retaliation.' That suggests that there had been a history of Soviet fighters attempting to engage UFOs, and that, at some point, there had been retaliation. Had such a circumstance not happened, then there would have been no reason to issue such an order."[26]

Moscow authorities were anxious to avoid any military clash with the off-world vehicles, which had often demonstrated their vast technological superiority over anything in the Russian arsenal. Provoking an incident with them might lead to consequences of the worst kind. At least whenever extraterrestrials were concerned, the Communists sincerely believed in peaceful coexistence.

The flying-saucer flap of 1952 at the nation's capital played itself out again in 1954, although with more serious consequences. Three hours after hundreds of persons stared up in awe at a formation of UFOs passing with impunity over downtown Washington, D.C., on the evening of October 28, a pair of large patrol planes flying out of Norfolk, Virginia (170 miles away), disappeared offshore into the night. In their last radio messages, the pilots of both aircraft reported no trouble of any kind. Search-and-rescue missions undertaken by U.S. Navy surface and air units over the next three weeks discovered neither survivors nor wreckage, even though the disappearance took place not far out over the Atlantic Ocean, but only a few miles from the East Coast. The two 32-ton *Neptunes,* with their twenty-two airmen, had utterly vanished without a trace. These were examples of the Lockheed P-2 that had searched for Transocean Airline's flight 512 the previous year.[27]

Earlier that same evening in 1954, a U.S. Navy pilot was rescued after ditching his fighter jet at sea for an undisclosed cause five miles outside Norfolk, in the general vicinity of where both patrol planes were lost shortly thereafter.[28]

On the morning of April 5, 1955, several dozen people in northern Illinois reported a brightly lit orb traveling the ten miles between Rockford and Cherry Valley, seventy-six miles northwest of Chicago. Shortly after 9:30, a trio of F-86s were seen in pursuit of the UFO. Their encounter was observed by numerous spectators on the ground, including John C. Gregory, executive secretary of the Winnebago County Civil Defense Council, from the top of the city hall building. He saw "another flat, spherical, brilliant-white object" fly past the USAF interceptors, which attacked the first target with a combined firepower of eighteen 12.7-millimeter Browning machine guns.[29] The spheroid instantaneously detonated in a thundering blast of flame, as its companion swiftly escaped through a vertical loop and climbed far beyond the top speed or maneuverability of the Sabrejets. Before they raced away, Gregory saw them circle the empty patch of sky, from which tiny pieces of the disintegrated UFO sprinkled earthward.

Reports of this mind-blowing action were embargoed by the entire Chicago press but covered in Rockford's small-circulation *Register* newspaper: "The jets were from O'Hare Field, in Park Ridge. Air Force officials at the field said that a weather balloon was sent up from Minneapolis."[30] No mention was made of the bright, white object Gregory and others observed streaking past the fighters. Nor did anyone call into question the preposterous explanation that a weather balloon had been brought down in flames as hot machine-gun rounds were fired over a populated area.

A more unique skirmish occurred six years later, in early 1961, when an off-world craft that had been buzzing around northern Europe for some weeks was finally intercepted by a pair of Saab J29Fs from the Swedish Air Force. Both pilots made visual contact of the silvery disk, from whose underside burned a wide mass of flames disgorging long, thick billows of ashen smoke.

The *Flygande tunnan,* or "flying barrels," eventually gained on the UFO to close within firing range. Just before their 75-millimeter, air-to-air missiles and combined eight 20-millimeter Hispano Mark V auto-cannons could be brought into play, the target suddenly shot a trailing line of "green, slimy goo" in the direction of its pursuers. The Saab jets executed an evasive maneuver, and the metallic disk flew off at several times the jets' maximum speed of 660 miles per hour.[31]

The most extraordinary and deadly extraterrestrial confrontations of the 1960s comprised a series of disasters at sea in which four submarines from different nations were lost in as many months at the cost of

Figure 13.5. *Swedish UFO Interception,* a depiction of the 1961 skirmish by Fredrik Alfredsson (fredrik.alf@gmail.com).

318 lives. Never before or since have so many underwater vessels been destroyed during peacetime in such a brief period.

On January 9, 1968, Israel's newly-purchased submarine *Dakar* (Hebrew for *swordfish*) left Portsmouth, England, under the command of Major Ya'acov Ra'anan. Sixteen days later, he informed Tel Aviv naval headquarters that he had entered the Aegean Sea earlier than expected, his vessel was performing satisfactorily, and all aboard were well. Nothing further was heard from the vessel until January 27, when a radio station in Nicosia received a distress call southeast of Cyprus on the frequency of *Dakar's* emergency buoy, which broke off when the submarine "dove rapidly through her maximum depth, suffered a catastrophic hull rupture, and continued her plunge to the bottom [at 9,800 feet]. The emergency buoy was released by the violence of the hull collapse," according to Wikipedia. [32] All sixty-nine men aboard perished.

Despite a five-nation search for the vessel, its wreckage between the islands of Cyprus and Crete was not located for more than

Figure 13.6. The recovered conning tower of INS *Dakar* at Israel's Naval Museum, Haifa. Photograph by Ido.

thirty years. "Her conning tower was snapped off and fallen over the side," Wikipedia writes. "The stern of the submarine, with the propellers and dive planes, broke off aft of the engine room and rests beside the main hull."[33] What could have caused such extensive damages remains unknown, because the *Dakar* evidenced no signs of having experienced an explosion.

The same day the *Dakar* was destroyed, another submarine was lost 1,560 miles away. At 7:55 a.m., Lieutenant André Fauve, commanding the French vessel *Minerve,* routinely notified his air escort, a Breguet Br.1150 Atlantic maritime patrol plane, that he would arrive at Toulon in about an hour. He was among the Marine Nationale's most experienced submariners, with over four years and more than 7,000 hours under water. Just 25 nautical miles from the south coast of France, the *Minerve,* along with her fifty-two crewmen, disappeared without a trace.[34] They have not been seen since, despite intense year-long searches undertaken by French and U.S. naval units, including the renowned oceanographer Jacques Cousteau. Nor had airmen flying the escorting Breguet observed

Figure 13.7. The French submarine *Minerve.*

anything at the time that suggested an explosion or anything out of the ordinary in the vicinity of the submarine.

The following February 24, K-129, a 330-foot-long, 2,700-ton Russian submarine reached deep water in the central Pacific Ocean, successfully conducted its test dive, and returned to the surface. Captain First Rank V. I. Kobzar reported by radio that all was well, then proceeded on his patrol. He and the other ninety-seven men aboard were never heard from again. The Soviet Navy deployed a huge flotilla of search-and-rescue ships, but they could not find K-129. But the Americans did. On March 8, after monitoring an underwater acoustic signal—the isolated, single sound of an explosion or implosion led them to the wreck lying approximately 600 nautical miles north of Midway atoll, between 16,440 and 16,500 feet down. Although U.S. Navy salvagers retrieved some or most of K-129, they were unable to determine the cause of its destruction. Subsequent theories suggesting a hydrogen explosion in the batteries while charging, collision with an American submarine, a leaking missile door seal, even mutiny, were all discarded in turn.[35]

On May 22, Commander Francis Slattery of the American submarine *Scorpion* radioed his position at 400 nautical miles southwest

Figure 13.8. The Soviet submarine K-129.

of the Azores, running at a steady 15 knots, 350 feet beneath the surface of the North Atlantic. Nothing further was heard from the ninety-nine officers and crew. After the *Scorpion's* broken wreckage was found at depths of 9,800 feet, Structural Analysis Group physicists concluded that an explosive event was unlikely to have caused the sinking, because the absence of a bubble pulse, which invariably occurs in an underwater blast, was absolute evidence that no torpedo explosion occurred outside or inside the vessel's hull. Hitherto a Russian attack had been suspected, especially in view of Commander Slattery's last message, which indicated that he was about "to begin surveillance of the Soviets." However, a U.S. Navy Court of Inquiry determined that USSR naval units were too far removed from the *Scorpion's* position to have intercepted her. "The certain cause of the loss of the *Scorpion*," the court ruled, "cannot be ascertained from evidence now available."[36]

The undersea disasters that occurred during the first half of 1968 had more in common than a shared time frame, although it was particularly remarkable that the *Dakar* and *Minerve* both succumbed on the same day. Probabilities against such a coincidence are astronomical, especially when one factors in two more such calamities within the next seventeen weeks. And the *Minerve's* complete disappearance—a

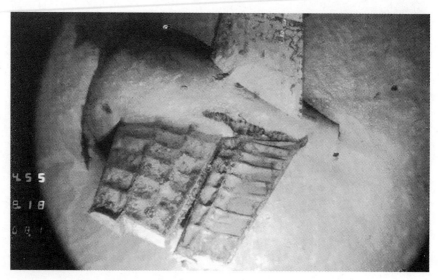

Figure 13.9. U.S. Navy photo of the *Scorpion's* wrecked stern.

mere 25 nautical miles off the French coast, in calm, clear conditions, while being escorted by ten observers aboard a low-flying aircraft—was not only unique in all history but utterly inexplicable. Her fate was no less baffling, however, than that of the other three doomed vessels: the causes for their demise equally eluded all investigating naval authorities.

Nonetheless, even after the passage of more than fifty years, clues exist in parallels among the submarines themselves. Each one was unusually ahead of its time and beyond the technological level of other submarines. These were, in fact, the leading undersea warships of their time. *Dakar* had been outfitted with a new radar-detection system that had not yet been tested. Lieutenant Colonel Benny Maimon, the engineer who developed it, was on board with his advanced equipment, which was never recovered from the wreck. The *Minerve* was an experimental missile-carrying submarine, while the U.S. Navy's *Scorpion* "specialized in developing nuclear submarine warfare tactics." Wikipedia relates how the submarine "entered an inland Russian sea during a 'Northern Run' in 1966, where it filmed a Soviet missile launch through its periscope before fleeing from Soviet Navy ships."[37]

K-129 carried an undetermined number of innovative SS-N-5 *Serb* rockets capable of lofting 1-megaton nuclear warheads more than a thousand miles; it was the existence of these superior weapons aboard the sunken K-129 that prompted America's Central Intelligence Agency to covertly salvage the Soviet submarine. But the singular capabilities of these warships appears to have engaged the interest of more than the CIA. On the dates they were lost, a dozen UFO sightings—most of them made at or near large bodies of water—were reported worldwide.

January 27, the day the *Dakar* and *Minerve* sank, a married couple walking along the southeast Florida shore of Lantana, just north of Miami, saw "a flying disc" at low altitude in clear weather not far out over the Atlantic Ocean, around 2:00 a.m. Beginning at 4:40 that same morning, Knoxville, Tennessee, police received telephone calls from nine witnesses describing a similar object hovering over the city. About 6:00 a.m., Keats Island residents off the coast of British Columbia reported seeing a white, starlike craft make "two, wide spirals [that] zig-zagged parallel to earth." Afterward it "changed color to yellow, then pink, [fading] into [the] distance." Two hours later, "an object larger than a star was observed" above San Antonio, Texas. "Electromagnetic effects [television, radio, and telephone interference] were noted." At 5:12 p.m., a flying disk "was sighted that had an appearance and performance beyond the capability of known earthly aircraft," and "observed by more than five witnesses from a building" in downtown Millington, in east-central Michigan, on Lake Huron. Around 9:00 that evening, in Modesto, central California, seventy miles from the Pacific Ocean, "an object the size of the moon [as it appeared in the night sky] was sighted that had an appearance and performance beyond the capability of known earthly aircraft." It was observed for twelve seconds by a man standing in his backyard.[38]

On March 8, as K-129 went down, "a flying disk was observed by three witnesses for five minutes" over Syracuse, New York, 34 miles from Lake Ontario, at 2:45 p.m. At 10:00 p.m., a single witness reported a trio of similarly disk-shaped objects flying over Rossington, in east-central England, thirty miles from the coast.[39]

An aerial disk "larger than a star was observed by two witnesses for two minutes" in Sherman Oaks, California, ten miles from the Pacific Ocean, at 11:40 on the morning of May 22, when the USS *Scorpion* disappeared. That evening, at 7:40, "three, cylinder-shaped UFOs flew to the south" of Bailesti, Romania, "emitting a strong light. A fourth object joined them, then vanished." Another (or the same) three objects "were observed by one witness for twelve seconds" at 10:22 p.m. over Greenwood, South Carolina.[40]

Although these reported observations were made far from the locations where the submarines vanished, at least one sighting was made in close connection with USS *Scorpion*. It was disclosed in March 2002, nearly thirty-four years after the event, to the National UFO Reporting Center by an eyewitness who, in his own words, "was involved in the actual incident" aboard the U.S. Navy vessel *Hyades* AF-28.[41] The *Hyades* was a combat-stores ship used to stow supplies and other goods for naval purposes. According to Wikipedia, she was "ordered to search the area for the doomed sub, and became the first to do so."[42] The eye-witness continues:

> The last known position report [of *Scorpion*] was in our area (just off the Azore Islands). We immediately commenced a search of the area, which for us lasted three days and nights. . . . On the second night of searching, an object was reflected in the searchlight (24-inch mercury arc light) I was on. (I was a signalman and my duty station was on the signal bridge running the light). As the ship turned toward the object, it went out of the "beam" and was lost due to darkness (it was a cloudy night with no moon or stars, pitch black). A few years later, I read about the aforementioned incident and that the object (which was lost in the beam) mysteriously lifted off the water and disappeared in the sky.[43]

These numerous sightings in conjunction with the lost submarines and their high technology suggest that the vessels were targeted by extraterrestrial intruders determined to blunt development of mankind's advanced weaponry.

Still more extreme was perhaps the single most terrifying Close Encounter of the Sixth kind in all ufology. Had its source and narrator been less credible, the account would have been deemed more worthy of inclusion in an anthology of the most gruesome horror stories. It derives instead from the Grudge 13 papers, a series of Project Grudge/Blue Book reports released over the years in connection with the USAF's investigation into UFOs. The original Project Grudge succeeded Project Sign in February 1949. Overtly concerned with debunking every aspect of the extraterrestrial problem to the American public, Project Grudge formally ended in December 1949, but continued in a minimal capacity until late 1951. After that, it was allowed to continue covertly in a phantom extension known as Grudge 13. Project Grudge was succeeded in turn by Project Blue Book, supposedly terminated with the release of the Condon report in the late 1960s.

Grudge 13's confidential findings remained unknown to the outside world until they were disclosed by William English, a former Green Beret captain in the U.S. Army 8th Special Forces Group. Following his Southeast Asian tour of duty in 1977, he was assigned to a U.S. security services command headquarters at an RAF base in Chicksands, England. As he stated in a Colorado radio interview broadcast on June 28, 1991:

> RAF Chicksands was a security listening post, and we monitored radio transmissions from Soviet Bloc nations. And those transmissions were translated, and then it was my job to take the information that was obtained and analyze it to try and make determination as to whether or not the information was factual. Specifically, my job was to analyze whatever came across my desk. I was a data analyst, and I was asked to analyze a document, which came across my desk entitled Grudge Blue Book Report Number 13. The report itself was about six hundred pages long.
>
> My job designation was to take information and analyze it for its validity, and on this particular day [in June 1977] the duty officer who brought us our daily assignments, which we signed for, brought this document in a diplomatic pouch and unsealed it there. I signed for it and I was in my little cubbyhole. [The document was] very much higher than top secret. I believe that there was a reason [for me to have been provided with the document], because there were some photographs [in it] which I had taken while in Vietnam.[44]

English's photos, made in Laos, showed the severely mutilated bodies of U.S. crew members still aboard a USAF bomber downed by UFOs in the early 1970s. He continued.

> It [the Grudge 13 file] clearly stated that this [wreckage] was material that had been recovered from various crash sites around the country and several South American and European nations. It very clearly stated that it was of alien origin, not of this Earth. After I analyzed the document, I turned in my report, as per regulations. Signed the

document back over to the officer of the day, and promptly forgot about it. We didn't discuss our work. You don't talk about things like that, and you just sort of mull it over, and then you get on with your life, as best you're able.[45]

Among the most disturbing things in the six-hundred-page Grudge 13 document were autopsy reports from hospitals, clinics, and even country doctors in the United States and various parts of the world, including the northern Ural Mountains of Russia (1959's Dyatlov Pass incident) of human beings mutilated by extraterrestrials.[46] One outstanding case was set in the White Sands Missile Range of New Mexico. At 3,200 square miles, it is the largest military installation in the United States.

In March 1956, Air Force sergeant Jonathan P. Lovette assisted Major William Cunningham of the United States Air Force Missile Command near Holloman Air Force Base in scouring the silent desert with flashlights for scattered debris from a recent rocket test. As their search carried them away from the launch sites, the two men wandered somewhat apart, and Sergeant Lovette temporarily disappeared over the ridge of a small sand dune.

Around 3:00 a.m., the major was shocked to hear a loud scream in extreme fright or pain. He assumed that Lovette had been bitten by a poisonous snake and sprinted over the sand dune to help him. Instead Cunningham saw a long, serpentine arm wrapped around the terrified sergeant's legs as it inexorably dragged him toward a silver disk hovering in the air fifteen to twenty feet away. The major froze in horror, staring dumbfounded as the hopelessly struggling Lovette was dragged inside the craft, which immediately thereafter rose vertically and speedily without a sound into the starry night sky. Cunningham stumbled toward the jeep that had carried them out into the desert and radioed missile control for assistance.

When security teams arrived, the major was so emotionally overwrought that they took him in charge and confined him to the White Sands Base dispensary for observation and treatment. No one could make much sense out of his rambling report, although Missile Control did confirm an unidentified radar contact near the base at the time Lovette vanished. Search parties went into the desert looking for him. After three days, they found his nude corpse some ten miles downrange. From all indications, the cadaver had been exposed to the elements from twenty-four to forty-eight hours. Where it had been for the extra day in between, no one could determine.

His autopsy proved shocking. It revealed that his body had been severely mutilated. The tongue had been removed from the lower portion of the jaw, while an incision beginning just under the tip of the chin extended all the way back to the esophagus and larynx. Lovette was castrated, his eyes were gouged out, and his anus was missing. In the Air Force's medical examination report, the coroner commented on the surgical skill evidenced in the removal of these organs, writing that the anus and the genitalia had been neatly extracted like a plug; in the case of the anus, it extended all the way to the colon. The sergeant's corpse had also been drained to the last drop of blood. Strangely, it showed no indication of vascular collapse due to death by bleeding. This was anomalous, because vascular collapse invariably results when a human body expires as a result of severe bleeding or complete blood loss.

No less unaccountably, the cadaver also appeared to have reached a fatal degree of toxicity. When it was discovered, security teams reported that it was surrounded by a number of dead birds that had collapsed after eating some of its flesh.[47]

Perhaps Major Keyhoe was aware of the White Sands incident when he declared:

> With control of the universe at stake, a crash program is imperative. We produced the A-bomb under the huge Manhattan Project in an amazingly short time. The needs, the urgency today are even greater. The Air Force should end UFO secrecy and give the facts to scientists, the public, to Congress. Once the people realize the truth, they would back, even demand a crash program, for this is one race we dare not lose.[48]

14

The Vietnam War Era

No UFO reported, investigated and evaluated by the Air Force was ever an indication of threat to our national security.

ROBERT C. SEAMANS JR.,
SECRETARY OF THE USAF, DECEMBER 17, 1969.[1]

William English told interviewer Rick Barbour on Radio KOA in Denver:

I was in Vietnam from 1970 to '72, and we had a recovery mission over in the jungles, in Laos—a downed aircraft [to] recover, [and] if possible, surviving crew members, [plus] what they told us were flight recorders, and those kind of things, and which we did. We went in and we found the aircraft [a Boeing B-52 *Stratofortress* jet bomber]. It had not crashed. It was an extremely unusual situation: there was no crash damage to the surrounding jungle.

The aircraft was not destroyed [minor damage was found only on the underside of the fuselage]. It looked as though it had been placed there in the jungle by a great, big, giant hand. [The B-52—all 133 tons of it, flying 525 mph at 50,000 feet—had been apparently abducted in midair, then set down at a remote spot of the tropical forest]. When we gained access to the aircraft—we went in through

Figure 14.1. A B-52D.

one of the hatches—the entire crew [of five men] was still in their seats, strapped in their safety harnesses, and mutilated.

English and his fellow rangers initially assumed that the airmen had been tortured by the Vietcong. But close examination of the mangled corpses' unusual condition soon convinced the men otherwise. Moreover, the immediate vicinity indicated that no outsiders had visited the downed aircraft.

The entire crew was still in their jump suits. We found no survivors. There were several hundred thousand tons of bombs on the thing. [The B-52 actually carried a maximum payload of 35 tons, something English, serving only in the Green Berets, would not have known.] A load of bombs [was] in the bomb bays. We were operating in enemy territory, and everybody [had to] get in and get out as fast as we could. I did take photographs. I collected dog tags. We recovered the black boxes that were on the aircraft, where we were told they were located. And then we placed satchel charges throughout the aircraft and destroyed it with the bodies in it. There was no possible way we could transport the bodies out. [The dead men aboard were subsequently listed as] "Killed in action."

We turned in the material that we got—the black boxes, the photographs, and the dog tags, and whatever records that we found on the aircraft to MAC-V [Military Assistance Command, Vietnam] headquarters in Saigon—and we forgot about it. When [five years later, as a data analyst in England] I viewed the [Grudge 13] report, there was a report attached to the photographs, which stated that the aircraft [a downed *Stratofortress*] had been in radio contact with its base, and that it reported that it was under attack by bright objects. And then, all of a sudden, the radio transmissions died. [The B-52 had been attacked by] very bright objects, bright, glowing objects.[2]

Accounts of alien atrocities committed against servicemen during the Vietnam War predated the grisly find English and his team made in Laos. "Rumors floated around that UFOs had kidnapped and mutilated two army soldiers," recalled Milton William Cooper, "then dropped them in the bush."

Cooper was captain of PB-44, a patrol boat that plied the Cua Viet River from 1967 to 1969, when he received the Silver Star, the U.S. military's third-highest decoration for valor in combat. Before his discharge in 1975, Cooper rose through the ranks of naval intelligence, where his prestigious citation granted him a kind of special clearance. Among the above-top-secret files open to him was a report about the outcome of a battle between the enemy and U.S. Marines for a village inhabited by some fifty Vietnamese, who could not be evacuated in time. As the fighting neared its climax, several metallic disks "were seen hovering above their huts . . . both sides had fired upon the UFOs, and they had blasted back with a mysterious blue light."

The guerillas fled as soon as they realized that their weapons, like those of the Americans, had no effect on the strange craft, which vanished away at high speed almost immediately thereafter. The Marines cautiously moved into the contested, strangely silent hamlet, only to find that "all the people of the entire village disappeared."[3]

Another mass disappearance involving extraterrestrials and U.S. elite forces occurred during August 1968, when members of a small ranger team were leaving enemy territory after completing a mission in North Vietnam, and were on their way to a prearranged helicopter pickup location. With National Liberation Front (NLF) forces gaining on them, the terribly outnumbered Americans climbed a high hill to gain some measure of defense. As they began digging in, the clatter of AK-47 assault rifles echoed from an adjacent hill just occupied by the pursuing Reds. Tracer rounds could be seen rising practically straight up into the sky, but not, as the commandos assumed, at their expected rescue helicopters. Instead, furious NLF fire concentrated on "a large, semi-circular object. One member of the team," as described by UFO historian Mack Maloney, "recalled that its color kept changing from light blue to bright red. It was making no noise. As soon as the enemy tracers got close to the object, it suddenly stopped in midair, just a few hundred feet from where the U.S. special ops team was hiding. The Americans saw a streak of light shoot out from the front of the object; then, there was nothing but silence. The UFO briefly lingered over the spot where the enemy had been firing at it, then turned and headed out to sea."

The rangers lay low for another half hour before moving out to warily reconnoiter the opposite hill. The Commies were nowhere to be seen. They had completely vanished. Only scattered about were their firearms, "and they'd been melted down to almost nothing, leaving a smell that was so bad, it stayed with the team members for hours afterward."[4]

In fact, 1968 was the most intense year for confrontations between Vietnam era earthlings and extraterrestrials. It began on January 31, as seventy thousand North Vietnamese and Vietcong forces launched a coordinated series of fierce attacks on more than one hundred cities and towns across South Vietnam. But something other than human was also involved in the Tet Offensive, named after Indochina's lunar New Year holiday. During one late-night operation, as a veteran recalls his experience, he and a few other Marines "went through the base gate [of the Red Beach Base Area, a complex of logistics and support bases, northwest of Da Nang], and marched into the jungle approximately three clicks [just under two miles] to a point where two of the uncounted trails, known as the Ho Chi Minh Trail, crossed, and set up our ambush, waiting through the long, hot jungle night for Charlie to come walking down the trail." (*Charlie* was U.S. slang for *Vietcong soldier*, from *Victor Charlie*, military communication code for *V.C.*, an abbreviation of *Vietcong*.) The veteran continues:

> We broke ambush early 'am, and had marched back down the trail, and had just entered a clearing, when suddenly, up in the sky, just above the jungle canopy, and slightly behind us, there it was—the UFO—visible for a short time. Apparently, Charlie saw it too, and opened fire with rpgs (rocket-propelled grenades) and small arms fire, with no effect on the UFO. We did not fire, but only watched, as it hovered over us for maybe five minutes, then seemed to drift sideways, and, as suddenly as it had appeared, it was gone. We started marching again toward Red Beach. Nobody said anything, but the Captain told us to forget about it. We got back to base without incident, but, to this day, I can still see it [the UFO], and so can the rest of us [in our memories].[5]

Three days in June, however, compressed more such activity than at any other time, beginning a world away from Southeast Asia, in another Communist country. On the 14th, a forty-two-year-old reservist in the *Ejercito Rebelde*, Fidel Castro's Revolutionary Army, was standing guard duty near Cabanas, a village on the northeast coast of western Cuba, when a bright object stealthily descended behind a line of trees about five minutes after midnight. When Isidro Puentes Ventura went to investigate, he stopped within 150 feet of a landed disk suffused with white light, surmounted by a dome and an antenna array. The silent, metallic craft, about the size of a large pickup truck standing on a kind of squat tripod, showed no other details, until Ventura blasted it with more than forty rounds from his Kalashnikov machine gun. The target responded by growing dark, while emitting an ear-shattering whistle.

The next thing he knew, Ventura awoke in a hospital bed after a coma lasting thirteen days. Although not physically injured, neurologists determined his condition had been induced by emotional trauma. Other reservists in the area heard the blast of his automatic weapon, came running, found him lying motionless outside Cabanas (but did not find a whistling disk) and carried him away to the naval hospital in Havana. After making his incredible report, he was subjected to fifty hours of continuous interrogation, followed by fifteen hypnosis sessions.

Meanwhile, state police investigating the scene of his alleged encounter recovered forty-eight spent cartridges from Ventura's Kalashnikov plus "fourteen bullets flattened as if they had been fired against an extremely hard surface," according to Hall. "A round depression was clearly visible in the soil with a hole about three feet in diameter in the middle and three indentations around it. Each of the three surrounding marks were rectangular in shape and measured one meter deep by forty centimeters wide, with the overall width across the three landing depressions measuring four meters. Intelligence officers discovered the area covered with a fine, grey dust spread fifteen feet across the circular depression. Soil samples were taken for analysis, showing that they had been subjected to a high degree of heat."[6]

Cuban radar operators additionally detected an unidentified aircraft in the Cabanas area shortly after midnight, June 14, before their contact was lost as a result of anomalous electronic interference.

Around noon the following day, two McDonnell-Douglas F-4 jet interceptors thundered low over Bong Son, a town in the south-central coastal region of Vietnam, hotly pursuing a large silvery disk. One of the Phantom IIs got close enough to get off a 20-millimeter shell from its cannon, and the strange craft "made a controlled crash landing in the middle of a firefight between a squad of American M-60 tanks and an undetermined number of NVA [North Vietnamese Army troops] and Viet Cong," according to a U.S. Army grunt who witnessed the attack.

> Things sort of stopped for awhile, until the NVA/VC fired an RPG [rocket-propelled grenade] at the UFO. The first RPG had no affect [*sic*], so more were fired.
>
> The UFO somehow neutralized the RPGs and started attacking the NVA/VC. [He does not indicate how the extraterrestrials defended themselves.] At this point, the American tanks opened fire on the UFO. The UFO could not stop the 90-millimeter tank rounds and was destroyed. The NVA/VC broke off and left. The Americans found several alien bodies and at least one survivor in the UFO wreckage.
>
> When the American commander, a major, called for a medevac, he was told nothing was available. Everything was being used in the search for the [other] UFO. He told them he had it, and a chopper was immediately sent. When it arrived, the CIA type in charge refused to take the wounded American GI's [casualties of alien counterfire] onboard. Instead insisting he would only take the aliens.
>
> At this point, the Major, shot the surviving alien, and had his tanks grind the wreckage and extraterrestrial bodies into the ground. The chopper pilot overruled the CIA type and medevaced the wounded.[7]

Word of the Bong Son incident spread rapidly among U.S. servicemen throughout the region, making them jumpy and primed to go off half-cocked at anything resembling a cross between Charlie and an alien. Just after midnight, Lieutenant Pete Snyder and the American crew of Swift boat PCF-12 set out under a brightly moonlit sky, down the Cua Viet, the same dangerous river where Captain Cooper earned his Silver Star for courage under fire. After approximately half an hour on the water, Snyder received an urgent message from another patrol boat not far away. Its commander, Lieutenant Richard Davis, requested immediate assistance against a pair of attacking "enemy helicopters."

Figure 14.2. A Vietnam War U.S. patrol boat.

During the Vietnam War, *enemy helicopter* was a U.S. military euphemism for *UFO*, because the North Vietnamese only operated fixed-wing aircraft. "They weren't called 'UFOs.' They were called 'enemy helicopters,'" according to General George S. Brown, commander of the 7th U.S. Air Force and deputy commander for Air Operations, Military Assistance Command Vietnam, from 1968 to 1970, who later chaired the Joint Chiefs of Staff.[8]

As Lieutenant Snyder's vessel approached the other boat, he and his three crew members observed two glowing spheroids poised motionless above its position. Moments later, a sudden flash of blinding light illuminated PCF-19, which was instantly engulfed in a terrific explosion, killing five of the seven-man crew, including Davis. The spheroids vanished before the thunder of the blast echoed away down the riverbanks. PCF-12 picked up two wounded survivors, the gunner's mate and seaman, who told how the UFOs had followed them for miles up the Cua Viet before attacking. Lieutenant Snyder radioed in a preliminary report to the U.S. Navy base at Saigon, and he received orders to complete his patrol. Just then, his second engineman, Jeff Steffes, frantically called out the appearance of two "enemy helicopters" silently but steadily approaching their vessel.

"We spotted two aircraft hovering on our port and starboard beams," said Steffes. "They were about three hundred yards away and one hundred feet above the water. As the boat swung around to put the aircraft ahead and astern of PCF-12, I could hear Mr. Snyder requesting air support and identification of these *helos* [short for *helicopters*]. The answer from the beach was: 'no friendly aircraft in the area; have contacts near you on radar and starlight scope.' The result was, 'no friendlies.' These had to be North Vietnamese."[9]

But they weren't. For the next two and a half hours—long beyond the operational range of any contemporaneous helicopter—PCF-12 played cat and mouse with the anomalous helos, opening fire on them at close range with twin .50-caliber machine guns from a forward turret, a pair of 7.62-millimeter machine guns mounted on the port and starboard sides, and an Mk 19 grenade launcher. But their combined firepower, as accurate as it was concentrated, had no effect on the incoming spheroids. One of them flew so close to the boat that Steffes could see they had "a rounded front, like an observation helo," and he saw what looked like "two crewmen sitting side by side."[10]

No pilot and gunner would fly an observation helicopter into combat "sitting side by side" behind a Plexiglas canopy. If they had, Steffes would have shot them down in a heartbeat. As Lieutenant Snyder repeatedly radioed headquarters for back-up, PCF-12 churned Cua Viet's murky waters at top speed in a desperate effort to escape its dogged pursuers. His pleas were finally answered around 3:20 a.m., when several Phantom fighter jets roared in low overhead, chasing off the menacing spheroids with six-barrel Gatling cannons clattering away and streaking AIM-9 *Sidewinder* air-to-air missiles.

By then, unknown to Snyder and his men, radar operators confirmed no less than thirty "enemy helicopters" of various dimensions—some of them as large as a warship—closing on Da Nang at 5,000 feet down Vietnam's east coast at 375 mph, more than twice the speed of any helicopter in the world at that time. When these contacts were visually identified by forward spotters along the eastern DMZ (demilitarized zone, a six-mile-wide strip separating North from South Vietnam), the entire Red Beach Base Area was thrown into full alert. More U.S. 7th Air Force interceptors were dispatched to engage the flying armada, which was additionally fired on by every antiaircraft gun at the Americans' disposal. Seemingly in the face of such resistance, the "glowing lights" veered away, out over the China Sea.

It was here that the U.S. naval fleet was stationed in company with a Perth-class guided missile destroyer of the Royal Australian Navy. Blacked out and maintaining radio silence, HMAS *Hobart* was patrolling near Tiger Island, about thirteen miles off Cap Lay, when her starboard side was struck by a guided missile. It penetrated the aluminum hull and exploded, killing Ordinary Seaman R. J. Butterworth and wounding two crew members. As *Hobart*'s deck gun got off five shots at her unidentified attacker, two more missiles slammed into her starboard side, killing Chief Electrician Richard Hunt and injuring several others.

After daybreak, military authorities were informed, to their horror, that the blacked-out Australian warship had been attacked by American fighter pilots, who had mistaken her in the dark for a UFO. They were

Figure 14.3. HMAS *Hobart*.

further mortified to learn that none of the thirty "enemy helicopters" had been shot down, for all the thousands of cannon shells and the dozen or so guided missiles expended during the incident.

"No physical evidence of helicopters destroyed has been discovered in the area of activity," reported the Royal Australian Navy News on August 1, "nor has extensive reconnaissance produced any evidence of enemy helicopter operations in or near the DMZ."[11]

Not a scrap of wreckage related to the events of the previous month was ever found. Air Force pilots, rattled by too many ferocious extra-terrestrial encounters, had become trigger-happy, mistaking the *Hobart* for an alien craft. Until the Royal Australian Navy News coverage, military spokesmen had been explaining how losses from friendly fire occurred in the midst of a confused skirmish with "enemy helicopters." When these proved too elusive, blame fell on faulty radar systems and pilot misinterpretation of radar returns, minus any mention of the mysterious "lights" that had outflown the USAF. Radar operator and ground observer veterans of the confrontation knew better, but said nothing.

Many years later, Jim Steffes, now retired, published his own eyewitness version. "I know what the 'official story' is," he concluded, "but this is mine, as true and complete as I can remember."[12]

The engagement and deadly confusion of June 15, 1968, may have represented less of a serious attack than a successful demonstration of otherworldly superiority. Two years before, an otherwise meaningless episode perhaps aimed at making a similar impression. It took place on the south-central coast of Vietnam, during mid-1966, in Nha Trang, then home to more than 40,000 troops, 2,000 of them U.S. GIs. Sheltering in a valley along the China Sea, the heavily defended base featured several warehouses and a fuel-storage area on the west, plus docks and equipment-storage facilities in the south.

On the evening of June 18, eight bulldozers were cutting roads by the light of their headlamps around Hawk Hill, less than half a mile west of the compound, while, under a mile to the east, two Douglas A-1 *Skyraiders*—piston-powered, propeller-driven anachronisms in the jet age—were warming up on their newly bulldozed airstrip. About a mile to the southwest, just off shore, a Shell Oil tanker rode peacefully at anchor in the bay. This tranquil scene was the last in more than a month of enemy inactivity, as a hundred or so soldiers casually gathered in an open area of the base to watch an outdoor movie around 8:00.

Less than two hours later, the film abruptly stopped, because the projector's power source—all six, new, independently-operated generators—ceased to function at that same moment, plunging all of Nha Trang into total darkness. About a half mile away, another Air Force base simultaneously experienced an identical electrical outage. The engines of both *Skyraiders* whirled to a stop, while the headlights and motors of all eight bulldozers switched off.

As someone who experienced the power failure explained, "There wasn't a car, truck, plane or anything that ran for about 4 minutes" after the sky lit up with an exceptionally bright light. "At first," the same observer recalled, "we thought it was a flare, which are going off all the time and then we found that it wasn't. It came from the North, and was moving from real slow to real fast speeds. . . . Some of the jet fighter pilots said it looked to be about 25,000 feet [in altitude] and then the panic broke loose. It [the light] dropped right towards us, and stopped dead still about 300 to 500 feet up. It made this little valley and the mountains around look like it was the middle of the day. It lit up everything. Then it went up and I mean, up. It went straight up, and completely out of sight in about 2–3 seconds."[13]

Extraterrestrial demonstrations of earthling inferiority were impartially carried out over North as well as South Vietnam. On September 29, 1972, a correspondent for *Agence France-Presse* published his personal account of an invulnerable spheroid he and thousands of residents in the North Vietnamese capital observed under bright daylight conditions. Jean Thoraval's feature article was carried around the world, including Lansing, Michigan's *State Journal,* beneath the headline, "What Was UFO over Hanoi?"

Watching the craft through binoculars, Thoraval reported that "a mysterious object appeared in the clear blue sky over Hanoi, Friday, attracting missile fire from the ground, but apparently remaining motionless. It was spherical in shape and a luminous orange in color, and was clearly at a very high altitude. . . . North Vietnamese air defenses fired three, surface-to-air missiles, [but they] were unable to reach the target. . . . The object remained in the same high spot for over one hour and twenty minutes, although, towards the end, it appeared less bright than before."[14]

Less than a month later, and half a world away from the war in Vietnam, a series of naval engagements took place with an extraterrestrial intruder north of Bergen, in Sognefjord, Norway's largest fjord at 127 miles long, though less than 4 miles wide. It was here, during the early morning hours of November 12, that a patrol boat on duty in the middle of the fjord, where its depths are greatest (4,291 feet) picked up what appeared to be a Soviet Whiskey-class submarine on its sonar scope.[15]

The Royal Norwegian Navy was alerted to arrive in a task force of destroyers, submarines, and an auxiliary aircraft carrier, which launched its attack helicopters. These were pairs of Westland WS-61 *Sea Kings,* each armed with four depth charges, which were dropped in the vicinity of the sonar contact. Shortly thereafter, all the *Sea Kings* experienced a variety of abnormal instrument failures that forced them to withdraw from further action, and they were replaced by land-based attack planes of the Royal Norwegian Navy Air Service. They too suffered from similar electromagnetic anomalies, but continued to fly cover for the growing number of naval units gathering below.[16]

Their target had meanwhile eluded them, so the western end of Sognefjord, which led out into the Atlantic Ocean, was tightly blockaded, trapping Norway's underwater intruder inside the narrow estuary. For more than two weeks, the fjord's depths were meticulously searched in a well-executed grid pattern that finally bore fruit after first light on November 26, when sonar rediscovered its lost contact near the mouth of Sognefjord, where the bottom rises abruptly to about 330 feet below the surface, in an apparent attempt at breaking out into the open sea.[17]

Destroyers closed in, dropping depth charges, which brought their evasive quarry to the surface. It was no Soviet submarine, however, but approximately twice as large as the USSR's 274-foot-long Whiskey-class boats, which bore no resemblance to the immense cigar-shaped vessel lacking a conning tower or any other physical details. The lead destroyer immediately opened fire with its deck guns on the motionless craft, to no visible effect.[18] The Norwegian submarine, KNM *Sklinna,* then launched a spread of torpedoes at the sitting-duck target, but all either malfunctioned or missed.[19]

Before another attack could be readied, the huge, unidentifiable vessel gradually slipped beneath the waves and yet again inexplicably vanished from every sonar scope.

Later that afternoon, civilians chanced to see the gargantuan object floating leisurely on the surface before it abruptly submerged near the island of Kraakenes, not far from the fjord's Atlantic entrance. Eighteen minutes later, five policemen from the village of Skjolden, on Sala Island, observed it surface, and informed the Navy. The distance covered by the object between these islands in the time separating both reports indicated it traveled at 124 mph, far beyond the performance of any known submarine.[20]

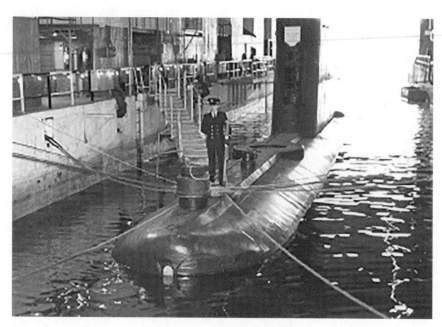

Figure 14.4. The KNM *Sklinna.*

Naval forces arrived too late for interdiction; the intruder disappeared yet again, but was finally cornered on the surface within forty-eight hours, and rapidly engaged with antisub missiles fired by destroyers and aircraft. The enigmatic vessel passed through this concerted fire unscathed, submerged in a controlled descent. It was never again detected by sonar or seen by eyewitnesses, much to the consternation of Royal Norwegian Navy commanders, who had deemed their blockade of Sognefjord impenetrable.[21]

The prolonged engagement had been far from secret, having been followed around the globe in the world press, including the *New York Times*. The *Times* assiduously avoided any references to extraterrestrials but was at a loss to explain just what the Norwegian naval authorities had been chasing and fighting for more than two weeks. A few months later, they found something on the bottom of the fjord that was and still is classified as top secret.[22]

In early 1973, a Royal Norwegian Navy Special Forces deep-sea diver was helicoptered without explanation from his advanced training at Bergen to Sognefjord, where he and another diver found themselves on a warship. There they were suited up with oxygen-helium equipment for a deep descent. Presented with state-of-the-art underwater military cameras, the two men were ordered to "observe, report, and debrief," and memorize every detail of what they found.[23] But they were not told what they were supposed to find or given any further knowledge about the operation.

The moment both divers simultaneously set foot on the midnight-dark bottom of the fjord at more than 300 feet beneath its surface, their subsurface lights revealed a pair of deeply grooved tracks obviously made by a belted vehicle of some kind, like a tank or bulldozer, that had progressed in a straight path through the ooze. Each track was 30 to 50 feet wide, and separated by a permanent 30–50-foot-wide gap. No other marks in the fjord bed suggested anything had been dragged or towed. But the vehicle that left the tracks had to have been an estimated 110–150 feet across, "something completely foreign to our technological capacity," one of the divers recalled more than forty years later, "both now and then. It looked like the object had been lifted off the sea floor," he said, after both men swam over the unvarying tracks, which suddenly terminated after nearly two miles. "There was no further trace of it further east of the fjord's entrance."[24]

Navy superiors provided their divers with no clarification about the nameless mission, and all photographs taken of the deep-water track were and still are classified. It had been doubtlessly left behind by the 500-foot-long vehicle that had been unsuccessfully hunted a few months before in that same location. The subsurface tracks were not publicly disclosed until the next century, by one of the divers. International attention shifted from the lengthy pursuit of what was, by all accounts, a USO, to headline-grabbing news about the increasingly costly conflict in Vietnam.

Even there, however, Americans were simultaneously fighting two enemies: the VC and the ETs. One of those Americans was Peter Mazzola, a forward observer for an Army platoon pinned down in tall elephant grass by enemy fire. His men lay low, hoping to find a way out of their encirclement, when several glowing spheres slowly and silently rose over the paddy fields and palm trees not far away. Assuming they were some kind of Vietcong reconnaissance craft, Mazzola radioed in their coordinates to U.S. Navy cruisers offshore.

In no time, shells hurled in from American warships in the south, and "then the objects began to receive artillery rounds from the other direction, from the north [the North Vietnamese position]. The shells never made the target. They all exploded short." Even though the gunfire of both the Vietcong and the U.S. Navy was right on target, neither side touched the objects. "We could see the black smoke puffs in the air."[25] The spheres continued to hover "silently, gracefully," but in less than five minutes, they "shot straight up in the air," and were gone.

Taking advantage of the confusion caused by such high strangeness, Mazzola and his comrades made good their escape. After the war, he became a New York City police detective, later founding Staten Island's Scientific Bureau of Investigation for the serious study of UFO phenomena.

Human soldiers continued to battle each other while confronting alien enemies until the fall of Saigon on April 30, 1975. The most notable extraterrestrial confrontation of the period occurred the previous June, when Japan Air Self-Defense Force commanders ordered a pair of F-4EJ *Phantom* jet fighters, flown by Lieutenant Colonel Toshio Nakamura and Major Shiro Kubuta, to intercept a presumed Soviet bomber near Hokkaido, the country's most northerly territory. Once airborne, they were informed that the intruder was actually a bright-colored UFO first observed by ground spotters, then tracked by radar operators. Vectored to their target at 30,000 feet, both pilots made visual contact with the red disk that Major Kubuta described as "made and flown by intelligent beings."[26]

As Kubuta and Nakamura came within firing range of the object, it began executing a series of evasive maneuvers, involving the *Phantoms* in a dogfight. After several minutes, during which neither pilot was able to score any hits on the disk, it collided first with one, then with the other aircraft. Both men successfully ejected, but Nakamura's parachute was set afire, and he fell to his death as the UFO sped away.

Figure 14.5. Two Japanese *Phantoms*.

While these confrontations were taking place in Asia, the Russians were waging their own War of the Worlds. Although the heavy hand of Soviet censorship erased many details, enough information concerning the premier military engagement of its kind survived the USSR's collapse for postcommunist researchers to reconstruct. They learned from fragments of original documents in *Stavka,* the Red Army's high command, that history's largest air battle between earthbound aviators and alien ufonauts occurred during early summer 1967. According to Stonehill, it took place "on the Soviet Union's border region with Iran and Afghanistan." Although the total number of combatants is unknown, "six modern Soviet aircraft were destroyed, and twelve pilots perished." Facts regarding their identities or the types of warplanes they flew are still missing. More certain, however, was Stavka's subsequent demand that "absolutely forbade any contacts with UFOs. Furthermore, military aviators were ordered not to approach the objects at less than six miles' distance."[27]

Such deadly confrontations were not limited to the USSR or Southeast Asia during the Vietnam War era. During the early evening of September 8, 1970, radar operators at Lincolnshire's Royal Air Force Station Binbrook, near the east coast of England, detected several unauthorized aircraft over Grimsby, a seaport in northeast Lincolnshire. At the same moment, "sightings of flying, transparent spheres," according to local newspaper coverage, were reported at the village of Flamborough, about fifty miles away, on the North Sea.[28] After the anonymous intruders ignored repeated radio calls for their identification, the RAF base commander assumed they were Russians, and ordered a Quick Reaction Alert fighter to intercept them.

At 10:06 p.m., twenty-eight-year-old U.S. Air Force captain William Schaffner took off from Binbrook in Foxtrot 94, a British-built Electric *Lightning* outfitted with a pair of 30-millimeter ADEN cannons and a quiver of air-to-air missiles. Ground-radar controllers vectored him to their mysterious scope contacts over the North Sea, where he soon made visual contact with something resembling "a flying cone."[29] While closing on it, Schaffner radioed that his avionics were going progressively haywire, and he was being outmaneuvered by one of Flamborough's "transparent spheres," despite the Electric *Lightning's* 1,300 mph top speed and 20,000 foot-per-minute rate of climb.

Shortly after 10:30 p.m., all communication with Foxtrot 94 failed, as ten crew members aboard a passing Avro *Shackleton*—a large maritime patrol aircraft—witnessed the jet lose control and fall into the sea about five miles offshore. Its wreckage was discovered on October 7 by Royal Navy divers operating from the minesweeper HMS *Kedleston*. They were surprised to find the aircraft in relatively good condition, sitting with the proper side up on the ocean floor. Greater surprise came early the following December when Foxtrot 94 was carefully brought to the surface by Royal Navy salvage workers. They found the plane's canopy still locked into position over the cockpit, but no one was inside.

"Captain Schaffner was declared dead," reported the *Grimsby Evening Telegraph*, "but his body has never been found."[30] Had he been atomized by an inconceivably powerful weapon, or teleported somehow out of his Electric *Lightning* and into the cone-shaped vehicle he had been pursuing?

Stateside U.S. military forces were no less under attack, although they were in grave danger of losing far more than a dozen men. Less than half a year before the Soviet air battle near the Afghanistan-Iran border,

Figure 14.6. An English Electric *Lightning* with open canopy.

a front-page story in the *Minot Daily News* for December 6, 1966, told of numerous eyewitnesses, including police and local government officials, who saw luminous, disk-shaped craft flying in the vicinity of Mohall, North Dakota, near the Minot Air Force Base, America's most important military installation, headquarters for a wing of B-52s loaded with atomic warheads and intercontinental ballistic missiles (ICBMs).

Captain David D. Schindele was the Minuteman I ICBM launch-crew commander there the following night, when a single UFO appeared over the facility. The extraterrestrial intruder destroyed no less than ten nuclear-tipped missiles in Captain Schindele's charge. Fortunately,

Figure 14.7.
A Minuteman I missile.

he disabled them in time to prevent a series of atomic explosions that would have otherwise decimated the Peace Garden State. He abided by Air Force suppression of all public knowledge regarding North Dakota's brush with catastrophe for more than fifty years, until the 2017 release of his appropriately entitled book, *It Never Happened.*[31]

Just eight months after Minot's missiles were taken down, the base was under siege again. On the night of July 26, 1967, Minot's executive officer received a red-alert notice from radar operators at the North American Aerospace Defense Command, located at Peterson Air Force Base, near Colorado Springs, Colorado. He was informed of an unidentified contact descending over one of Minot's missile silos. He immediately scrambled two specimens of the Convair F-106 *Delta Dart,* then regarded as the ultimate interceptor.

As the fighters were getting airborne, heavily armed members of a security team dispatched to the silo in question were astounded to behold a metallic disk, about 50 feet across, its rim encircled by a garland of bright lights, slowly moving approximately 100 feet above the facility. The apparition stopped suddenly in midair, then ascended vertically another 400 feet to hover briefly before vanishing away at the sound of the approaching jets.

The next night, what appeared to be the same disk was observed drifting over each ICBM emplacement.

"Within an hour," writes UFO historian Mack Maloney, "all of Minot's launch facilities had reported that a UFO had been over their location," until—like a bee singling out a special flower—it seemed to select a particular silo, pausing there about 40 feet in the air. Moments later, the missile's emergency indicators began to repeatedly flash in big, bright, red lights, "LAUNCH IN PROGRESS!" accompanied by the wail of doomsday sirens blaring across the whole base. Horrified control-room directors and personnel fell over themselves trying to deactivate the nuclear-tipped missile before it shot off on its irrevocable course toward Moscow. With only moments to spare, they succeeded in canceling the launch sequence, and the awful emergency indicators went abruptly dark.

As the chorus of sirens echoed away, the illuminated disk escaped unnoticed in the confusion. "But it was apparent to all concerned," Maloney concludes, "that the UFO had probed the missile's controls, and had somehow switched them on. Had any of the inhibit commands failed, the missile would have launched."[32] Clearly the aliens had attempted to precipitate nuclear war.

Even that near miss was perhaps less compelling than a discovery made by Sergeant Karl Wolfe while he and his fellow electronics experts were compiling surveillance data for an escalating Vietnam War. He was a color-laboratory photographic technician trained in electronic-photographic repair at Colorado's Lowry Air Force Base. During July 1965, Wolfe was issued a top-secret "crypto-security clearance" to the Tactical Air Command at Langley Air Force Base, Virginia, in the 44th Reconnaissance Technical Group, then involved in photographic reconnaissance and spy-satellite photography.

Some computerized contact-printing instrument there was not functioning properly, and Sergeant Wolfe was called over to fix it. When admitted into the equipment room, he found another airman second class technician at work on the printer, which was about the size of a small apartment refrigerator.

"He showed me the equipment where the digital information came in," Wolfe recalled, "where it was converted to photographic images. They were doing 35-millimeter strips of film at that time, which were then assembled into 18.5-by-11-inch mosaics . . . those strips were from successive passes around the moon, and they would take and build up a photograph by scanning one section of the moon and then another and another; and then they would get a larger image. So, this mosaic then would be put into that contact printer, and that was then a print."[33]

Because the darkroom in which the printer had been installed was unsuitable for repair work, Sergeant Wolfe telephoned guards for removing the equipment to a larger, better-lit area. While waiting for them to arrive, Wolfe and his colleague

walked over to one side of the lab, and he said, 'By the way, we discovered a base on the backside of the moon.' . . . And then he pulled out one of these mosaics that showed this base, which had geometric shapes that were towers; there were spherical buildings; they were very tall, thin towers . . . they were massive. Some of the structures are half a mile in size . . . And they're all different structures in different-size photographs; there were angular shots with shadows. I try to relate them in my own mind to structures here on Earth, and they don't compare to anything you see here in scale and structure. Not metallic, they're more like a stone structure, but fabricated stone. Some of the buildings seemed to have very reflective surfaces on them. A couple of structures I saw reminded me of cooling towers at power plants; they had that sort of a shape. Some others were very straight and tall with a flat top. Some of them were round. Some of them looked like a Quonset hut . . . like a greenhouse . . . In the photograph that I saw, they were fairly clustered together over a fairly large landscape. There was one building that had a dish-like shape to it, but it was very large. It looked like a radar dish, but it was a building. There was another building near it with an angular top that was truncated.[34]

All this four years before Neil Armstrong was the first man to walk on the moon. But the extraterrestrials operated more than lunar installations, according to Clifford Stone, a former U.S. Army sergeant first class attached to the 96th Civil Affairs Group, 6th Civil Affairs Company, NBC (nuclear-biological chemicals) Com (communications), with a nuclear-security clearance, stationed at Fort Lee, Virginia. In winter 1969, Stone was the noncommissioned officer in charge of measuring surface readings of a crashed off-world vehicle outside Indiantown Gap, Pennsylvania, with his Geiger counter. While examining the wedge-shaped craft, he observed the corpses of several occupants.

Over the next ten years, Sergeant Stone was engaged in another eleven related investigations for the Army, where he learned shocking news about the aliens: "We [U.S. military forces] were involved in a major engagement in 1970 in one of their bases at a place called

Duibadiem, Tiền Province [Tiền Giang, in the Mekong Delta region of southern Vietnam], approximately seven miles from the Cambodian border."[35]

A similar confrontation was described by Phil Schneider, a certified geologist, structural engineer, and explosives expert. It took place at a subterranean federal-government installation he helped construct in 1969 on the Jicarilla Apache Indian Reservation, under Archuleta Mesa, on the Colorado–New Mexico border, northwest of Dulce, a small New Mexico town. Schneider claimed during his June 15, 1995, Preparedness Expo lecture at California's Orange County Convention Center that he was one of only three survivors from a vicious firefight that occurred in late August 1979 with tall extraterrestrials at the underground facility. Although he did not specify how many aliens died, sixty-six U.S. Air Force and NATO Delta Force personnel were supposedly killed. After publicly describing the incident, Schneider claimed to have been repeatedly threatened by unknown persons who made him fear for his personal safety.[36]

Although many listeners found Schneider's unsubstantiated account difficult to accept, they were shocked to learn that just seven months later, on January 17, 1996, his dead body was found in his Wilsonville, Oregon, apartment, a rubber catheter hose wrapped three times around his neck and half-knotted in front. The victim of an execution-style murder, he had been tortured to death. Marie, his grieving widow, told newspaper reporters that Phil had no known enemies and was not in serious debt to anyone. She emphatically denied police accusations that her husband committed suicide—a physical impossibility in any case, given the mutilated condition of his corpse.[37]

PART FIVE

Modern Sightings, Modern Conflict

15

Conflict in the Late Twentieth Century

I occasionally think how quickly our differences would vanish if we were facing an alien threat from outside this world . . . if suddenly, if there was a threat to this world from some other species from another planet outside in the universe. Well, I don't suppose we can wait for some alien race to come down and threaten us. And wouldn't we come together to fight that threat?

U.S. President Ronald Reagan,
addressing the General Assembly of
the United Nations, September 21, 1987.[1]

The same "alien race" that came within seconds of triggering an atomic holocaust at Minot Air Force Base in North Dakota endeavored to achieve similar results at the Byelokoroviche missile base in the Soviet Ukraine. It was here that Lieutenant Colonel Vladimir Plantonev was in local command of fully functional nuclear warheads for deployment against targets in the United States. He was under orders to launch them only after he received direct telephoned orders from the highest authorities in Moscow. As an eyewitness to the events of October 4, 1982, he testified that an object "of perfect geometrical shape and 2,900 feet in diameter" appeared over the installation. "According to him," writes Stonehill, "the UFO was a noiseless, disk-shaped craft; it had no portholes, its surface completely even."

Just then, signal lights on both the control panels in the operational command room lit up bright red, indicating that the launch sequence for Byelokoroviche's ICBMs had been initiated. "But no order came from Moscow, and no one at the base pushed any buttons. For fifteen long seconds, the base simply lost control of its nuclear weapons, much to the subsequent alarm of Moscow." When precautionary backup measures automatically kicked in to cancel the unauthorized launch sequence, or whether the immense intruder that had initiated it was responsible, Lieutenant Colonel Plantonev never indicated. He remarked only that the seamless disk disappeared at great speed, after having sparked an "incident that almost unleashed a nuclear war."[2]

Were the events in North Dakota and Ukraine separate, but fundamentally similar warnings? Or were they narrowly failed attempts to consume both nations in mutual destruction?

These incidents were by no means unique, nor were they the first accounts of off-world beings intruding at nuclear facilities. On the morning of March 16, 1967, remote electronic sensor alarms were triggered by something violating security at ICBM launch-control facilities located fifty miles south of Lewiston, Montana. According to procedure, a security helicopter was dispatched, together with a pair of Convair F-106 fighters from Great Falls, while security alert teams, consisting of four to six armed guards, rushed to the compromised section.

Closing to within half a mile of the missile site where the K-7 was located, they radioed central command headquarters that the missile site in question was brightly lit by a glowing orange disk, about as large as a football field (160 feet wide by 360 feet long), hovering above the installation at no more than 200 feet. Security alert team members were ordered to proceed at once into the violated location but categorically refused, as the immense craft began to rise with gradually increasing speed. By the time the Convair jets arrived overhead, the intruder was lost to view and never intercepted.

Targeting specialists and computer analysts later found that K-7's guidance system had been reconfigured to attack an objective other than the target preprogrammed by launch-control officers. The identity of either objective was never declassified, though rumors persisted that the original setting had changed directional course from Kiev to New York City. Meanwhile, the Minuteman II missile was complexly modified—in effect, sabotaged—necessitating removal from its silo and replacement with a fresh missile.[3]

The cold war of UFO activity at military installations turned suddenly hot on January 18, 1978. Early that morning, glowing spheres buzzed the U.S. Army's Fort Dix and the adjacent McGuire Air Force Base, located about sixteen miles south-southeast of Trenton, New Jersey. Some hours later, a military policeman "was pursuing a low-flying object that had hovered over his car," writes UFO historian Richard H. Hall, "then a small being with large head and slender body appeared in front of his car. The MP had panicked and shot the alien several times with a .45 automatic. The being had fled over the fence between the two bases, before falling and dying on the deserted runway."

A sergeant on duty and other soldiers "found the body lying on the runway . . . and roped off the area of the 'crime scene.'" The sergeant told Hall that "under the glare of truck headlights the skin of the unclad, hairless body was wet, shiny, and snake-like. As reported in his initial letter, the entity was about 4 feet in height, with large head, slender torso, thin arms and legs, and, overall, of grayish-brown coloration. Unquestionably not human, it was however of humanoid stature . . . attributed to the presence of the body was the strong smell of ammonia in the cold, night air . . . the same odor has been present at other crash sites."

The sergeant adamantly stated that "a UFO had not crashed or been disabled nearby, requiring close tactical air support. But what of a landed craft, perhaps one that touch-landed earlier at Ft. Dix? Could it have deployed one or more of its kind to perform a duty, forever unknown," Hall wondered, "at one or both of the adjoining military installations?" Sitting alone in his patrol car not far from the alien corpse, the sergeant "received word by radio that a state of alert was in effect at McGuire, as a result of the shooting incident." The sergeant said, "It was maximum security. . . . At least a dozen men, armed with M-16s were assigned to guard at the ropes, and no one was allowed to enter, except the base commander, the security police squadron commander, 1st Lt. WS of the security police squadron, and a base photographer."

Unidentified specialists wearing blue berets arrived to "spray the corpse from a portable tank and cover it with a white sheet. Before daybreak, the body was carefully placed onto a platform and a wooden frame built around it. This was finally placed into a large square silver metal container, about ten-by-ten feet, with undistinguishable blue markings." The sergeant "and others watched the silver box fork-lifted into a C-141 [Lockheed C-141 *Starlifter,* a four-engine cargo jet], which arrived about 7 a.m. from Wright-Patterson AFB (identified by special markings), and, later at a distance, he said he watched the plane and its secret cargo soar aloft into limbo, presumed destination, Dayton, Ohio [location of the air base]." Witnesses "were warned not to talk about the incident, or they would be court-martialled."[4]

Despite occasional casualties, the aliens were persistent if impartial observers (and sometimes saboteurs) of weapons facilities on either side of the Iron Curtain. Three months after the Fort McGuire fatality, a UFO slowly circled at low altitude (beneath 1,000 feet) above an AA-class (top-priority) air-defense installation located between Urdzhar and Alekseevka, in Kazakhstan, not far from Likhanova, in Russia. On the night of March 3, 1978, against standard operating procedures, the base commander ordered a new ABM-1 *Galosh* fired at the extraterrestrial spy-craft. The surface-to-air, antiballistic missile detonated close enough to bring down its target, which crashed nearby.

The silvery disk, thirty to fifty feet in diameter, was surmounted by a dome, part of which had been damaged by the interception blast, along with the upper side of the hull. Two four-foot-tall humanoids with large, bald heads, were found dead inside the vehicle. Preliminary autopsies were performed on location by medical personnel. The bodies were then removed to an underground holding area west of Moscow. Wreckage of the disk was transported to the Semipalatinsk State

Figure 15.1. A Soviet *Galosh* antiballistic missile launcher.

Nuclear Test Range, where it is still allegedly stored in another sub-terranean facility.[5]

The following October, an American interceptor skirmished with an off-world craft in the air above Washington State, as closely observed by a highly credible witness. During late 1960s, Donald Bockelman had been a U.S. Army launch-area electronics technician and systems analyst assigned for two and a quarter years to integrated fire control at *Nike-Hercules* batteries in Western Europe. He later worked in Seattle for Honeywell International, which provides engineering services and aerospace systems for major corporations and governments. Bockelman said of the UFO, "Then this jet came from due west. I saw this object while I was standing on the back porch of my house, and it was then attacked and fired on by an Air Defense missile. As it turned out, it was a high-explosive missile right at the target. Shrapnel was falling to the ground. It [the missile] had exploded, and the object was accelerating away at a mind-boggling speed, away from where the attack occurred. The actual attack on the craft occurred . . . I would say about three miles north of the area called Lyman [and] Hamilton [on the Skedge River, in north-west Washington State]."[6]

ABDUCTIONS

By the last decade of the twentieth century, military confrontations between earthbound defenses and extraterrestrial intruders had mostly shifted back behind the Iron Curtain. Stonehill writes, "A UFO was sighted by numerous witnesses" as it hovered over the Baikonur Cosmodrome, a Soviet launching site for spacecraft, in the town of Leninsk, less than fifty miles east of Volgograd, the former Stalingrad.

"The sighting caused panic in the base, and several of the alarmed sentries fired at it." Communications at the facility failed and the lights went out shortly following the intruder's rapid departure. Not far from the disabled cosmodrome, screens at a Volga-Ural radar station went blank almost as soon as they detected an incoming UFO on September 13, 1990. When watch commander Major A. Tuplin emerged from the underground installation to determine a cause for the breakdown, he observed a delta-shaped craft moving very slowly overhead.

"It was black," Stonehill reports, "each side measuring some fifty feet, with no doors or portholes anywhere." Vertically emitting three bright beams of blue light, the silent triangle gradually settled to the ground in a soft landing not far away. "Then a blast from its side was followed by a ray, and the steely antenna of the station was set ablaze. Corporal Dudnik stopped soldiers from firing at the UFO," which remained in place for more than an hour, refraining from further attack, before departing skyward at high speed.[7] The Volga-Ural radar station escaped destruction but remained disabled for some weeks.

No casualties were sustained, but two men appear to have been abducted during the incident. Corporal Blazhis and Private Varennitza were unaccounted for until hours later, although they were unaware of any lost time. Investigators found that the wristwatches of both AWOL soldiers had stopped at precisely the same moment of their disappearance, and the serial numbers of their rifles were inexplicably missing.

Their experience resembled the encounter of an unidentified sentry in Jian-Shui County, Yunnan Province, China, whose wristwatch had stopped on an evening in October 1975 just when he disappeared from the front of his barracks. He had been stationed there on guard duty with one other soldier, and both men saw a huge metallic disk circling low over an installation of the Chinese People's Liberation Army. While his comrade ran off to sound a general alarm, he stayed to observe the saucer-shaped object emit beams of soft, orange-colored light in its slow circuit over the base.

The sentry had vanished and could not be found by the time the camp commandant arrived at the barracks with a dozen armed men, though they thoroughly scoured the facility for any trace of his whereabouts. Several hours later, four replacement sentries posted to his barracks—which had been repeatedly searched—found him moaning, as if in a deep, troubled sleep. As he regained full consciousness, he realized that most of his memory was gone. His eyebrows, beard, and hair, however, had grown excessively long, while his rifle—like his stopped wristwatch—was slightly magnetized.[8]

Another abduction that took place in the USSR was of an entirely different character. It occurred during the flight of a new aircraft over the Russian Far East, sometime in early 1992. The Sukhoi Su-27 was then the world's foremost jet fighter, with heavier ordnance, more sophisticated avionics, and higher maneuverability than anything comparable

Figure 15.2. Sukhoi Su-27s at an airshow. Photograph by Alexander Mishin.

in the American arsenal. Specifically designed for air-superiority missions, the Sukhoi could perform virtually all aerial warfare operations and therefore embodied the accumulative best of everything envisioned concerning an interceptor. Because this state-of-the-art masterpiece represented military aviation's supreme achievement, the aliens needed to take possession of a specimen as part of their efforts at keeping themselves abreast of current developments in human arms production.

A single Su-27 was being closely monitored by ground-radar operators when it unaccountably vanished from their screens in the blink of an eye. They assumed it had blown up for some accidental cause, but no explosion was heard, and no debris was ever found. After more than a month of concerted search efforts undertaken by hundreds of rescue workers over a wide area, not a trace of the pilot or a scrap of the plane was ever found. "Intriguingly," observes Stonehill, "the territory's air defense HQ reported that a UFO had been sighted in the area at the time of the disappearance."[9]

EXTRATERRESTRIAL INTERFERENCE

In a set of interdictions related to extraterrestrial activity at military bases in the East as well as the West, ufonauts occasionally destroyed both Russian and American missiles before either Minot or Byelokoroviche were temporarily taken over by "some other species from some other planet." These creatures appear to have been on hand sometime during 1978 in Kazakhstan, where the latest Soviet ICBMs were about to be put through their paces for the first time. Alarmed by the abrupt appearance of a 1,640-foot-wide flying saucer hanging stationary in the air above a supposedly secret facility, Emba 11 Air Defense and Anti-Missile Testing Range's commanding general—against Soviet Army directives—ordered the uninvited visitor destroyed. The antiballistic missile he launched had no sooner blasted off than it was struck and obliterated by a thin ray that shot from the immovable UFO.[10]

Similar shoot-downs occurred in the United States from the beginning of American missile testing. As long ago as May 15, 1949, a

German V-2 was test-fired from White Sands Proving Ground in the American Southwest. All went well until the unguided missile attained an altitude of 40 miles, then suddenly altered course northeast at the same moment it was intercepted by an intelligently controlled, silver disk keeping pace at the speed of sound. As horrified ground observers watched through tracking telescopes, the 12-ton projectile was now headed on a collision course for the town of Alamogordo, with 20,000 residents, just as its Second World War predecessors had targeted London several years earlier.

The unidentified object continued to fly escort, veering away just a moment before launch command officers remotely detonated the rogue rocket, as though their minds had been read by the alien pilot.[11] He could have probably downed the V-2 harmlessly anywhere in the vast New Mexico desert. Instead it was aimed at a human population center. Whether he really intended to strike Alamogordo or was aware somehow that the missile would be aborted in time, the hijacking of such a high-priority project by an unknown outside power sent shock waves of alarm throughout the upper echelons of America's armed forces. The off-world aviators had the advantage, it seemed.

Fifteen years later, in 1964, USAF first lieutenant Robert Jacobs was the photo instrumentation officer at Vandenberg Air Force Base, nine miles northwest of Lompoc, California, where he photographed missile launches going down the test range. Jacobs made an extraordinary film documentation of an Atlas rocket flight, which proceeded according to plan until something resembling one saucer topped by another circled the dummy warhead, shooting it four times, in as many directions, with what appeared to be a plasma beam from one of several bulges or domes attached to the craft. As some measure of its controlled performance, the object moved with ease in front of the missile, which was traveling between 11,000 and 14,000 miles per hour. After a final ray burst from the UFO, the Atlas warhead tumbled to its destruction.[12]

Shortly before his death in 2007 at eighty-nine years of age, a far more significant interception was made known by Colonel Ross Dedrickson, USAF (ret.). Attached to Washington, D.C.'s Chief of

Staff Office forty years earlier, his duties covered the inventory, security, and accountability of America's nuclear-weapons stockpile. While serving as a liaison between the secretary of defense and the Atomic Energy Commission, Dedrickson administered Nevada test sites and supervised nuclear-weapons manufacturing and quality assurance in Albuquerque, then managed the Pacific Nuclear Test Area west of Hawaii. As such, he was eminently placed to learn about a mind-boggling event that was kept secret from the outside world for a quarter of a century.

"The very end of the '70s or early '80s," Dedrickson stated, "we [the USAF] attempted to put a nuclear weapon on the moon and explode it for scientific measurements and other things, which was not acceptable to the extraterrestrials. . . . They destroyed the weapon before it got to the moon."[13]

The incident he described did not take place in a historical vacuum. As long before as 1958, the USAF planned to atomically bomb the lunar surface. Known as Project A119, it was initiated by a ten-member team of enthusiastic physicists—among them a young Carl Sagan—at Chicago's Illinois Institute of Technology, where a more powerful hydrogen bomb was originally envisioned for the project but subsequently discarded, because it would have been too heavy for any missile then available. They decided instead to use a W25 warhead with a 1.7-kiloton yield. Their ostensibly scientific interest in atom-bombing

Figure 15.3.
Colonel Ross Dedrickson, USAF (ret.).

was public cover for Project A119's real objective—to intimidate the Soviets, who were then ahead of America in the space race.[14]

Fears of unpopular reaction, both in the United States and among its allies—together with 1963's Partial Nuclear Test Ban Treaty and, four years later, the Outer Space Treaty—made it impossible to target Earth's satellite. But a recrudescence of Cold War tensions late the following decade emboldened Air Force commanders to actually launch an atomic warhead at the moon. By then they knew about the alien base there (as recounted in chapter 14), and may have targeted it.

EXTRATERRESTRIALS AROUND THE WORLD

About the same time extraterrestrials destroyed America's attempt to bomb the moon with a nuclear weapon, they engaged in a high-altitude dogfight in the skies over Peru. On the morning of April 11, 1980, a ball-shaped object hovered around 1,800 feet above La Joya Air Base, at Arequipa. Visual sightings confirmed by radar at 7:15 a.m. made local commanders suspect that the unknown contact was an Ecuadoran espionage balloon equipped with cameras for photographing sensitive military material at their base. (Indeed, the two South American neighbors would go to war the following year, after the Peruvian Army seized three of Ecuador's military outposts on the eastern slopes of the Cordillera del Cóndor mountain range.) To confirm or deny official suspicions, First Lieutenant Oscar Santa Maria Huerta was ordered into his Sukhoi Su-22 fighter armed with a pair of Nudelman-Rikhter NR-30 cannons. Just minutes after takeoff, he spotted his target.

"I approached within shooting range, and shot around sixty 30-millimeter shells at the 'balloon,'" Huerta said. "It had no effect at all. One of those rounds would have blown up a truck," but none made so much as a dent in the object, which "seemed to absorb the shots." After Huerta made several firing passes, as accurate as they were ineffectual, the hitherto stationary intruder began to ascend rapidly, the lieutenant in hot pursuit, until, about fifty miles from La Joya, it came to a dead stop in the middle of the sky, and he banked sharply to avoid collision. "I decided to ascend quickly and get in an attack position, vertically," Huerta explained, "but I was not able to get it in my sights to fire," because the object invariably spoiled his aim by turning, climbing, or descending beyond the capabilities of his Sukhoi jet. "The total 22 minutes of maneuvers is clearly etched in my brain," he said.[15]

Obviously the object was no balloon. In his high-flying dogfight, Huerta twice had the target locked in to fire, but each time it side-stepped his intentions before he could pull the trigger, quickly rising level with his own aircraft. The object, he felt, seemed to anticipate his every move. Their indecisive dogfight spiraled ever higher, rising to around 63,000 feet, dangerously above the Su-22's service ceiling of 46,590 feet. What was the UFO pilot trying to do? Lure Huerta into a fatal stall? Nearing the performance limits of his airplane, the strange object came close enough for the first time for him to get a long, clear look at it.

About thirty feet in diameter, the craft featured an enameled, cream-colored dome atop a wide, circular, silver-metallic platform. Its overall surface was smooth, seamless, and without insignia, canopy, portholes, antennae, wings, exhaust, or visible means of propulsion. Running low on fuel and still climbing beyond the altitude restrictions of his fighter, Huerta broke off the pursuit by heading back to Arequipa. The mysterious intruder did not follow, but rapidly accelerated its ascent and was lost to view within two seconds. The entire encounter had been witnessed, either visually through binoculars or electronically on radar, by all eighteen hundred personnel at the La Joya Air Base.

Just four days later, on April 15, a quartet of UFOs was tracked by Russian radar somewhere near the Mongolian frontier. At 11:50 p.m., twice as many MIG fighters were dispatched to intercept them. The new Mikoyan MIG-31 seemed ideal for just such a mission, because it had been designed to detect and destroy low-flying cruise missiles with its twenty-two air-to-air guided missiles and single 23-millimeter cannon. As usual, the luminous spheroids outmaneuvered their earthly pursuers until one pilot got off two AA-9 *Amos* rockets that detonated simultaneously on either side of one of the extraterrestrial targets, sending it into a fatal dive. Its three companion spheroids disengaged to quickly vanish among the stars.

Several search helicopters carrying twelve-man contingents of retrieval experts came to the crash site. They were fitted with full-body environmental suits equipped with air tanks, anticipating dangerous levels of radioactivity sometimes encountered at UFO crash sites. This one was no different, as evidenced by its excessive radiation count. The relatively well-preserved object was disk-shaped, approximately 15 feet tall from the top of its gently sloping cupola to the object's featureless underside. The investigators entered through a gaping fissure—the only apparent damage—at the center of the vehicle's 85-foot diameter. Inside, they recovered a pair of small, dwarflike corpses amid fractured devices "without the least sign of anything resembling wire, printed circuitry, or bracing struts. An opaque, glass-like material was found. Some type of ornamental inscription was also found inside the craft."[16]

Soviet airmen were not invincible, however. Just one year later, in October 1981, a much smaller spheroid materialized directly ahead of a MIG fighter on patrol at 23,000 feet above the city of Yekaterinburg. First Lieutenant V. Korotkov was just barely able to avoid colliding with the 16-foot-wide spheroid as it closely missed his canopy in a bright, orange glow, then circled around in a tight 360-degree turn to chase him from behind. It quickly overtook the 1,860-mph fighter to pull up off the starboard wing, when Korotkov's radio filled with disabling static and both of his engines shut down.

"Then the sphere shifted toward the tail unit," writes Stonehill. "There was an explosion that damaged the fin, and, after that, the sphere vanished from view. The engines began again, and the pilot landed safely."[17] While the ufonaut could have downed the interceptor by merely continuing to fly alongside it, keeping the turbojets inoperative, perhaps he only wanted to put the Soviets in their place by demonstrating how, despite some losses, he and his fellow aliens still held the upper hand.

If so, they reaffirmed their point when Maxim Churbakov took off on an August 28, 1991, training flight in a Yakovlev Yak-18. At 5:31 p.m., some 13,000 feet above the Yeisk military-aviation school, located near the Sea of Azov, he radioed his observation of a bright orange light like the spheroid Lieutenant Korotkov encountered, traveling parallel to his right, above cloud cover. The air cadet no sooner transmitted his sighting when the luminous object swooped down to only a few yards off his right wing.

"At first, I felt curious," Churbakov said, "but then I felt dread," as the six-foot-wide globe began to set his aircraft on fire. He bailed out of the flaming Yak, but was not pursued by the orb, which immediately disappeared. He was arrested by Soviet secret police, who, unimpressed by his report of an aggressive light, charged him with sabotage. At the young recruit's trial, his superior officers told how "during the flight, there was a typical encounter with a UFO," and charges against him were dismissed.[18]

Nearly two dozen of his fellow recruits were less fortunate two years later, while training in a remote area of Siberia, where they were approached by a slow-moving, low-flying saucer. Defying Army protocol for such encounters, one of the young soldiers panicked and fired a Strela surface-to-air missile at the UFO. Immediately after it crashed a short distance away, "five short humanoids, having large heads and huge, black eyes, emerged," according to the March 27, 1993 edition of *Ternopil vechirniy* (the Ternopil chronicle), a Ukrainian publication translated by the U.S. Central Intelligence Agency in a paper that remained classified for the next twenty-four years.[19] The aliens then combined themselves into a white sphere of bright light that buzzed, hissed, and finally exploded, transforming twenty-three of the enlisted men into stone. Two survived in a shaded area to later make their report.

Ternopil vechirniy explained how "the remains of the petrified soldiers were transported to a secret research institution near Moscow."[20] They were unlike statues, appearing more like roughly hewn, dark-gray pillars with no resemblance to human forms. The Soviets' original 250-page file "contains not only many documentary photographs and drawings," according to the CIA report, "but also testimonies by actual participants in the event. One of the CIA representatives referred to this case as 'a horrific picture of revenge on the part of extraterrestrial creatures, a picture that makes one's blood freeze.'"[21] What became of the five aliens and their disabled craft was not disclosed.

The Russians were not alone in downing UFOs during the last decade of the twentieth century. In March 1997, Lance Corporal Jonathan Weygandt was sent from North Carolina's 2nd Marine Air Wing, Marine Air Control Group 28, to Peru as part of international narcotics-trafficking countermeasures. His assignment included providing perimeter security at a radar installation tracking drug-smuggling aircraft. While on guard duty at the station's command center, he overheard two USAF women discussing the recent appearance of aerial targets flying in and out of South American airspace at speeds above Mach 10—that is, in excess of 7,673 mph, far faster than any known aircraft.

A few days later, around 4:00 a.m., Weygandt was ordered to accompany rescue-team members in their investigation of a remote crash site. After penetrating the Peruvian jungle as far as possible in half a dozen Humvees, they proceeded on foot with Weygandt and three sergeants in the lead. In the early morning light, around 6:00 a.m., just before dawn, they came upon "a huge gash in the land where something had crashed," Weygandt said. "It didn't break anything . . . everything was *burned,* and it was almost as like you had cut warm butter with a knife."[22]

At the far end of this incinerated swath was a large object that had apparently careened off the side of a hill and into the side of a 200-foot ridge, where the nose section was partially buried at a 45-degree angle in the side of a cliff. The teardrop or egg-shaped craft was about 60 feet long, with an approximate diameter of 30 feet. The vehicle was metallic, but not reflective, with large, gill-like vents at what may have been the vehicle's aft section, and three dorsal hatches, one of which was half open. As Weygandt and the three sergeants came closer, they observed a light, dimming as its rotation slowed, accompanied by a diminishing, deep bass sound, like a decelerating gyro winding down from the crash site, then silence.

The object appeared more organic than manufactured, an impression underscored by a syruplike, purplish-green liquid dripping from it and scattered over the immediate vicinity across plants, trees, and rocks.

After Weygandt inadvertently got some of the fluid on his uniform, his sleeve partially dissolved and the hair on his arm was eaten, as if by acid.

Great gashes in the rear of the craft indicated that it had been deliberately attacked. Familiar with such telltale damage, having been trained at Fort Bliss in El Paso, Texas, as a gunner on FIM-90/92 *Alpha Stinger* missiles, Weygand concluded the Peruvians shot down the craft. Batteries of similar surface-to-air *Hawk* weapons were operating in Peru at the time.

Four or five of the vehicle's extraterrestrial occupants had survived its crash and appealed—telepathically, he claimed—to Weygandt for help. Within fifteen or twenty minutes after his arrival at the site, a pair of large Boeing CH-47 *Chinook* helicopters landed nearby to disembark dozens of military personnel, some of them Department of Energy specialists in containment suits, to secure the area and arrest the corporal. He was bound hand and foot, immediately evacuated by one of the departing *Chinooks,* and threatened with death if he ever disclosed to anyone what he saw in the jungle.[23] Only after he had left the Marine Corps did Jonathan Weygandt enter his life-changing experience into the public record.

Figure 15.4. A Raytheon MIM-23 *Hawk* missile battery of the type used to down a UFO in 1997.

16

From Iran and South Africa to the Gulf War

I believe that UFOs are spaceships or extraterrestrial craft. . . . The nations of the world are currently working together in the investigation of the UFO phenomenon. There is an international exchange of data. Maybe, when this group of nations acquires more precise and definite information, it will be possible to release the news to the world.

GENERAL CARLOS CASTRO CAVERO,
SPANISH AIR FORCE,
AND FORMER COMMANDER OF
SPAIN'S 3RD AERIAL REGION, 1976.[1]

As the twentieth century entered its last decades, the predominance of military clashes between extraterrestrials and superpowers began to noticeably shift to other nations. "UFOs sighted in Indonesia are identical with those sighted in other countries," claimed the Indonesian Air Force commander-in-chief, Air Marshal Roesmin Nurjadin, back in 1967. "Sometimes, they pose a problem for our air defense. And once we were obliged to open fire on them."[2]

ENCOUNTERS IN IRAN

But the first truly significant indication of a transition began on September 18, 1976, when Hossian Pirouzi, the night supervisor of Tehran's Mehrabad International Airport, picked up a ringing telephone around 10:30 p.m. A woman caller told him about an unusually bright light that was changing colors as it hovered a few thousand feet above the Iranian capital's Shemiran neighborhood. Pirouzi explained that she was probably seeing a star, but assured her that he would check into her sighting. Within the next forty-five minutes, Pirouzi received three more calls, all of them describing the same multicolored light. Intrigued, he stepped outside and into the night air, onto the balcony that surrounded the control tower. Searching the clear sky, he saw nothing unusual, except for what appeared to be the star he suggested to the evening's first caller. But raising a pair of high-powered binoculars to his eyes revealed something altogether different. "I was amazed," he later said, "flabbergasted" at seeing a luminous rectangle, rotating and oscillating at an estimated altitude of 6,000 feet.[3]

After four civilian pilots flying over the city transmitted their observations of the kaleidoscopic object, sometime after midnight Pirouzi contacted the duty officer at the Shahrokhi Air Force Base, headquartered southwest of Tehran. General Parviz Youssefi, the base commander, was informed and walked out onto his porch to see for himself. As soon as he saw the light—several times the magnitude of the brightest star—he ordered Lieutenant Yadi Nazeri to intercept but not attack the object unless clearly threatened. The two-man F-4D *Phantom,* with the radar operator seated behind the pilot, got airborne at 1:30 a.m., followed ten minutes later by another *Phantom* jet piloted by Major Parviz Jafari, Shahrokhi's squadron commander, at that time the third-highest-ranking officer in the Imperial Iranian Air Force, which years later he would command in its entirety. Nazeri was the first to make visual contact with the target, which he described as a revolving combination of violet, orange, and white lights.

"The sequence of the lights was so fast," according to a U.S. Defense

Figure 16.1. Major Parviz Jafari.

Intelligence Agency (DIA) report, "that all the colors could be seen at once."[4] Nazeri's radar operator informed him that the object was about twice the size of a Boeing 707 tanker—300 feet long, with a wing area of 6,000 square feet. Closing in at nearly the speed of sound on the strobing rectangle, now about thirty miles away, the jet fighter's avionics and internal navigation instruments were abruptly disabled. The *Phantom* banked away, and its electronics steadily revived the farther Nazeri flew from the object. He doggedly resumed pursuit but ran into trouble again.

"When I get closer to the object," the persistent pilot radioed, "my systems shut down."[5] Low on fuel now and straying close to the Afghanistan border, he was ordered by Major Jafari to return to base. Nazeri obediently completed his 180-degree turn away from the object, but was shocked to see it again, this time directly ahead of him. It had jumped from one directly opposite position to another within seconds. After completing this impossible maneuver, the blindingly illuminated craft seemed to step aside, as though to avoid collision, and was visually spotted by Jafari.

"It shifted, all at once," Jafari said, "one full degree on my canopy delineators. That means, it jumped twenty-six miles—I won't say in one second, but in less than one second. When I got closer than twelve miles [from the UFO], my emergency light came on."[6] It indicated that his aircraft was experiencing progressive instrument failure, beginning with radio reception, which became garbled with static interference. Stopping on a dime at 23,000 feet in the middle of the night sky, the colossal rectangle disgorged four much smaller lights, one of which made a beeline for the F-4. Assuming it was a heat-seeking missile, Jafari squeezed the trigger that would fire an anti-missile missile. He was horrified to see that its arming lights were off, and the firing panel went dark. The AIM-9 *Sidewinder* refused to engage, just as UHF (ultrahigh frequency) and interphone communications quit. Jafari told his radar operator that they were bailing out, but even backup systems for their ejection seats failed.

As a desperate evasion maneuver, Jafari pitched the jet forward into a steep, negative-G-force descent. The DIA report tells how "the object fell in trail at what appeared to be three to four nautical miles," as "the second object [smaller orb] went to the inside of his turn [nose dive], then returned to the primary object [the large rectangle] for a perfect rejoin."[7]

About the same time, another of the smaller globes dropped like a stone toward the Earth. Observing its meteoric fall from Shahrokhi, Vice-Commander Mahmoud Babahat held his breath in anticipation of a substantial explosion. Instead, the object rapidly decelerated just above the ground, gently settling into a dry lake bed. After descending to 15,000 feet, Jafari could see its sandy bottom perfectly illuminated by the very bright light, which cast a radiance of one or two miles. He turned to investigate further, but his avionics, which had come back on line after the other pair of orbs terminated pursuit, were once more deteriorating, so Babahat ordered him back to Mehrabad.

The major had flown in, out, and over the base on hundreds of occasions, in daytime and in after-dark conditions. He was no less familiar with the landing strip from the air than he was with his own home. Yet on this night he could not find his way. When, after some long, anxious moments, he finally did locate the airdrome and began making his final approach, the huge multi-light rectangle came after him at high speed. Observed by dozens of personnel on the ground, it passed him in a low, silent pass above the airport, temporarily shutting down all power and bathing it in darkness before rising and disappearing into the west.

Twenty-five minutes later, the object was spotted by an Egyptian Air Force pilot over the eastern Mediterranean Sea, off the mid-Egyptian coast, as was later verified by a Cairo government spokesman. Traveling the 1,230 miles separating Tehran from Egyptian airspace meant that the UFO averaged a speed of approximately 2,250 mph (still far slower than the 25-mile-per-minute jump Jafari saw it make). The rectangle nevertheless must have maintained this speed of plus-Mach 2, because it was last seen about forty minutes later by the passengers and crew of KLM Royal Dutch Airlines Flight 241 over Lisbon, some 2,359 miles from the Egyptian pilot's sighting.

During Major Jafari's medical debriefing following his Close Encounter of the Eighth Kind, he was found to have suffered partial short-term memory loss, plus temporary hemophilia. Within days, his blood began to clot properly again, but perhaps the UFO's incapacitating effect on the electrical systems of both Iranian jets and the Shahrokhi base may have also interfered with his body's ability to function properly. Blood contains hemoglobin, an iron with magnetic properties, which, if affected by too strong an electromagnetic field, can adversely affect biocircuitry.

As soon as the mothership rectangle dropped one of its four smaller lights into the lakebed outside Tehran, an anomalous signal was picked up over the radio receivers of military and commercial pilots alike for the next forty-eight hours. Major Jafari described it as similar to the wail of an ambulance siren. On the morning of September 20, he and other investigators helicoptered out to the lake bed, the presumed location of the landed orb and the source of the mysterious signal, but they detected no trace of either. A couple living nearby saw a bright flash and heard some thunder the night before, but nothing more.

The DIA report (obtained through the diligence of investigators Lawrence Fawcett and Barry Greenwood through the Freedom of Information Act) concluded that the Tehran incident, especially given the credibility and multiplicity of its witnesses, backed up by radar contacts, "is a classic that meets all the necessary conditions for a legitimate study of the UFO phenomenon."[8]

RETRIEVAL IN SOUTH AFRICA

While the aliens dominated Iranian airspace, they were less fortunate in South African skies. Although the following document is still controversial among ufologists, J. J. Hurtak, Ph.D., assistant professor of anthropology at California State University, Northridge, from 1968 to 1970), and respected German researcher J. von Buttlara independently conducted their own inquiries to conclude that its description of events, as excerpted below, is correct. It was additionally confirmed by Dithoko Seiso, Botswana's environment minister, in his 1993 report for the *Argus,* a Cape Town daily newspaper.[9]

Around the turn of the twenty-first century, Anthony Dodd used his investigative skills as a twenty-five-year veteran in British law enforcement to confirm the document's credibility.[10] It was also closely examined by Leonard Stringfield, among the most cautious and widely regarded ufologists of the time, who studied "several versions of the so-called five-page document with the code names either deleted or changed,"[11] as were the identities of persons involved. He eventually published "a retyped 'uncensored' copy of the original," which follows. Here, the squadron leader is identified as Goosen. His identity has been crossed out in various reports to protect his identity.

At 1:45 p.m., on May 7, 1989, the naval frigate [SA *Tafalberg*] radioed Cape Town Naval headquarters to report an unidentified flying object that appeared on radar scopes, heading towards the African continent in a northwesterly direction at a calculated speed of 5,746 nautical miles per hour. Naval headquarters acknowledged and confirmed that object was also tracked by airborne radar, military ground radar installations, and D. F. Malan International Airport at Cape Town.

The object entered South African airspace at 13H:52 GMT [1:52 p.m.]. Radio contact was attempted with object, but all communications to object proved futile. Valhalla Air Force Base was notified, and two, armed *Mirage* fighters were scrambled. The object suddenly changed course at great speed, which would be impossible for military aircraft to duplicate. At 13H:59 [1:59 p.m.], squadron leader [Goosen] reported that they had radar and visual confirmation of the object. The order was given to arm and fire the experimental aircraft-mounted *Thor Two* laser cannon at object. This was done.

[Goosen] reported that several blinding flashes emanated from the object. The object started wavering whilst still heading in a northerly direction. At 14H:02 [2:02], it was reported that the object was decreasing altitude at a rate of 3,000 feet per minute. Then at great speed it dived at an angle of 25 degrees and impacted in desert terrain 80 km north of South African border with Botswana, identified as the Central Kalahari Desert. Squadron leader [Goosen] was instructed to circle the area until a retrieval of the object was complete. A team of airforce intelligence officers together with medical and technical staff were promptly taken to area of impact for investigations and retrieval.

[The officers found] a crater 150 meters in diameter and twelve meters in depth; a silver-coloured, disk-shaped object, forty-five degrees embedded inside of crater. The vehicle was approximately 60 feet across, with flawless, polished, smooth, silver color. No visible seams noted inside or on outer surface. . . . Perimeter showed twelve, unevenly spaced, flush with outer surface, oval-shaped portholes. A hydraulic type landing gear was fully deployed. . . . Around the object, sand and rocks were fused together by the intense heat. An intense magnetic and radioactive environment around the object resulted in electronic failure of air force equipment. . . . The terrain of impact was filled with sand and rubble to disguise all evidence of the event having taken place. . . .

While the investigation team observed the object at a classified air force base a hatch on the lower side of the craft had opened slightly and appeared to be stuck. This opening was later forced with the use of hydraulic pressure equipment, at which point two humanoid entities in tight-fitting, grey suits emerged and were promptly apprehended. Height: 4–4.5 feet. [Their complexion was] grayish blue; skin texture [was] smooth, extremely resilient. Hair: totally devoid of any bodily hair. Head: oversize in relation to human proportions. Raised cranium with dark blue markings around head. Eyes: large and slanted upwards, toward side of face. No pupils seen. Nose: consisting of two nostrils. Mouth: small slit devoid of lips. . . . Body/ arms: long and thin, reaching just above knees. Hands: consisting of three digits, webbed, claw-like nails, Torso: chest and abdomen covered with scaly ribbed skin. Hips: small, narrow. Legs: short and thin. Genitals: no exterior sexual organs. Feet: consisting of three toes, no nails, and webbed. Due to aggressive nature of humanoids, no samples of blood or tissue could be taken. . . . When offered various foods, refused to eat.[12]

The report concludes by stating that high-ranking military officers from America's Wright-Patterson Air Force Base arrived in South Africa on June 23 to take charge of the wreckage and the extraterrestrial survivors. In exchange, the Americans arranged for the transfer of advanced, classified weapons systems and communications to the South African Air Force.[13]

BREACH IN COMMUNICATIONS

Five months later, the U.S. Navy experienced its own, less successful clash with an off-world vehicle. A veteran of that confrontation recalled, "I was assigned to USS *Memphis* (SSN-691), Homeport: Titusville (Cape Canaveral)." The atomic-powered, 362-foot-long *Memphis* submarine carried a complement of twelve officers and ninety-eight enlisted men. The veteran continued:

Our mission was Special Assignments, which meant we protected the Space Program. We would go to sea and patrol while the shuttle was on the pad. On October 24 and 25, 1989, my ship was on patrol about one hundred fifty miles off the Florida coast. We were cruising at about five hundred feet [beneath the surface], when the submarine started experiencing electronics problems. The ship was malfunctioning, our tanks were blowing out of control, we were losing navigation ability, and the communications area was totally lost. We went to all-stop and tried to assess what was happening. The controls in the reactor area started to malfunction. This presented a serious danger to our safety, so the captain [Commander Gary E. Williams] ordered us to shut down the reactor, surface, and go to diesel motors.

When the ship surfaced, I went to my watch station. The ship was still experiencing electronic difficulties, but the mechanical devices, such as diesel engines, cook stoves, and turbines, were fine. It was raining, and the entire sky was red like a red neon sign. I saw a large, inverted, V-shaped UFO off the port side. The executive officer told me to stand fast, and he would speak to the captain. In a minute, the captain appeared on the tower, and asked me for a distance to the craft. The laser range-finder determined the closest point was two hundred meters [656 feet], and the farthest point was one thousand meters [3,281 feet] off the port. The UFO was not perpendicular to our ship, but at about a forty-five-degree angle. This huge vessel was over a half mile across.

The UFO made a half circle around our ship, then passed across the stern, causing our electronics systems to go crazy. We had permanent damage in communications and the sonar room. As the craft flew over the stern, I could see the rain stop under its red glow. The water seemed to rise almost a foot as the UFO passed over silently. When the UFO finished its swing across the stern, it paused—the sky got brighter red, and it simply moved off at tremendous speed inside fifteen seconds.

When the UFO left, our boat returned to normal, with the exception of the radio and sonar. We did a quick system check and the captain ordered us to return to reactor power and get underway. . . . We reached port in about seven hours, where I was taken into "protective custody."

Other shipboard witnesses of the UFO were also arrested for special debriefing.[14] Thereafter, Captain Williams was relieved of command, and his crew was untypically broken up and dispersed among other vessels throughout the fleet. The 1989 entry in the official history of the USS *Memphis* states only that the vessel was "Underway for a Dependent's Cruise on Oct. 2."[15] All other references to that cruise, including the events of the twenty-fourth and twenty-fifth, have been deleted.

Figure 16.2. The USS *Memphis*.

GULF WAR INTERCEPT

Nine months after the *Memphis* returned to Florida, war erupted in the Persian Gulf. So-called coalition forces there made regular UFO sightings as numerous as they were unofficial between early August 1990 and late the following February. These visual experiences were invariably classified by U.S. commanders because of the ultra-high-tech weaponry involved. Thereby virtually all information of the kind was censored and suppressed, save on those rare occasions when such off-world encounters were described by someone the Americans could not control.

A case in point was Colonel Gregor Petrokov, a senior Russian official appointed to Riyadh as military adviser with the Saudi Army. In this capacity, he learned firsthand of an aerial firefight involving an alien craft that occurred during Operation Desert Storm. Saudi communications experts who were closely monitoring hostilities told him how, before noon on January 21, 1991, an unidentified blip sped across the radar screens of four General Dynamics F-16 Fighting Falcons during a mission to Baghdad. After reporting their contact to base commanders, the pilots were diverted to intercept it. Minutes later, they caught up with and visually confirmed a vehicle of indeterminate nationality or type flying just under 20,000 feet almost beyond the F-16's maximum speed of 915 mph.

Going to afterburners, the lead jet approached it within three miles, as a small, exceptionally bright orb shot at high velocity from the larger object on a collision course too fast for the pilot to avoid with an evasive maneuver. After it narrowly flashed by the right side of his Plexiglas canopy, he returned fire with two air-to-air missiles. Both scored direct hits on the craft, which exploded and dove in flames toward a barren desert region some 250 miles northeast of the Saudi capital. Petrokov was among a handful of Russian investigators allowed by the Saudis to visit and inspect the wreckage. He stated:

> The craft was circular, and made of a material I've never seen before. About a third of it seemed to be missing, possibly blown away by the

American missiles. The Saudis wouldn't let us touch anything, but we saw instruments, machinery, and other things that completely baffled us. It seemed to be a relatively small craft, maybe fifteen feet across.[16]

Its interior was exposed by gaping holes in the upper structure, through which the colonel and his associates discerned some details, including an apparent instrument panel covered with indecipherable text.

There were three chairs, probably for crew-members, but they were so small, they seemed to have been made for children. Evidently, space aliens are only about three feet tall. Most amazing, though, is the fact that there were no bodies at the crash site, nor did there appear to be an engine in the craft. Search helicopters were all over the area, which is a desert, and they did not spot any survivors in the vicinity of the crash. The Saudis with me were so frightened that they asked American, British and French investigators to come to the crash site immediately.[17]

As soon as U.S. Army engineers arrived, the Russians were hustled off. The Americans quickly gathered up all debris and carted it away for shipment to their country. "There were things they didn't want us to see," said Petrokov. "It is a cover-up waiting to explode."[18]

At least one engagement between coalition naval forces and an extraterrestrial intruder involved too many witnesses for a cover-up. During the early afternoon of January 24, 1991, just three days after the Saudi crash, American and British warships in the upper Persian Gulf were supporting combat operations onshore in Kuwait when sonar operators tracked a submerged object traveling 152 knots—an impossible 175 mph—at about 200 feet down.

As sonar instruments were checked for presumed malfunction, a 100-foot-wide disk floated to the surface—"apparently," as described by investigator John Kettler, "boiling the water off its hull, once it emerged"—in plain sight of officers and crew members aboard five surrounding vessels.[19] These included the 52,000-ton, 880-foot-long battleship USS *Wisconsin,* escorted by vessels including a cruiser, USS *England,* and the destroyer USS *O'Brien.* They were joined by two frigates of the British Royal Navy, HMS *Battleaxe* and HMS *Jupiter.*

Paralyzed with awe at the sight of a huge flying saucer slowly rising to hover some 2,000 feet above their battle group, not a man aboard moved a muscle, until the object began emitting an ear-splitting sound. The high-pitched resonance may have been in response to the continuous, perhaps disruptive pinging generated by coalition sonar sweeping Persian Gulf depths for enemy submarines.

In any case, the *Wisconsin*'s commander, after confirming that no allied planes were in the vicinity, ordered every warship within range to commence firing on the stationary vehicle with conventional ordnance. More costly surface-to-air missiles were held in reserve. Ammunition for twenty-two 5-inch artillery, plus five 54-caliber and two 40-millimeter antiaircraft guns was almost entirely depleted after

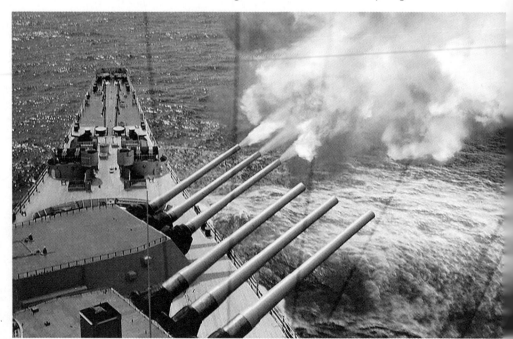

Figure 16.3. U.S.S. *Wisconsin* in action.

nearly twenty minutes of constant, accurate shooting failed to silence the noisy but inert UFO. In a controlled descent, it gradually slid to resume hovering at 500 feet, 1 nautical mile (6,076 feet) off the battleship's starboard side. The *Wisconsin* opened up on the immobile target from her two forward turrets.

Of the nine 16-inch, 2,700-pound, armor-piercing shells the *Wisconsin* fired at 2,500 feet per second, two struck the UFO, apparently penetrating its hitherto impenetrable, invisible shield. The large disk erupted in a devastating explosion, "blowing it to smithereens," according to Kettler, in "pieces so small no debris recovery effort has been mounted to this day."[20]

As with the submarine *Memphis* the previous year, any mention of USS *Wisconsin*'s successful engagement with an off-world craft during the Gulf War was deleted from her official record.

17

UFO Espionage

Significantly, the UFO activity occasionally transcends mere surveillance and involves direct and unambiguous interference with our strategic weapons systems. Numerous cases include reports of mysterious malfunctions of large numbers of nuclear missiles just as one or more UFOs hovered nearby.

DECLASSIFIED SOVIET
MINISTRY OF DEFENSE DOCUMENT[1]

A worldwide shift in the extraterrestrial phenomenon occurred around the turn of the present century. This change was characterized by increased alien interest in our development and application of atomic power, as manifested by more UFO incidents at nuclear sites than at any other previous period. While otherworldly spies have been shadowing these facilities as long ago as early 1945, at Washington State's Hanford plutonium manufacturing plant, the frequency and extent of their espionage from 2010 to 2015 was unprecedented. And the installations reconnoitered during those years were no longer located exclusively in the United States or Russia but were additionally found in Canada, South America, Western and Eastern Europe, the Near East, and Asia. The fundamental similarity of these individual experiences reinforce the trustworthiness of these reports.

These encounters began on the evening of March 29, 2010, when a photographer "using a Panasonic HD 1080p handheld cam" visually captured a luminous disk "hovering for almost two hours" at some 300 feet above the Pickering nuclear power plant in Ontario. He was among several civilian spectators who clearly observed the 50-foot-wide vehicle "before it disappeared into the night."[2]

Three days later, another, similar disk hovered silently at low altitude above the Cattenom Nuclear Power Plant, in Lorraine, in the east of France. "I was on the balcony," reported one of numerous eyewitnesses, "when I saw this very odd object, which moved in all directions. I have never seen an object like this one before. There was no noise coming from the object. This happened at the Cattenom Power Station, and lasted about one minute. It then made an erratic move toward the clouds" and was gone.[3]

The following May 8, at 7:23 p.m., a large, flat triangle was spotted, photographed, and filmed by an airline passenger flying parallel to his plane at about 25,000 feet over the Clinton Nuclear Generating Station, in central Illinois, 170 miles south of Chicago. His encounter was duplicated by the separate sighting of an identical object that same day.[4]

As reported by Argentina's *Diario Popular,* several glowing spheres were repeatedly observed over the Atucha Nuclear Power Station in Zárate, a port city in the northeast of the province of Buenos Aires, on July 1. The article cites Cristian Soldano, a field researcher familiar with Atucha, who stated that the area had become "a place for constant phenomena" of the kind since early summer.[5]

On October 23, one-ninth of America's nuclear arsenal went offline for more than a day at the 90th Missile Wing headquarters, described by *Atlantic* reporter Marc Ambinder as "a main locus of the United States' strategic nuclear forces." Three technicians at Wyoming's Francis E. Warren Air Force Base independently described "multiple sightings by 'numerous [Air Force] teams' of an enormous, cigar-shaped craft" above the 9,600-square-mile missile field, where the 319th Strategic Missile Squadron is in charge of one hundred fifty Minuteman III ICBMs.[6]

The eyewitnesses spoke with researcher Robert Hastings on condition of anonymity, because "the military has kept UFO sightings that occurred during the power outage under wraps."

"Since 1973," writes Hastings, the son of a USAF special weapons senior master sergeant at Malmstrom Air Force Base, "I have been interviewing former and retired U.S. Air Force personnel—from retired colonels to former airmen, [who] held positions ranging from nuclear missile launch and targeting officers, to missile maintenance personnel, to missile security police—regarding their direct or indirect involvement in nuclear weapons-related UFO sighting incidents. To date, I have interviewed over eighty individuals, who were involved in various UFO-related incidents at Strategic Air Command bases or remote sites."

Hastings tells how the Warren technicians "agreed that what they saw 'was not a commercial blimp. It had no passenger gondola and no advertising on its hull.' Further, its aspect ratio (length to width) was very similar to a World War I Zeppelin: long and thin, and not at all like the squat shape of a corporate blimp."[7] As the craft drifted over the base, "intrusion alarms and warhead separation alarms were offline," according to Ambinder, while control officers "in their bunkers could no longer communicate with the missiles themselves. . . . More and more missiles began to display error settings that left fifty missiles in the dark. . . . A half dozen individual silos were affected by Saturday's failure. . . . The five Missile Alert Facilities responsible for launching those ICBMs in time of war—Alpha through Echo—would have been unable to do so during the period of the disruption." Had an enemy strike occurred during the nearly twenty-six hours when the missiles were deactivated, American defense would have been at a distinct disadvantage. During that time it would have been impossible to fire the missiles from the ground. They remained "technically launchable," but only from "an airborne command and control platform like the E-4B NAOC aircraft, or perhaps the TACAMO fleet, which is primarily used to communicate with nuclear submarines."[8]

The E-4B NAOC, or the E-4 Advanced Airborne Command

Post, is a specially modified Boeing 747-200B known as "the dooms-day plane" for its proposed use as America's last-ditch communica-tions center in the event of the country's devastation by atomic attack. TACAMO is an acronym for "Take Charge and Move Out," a U.S. military system of communications links designed to be used, in the event of a nuclear hit on the United States, for maintaining contact among surviving decision makers of the National Command Authority. Ambinder quoted a base commander as saying, "We've never had something as big as this happen. Occasionally, one or two might blink out," In addition, several warheads are routinely out of service for maintenance. At an extreme, he added, "we can deal with maybe 5, 6, or 7 at a time, but we've never lost complete command and control and functionality of fifty ICBMs."[9]

Less than two months later, on December 16, radar operators desig-nated a no-fly zone over the Negev Desert on full alert after detecting a single, low-altitude, unidentifiable aircraft heading for Israel's Dimona nuclear plant. An F-16 was scrambled to intercept the intruder, which the Israeli Air Force pilot visually contacted and described as a spheri-cal, silver metallic "motor-driven object" with neither apparent means of propulsion nor insignia; traveling approximately 400 mph at 7,000 feet. Although it made no evasive or aggressive maneuvers, he fired several 20-millimeter rounds from his M61A1 *Vulcan* six-barrel, rotary can-non. The globe exploded into a cloud of small fragments, but no wreck-age was ever found.[10]

Perhaps the most devastating alien intervention in atomic affairs was the Fukushima Daiichi disaster of March 11, 2011. Emergency generators that provided power for cooling the nuclear power plant's reactors were destroyed by the tsunami that demolished more than 130,000 buildings and killed 18,456 people. As a result, the facility's internal temperatures rose to trigger three meltdowns, followed by hydrogen-air chemical explosions that released radioactive materials over the next four days.

During that period, a Japanese Television crew circling close to the disabled factory in a news helicopter documented a large, bright-white,

cigar-shaped craft moving very slowly, low above the stricken installation's tottering towers.[11] The clip was aired first nationally, then
worldwide, but the object it featured was characterized by Japanese government representatives as a passenger train that only gave the illusion
of floating over Fukushima Daiichi, because the locomotive and its cars
traveled some distance in the background. This transparent fabrica-
tion was debunked by skeptics, who pointed out that the site had been
declared off-limits as a no-go zone for twenty miles around days before
the sighting was videotaped. Subsequent analysis of the news clip determined that its controversial object was not a train.

Were the Daiichi UFO's occupants surveying the damage there, or
did they cause the earthquake and tsunami that destroyed it? Among the
investigators probing this question, Britain's Scott C. Waring concludes
from hundreds of close encounters he has chronicled around the world
that off-world vehicles do indeed occasionally initiate seismic activity.
He cites November 14, 2016's geological violence at Christchurch, when
a number of New Zealand cliff sides tumbled into the sea, following
"a giant UFO" reportedly observed exiting an underground location
nearby.[12]

Waring's statement that such craft "are often seen during and after
earthquakes" is supported by statistical studies carried out by Canadian
geologists Michael Persinger and Gyslaine Lafrenière. In their book
Space-Time Transients and Unusual Events, they correlate "flying saucer sightings" with seismic-related locations and events.[13] Underscoring
their findings, other unaccountable lights were photographed in the
skies just before and during the Tohoku earthquake. But the question still remains: Was the craft videotaped there benignly surveilling
the ravaged plant, or could it have brought about the worst disaster in
Japanese history since the bombing of Hiroshima and Nagasaki?

On September 19, 2012, a pair of large, peculiar vehicles appeared
over Montana's Malmstrom Air Force Base, previously the target of
numerous extraterrestrial visitations. About 9:45 that night, the luminous objects flew swiftly but silently from the northwest to pause
briefly at very low altitude over the command and control center for

one hundred fifty Minuteman III nuclear missiles operated by the 341st Missile Wing. Flying closely together, both craft were identically V-shaped, with bright orange lights on each of three extended legs. After a few minutes, the objects sped off into the southeast.[14]

In another corner of the world, around 10:00 a.m., on January 26, 2013, several eyewitnesses saw an undetermined number of bright lights hovering in the night sky perhaps 200 feet above the Krško Nuclear Power Plant, Slovenia's only atomic station. The silent objects disappeared within forty-five minutes.[15] Just as the eyewitness merely watched the bright lights, so too did the extraterrestrials evidently watch the observers below.

Other UFOs were caught spying on a nuclear plant. Between the first week of October and early November 2014, dozens of persons observed illuminated disks apparently monitoring nuclear facilities across France and Belgium on eighteen separate occasions. A typical

Figure 17.1. The Krško Nuclear Power Plant.
Photograph by the Ministry of Defense of the Republic of Slovenia.

sighting was made by security guards, who reported "two flying objects" lingering at only one hundred feet above the Nogent Nuclear Power Plant, southeast of Paris, on November 7. French government spokesmen repeatedly insisted that antinuclear protesters had been operating remotely controlled drones over all the facilities visited. But no activists claimed credit for the flyovers, nor was anyone ever arrested in connection with them.

Moreover, the observed craft was, in every instance, utterly silent and bore no physical resemblance to a drone. One day after the Nogent sighting, Pascal Pezzani, director of the Blayais Nuclear Power Plant in southwestern France, personally observed the same "flying objects" poised, "as though nailed in the evening sky," for nearly an hour at low altitude over his reactor. "Here, we have not seen a drone," he was quoted by the local newspaper, *Sud Ouest*. "We saw a UFO."[16]

On the other side of the world, in the United States, a "bright, flashy, platform-like object" was hovering over Arkansas Nuclear One, a two-unit pressurized water-reactor atomic power plant located just outside Russellville. ANO is the only atomic facility in Arkansas. The craft took up station over the plant around 1:00 a.m. on November 8, 2014, according to area witnesses. Among them was a man who preferred not to be identified, a resident of Dover, a small town less than twenty miles from Russellville. "It emitted multi-colored lights," he said, "as it stayed stationary in the sky. For the next two hours, I would check on it periodically. It ascended a flight path [about 3:00] over my house, and was completely out of view within three minutes. The object had no sound, and had a strange, electromagnetic-like feeling pulsate through my body, as it flew over me."[17]

England's *Worthing Herald* reported that aviation enthusiast Elaine Costello was videotaping the July 19, 2015, flight—the last—of an old Hawker Siddeley *Vulcan* B2, operated by the Royal Air Force during the Cold War.[18] As the jet-powered, tailless, high-altitude strategic bomber lumbered into Saturday afternoon's cloudy skies over Fairford, Gloucestershire, a much smaller disk topped with a dome zipped past the tip of the Vulcan's starboard delta-wing. The B2, according to

Figure 17.2. A Hawker Siddeley *Vulcan* B2.

Wikipedia, "is linked with early British atomic weapon programme and nuclear deterrent policies," and "carried Britain's first nuclear weapon."[19] The bomber and the accompanying UFO documented by Costello flew close to the Berkeley nuclear power station, situated on the bank of the River Severn.

On September 2, 2015, the "distended skull, elongated body and talon-like feet" of "an alien corpse," according to Britain's *Daily Mail,* was "found by two residents next to the River Kovashi, in the Russian town of Sosnovy Bor, which was built in the 1950s to serve the Leningrad nuclear power plant."[20] The tiny cadaver—about four inches long—was initially misidentified as a mutant chicken embryo. Britain's Yahoo News added, "Scientists believe that if it is a corpse, it isn't from any known animal on the planet. One said: 'It seems that this body is neither fish nor fowl—this creature has a mysterious skull, no neck and wings.' Experts from the Institute of Biophysics in Krasnoyarsk, where the body was taken for more tests, are equally baffled. Biologist Yegor Zadereev said: 'Extensive studies are needed to determine what kind of creature or organism it is.'"[21]

18
Intruders in the Early Twenty-First Century

The study of UFOs is a necessity for the sake of world security in the event we have to prepare for the worst in the Space Age, irrespective of whether we become Columbus or the Indians.

AIR COMMODORE J. SALUTUN,
NATIONAL AEROSPACE COUNCIL OF INDONESIA,
AND INDONESIAN PARLIAMENT MEMBER[1]

A long-contentious relationship between the all-too-human operators of atomic power facilities and their off-world critics bridged the late twentieth and the early twenty-first centuries. On November 9, 2004, ground radar picked up a UFO over Arak's heavy-water plant in northwestern Iran. A U.S.-built, twin-engine, two-seat Grumman F-14A *Tomcat* was vectored toward the intruder, and caught up with it at approximately 25,000 feet.

"The pilot described the object as being spherical," according to an article in an American aviation magazine, "with something like a green afterburner, creating a considerable amount of turbulence behind it."[2]

The pilot initiated his interception in a steep climb. But when the aircraft's radar beam began to "paint" the luminous target (i.e., sweep a returning signal across it), the scope faltered. It was as though the object was emitting high electromagnetic energy that was multiplying the amplitude of reflecting radar waves to interfere with and jam the fighter's receiving instrument. When the F-16 drew level with the object on a linear and constant flight path, however, radar-weapons lock-on clicked in. The pilot had no sooner selected an AIM-7E-4 air-to-air missile to launch against it than the unidentifiable vehicle suddenly increased its speed. Although it was capable of flying Mach 2.34, or 1,544 mph, and of climbing 45,000 feet per minute, the *Tomcat* was left behind, as though standing still, by the intruder, which "disappeared like a meteor," according to Iranian crew members. Their encounter was additionally remarkable for its straightforward description by *Combat Aircraft Monthly,* a prestigious military aviation periodical not otherwise given to discussion of UFOs.[3]

Five days after the Iranian incident, U.S. Navy Air Force Commander David Fravor and Lieutenant Commander James Slaight were flying a routine training mission over the Pacific Ocean, about one hundred miles southwest of San Diego, California, between "America's Finest City" and Ensenada, Mexico, when they were radioed by an operations officer aboard the USS *Princeton.* He inquired whether their F-18 *Super Hornet* jets were armed, but they carried only two CATM-9 dummy missiles that could not be fired. The operator then explained that his cruiser was still being tracked by unidentified aircraft after two weeks of radar monitoring.

"The objects appeared suddenly at 80,000 feet," reported the *New York Times,* "and then hurtled toward the sea, eventually stopping at 20,000 feet and hovering. Then they either dropped out of radar range or shot straight back up."[4]

"There's a whole fleet of them!" cried one of the Navy officers observing the objects. "Look on the ASA!"—one of the warship's dozen different sonar and radar sensors and processors that made the 9,800-ton *Princeton* the world's most sophisticated air-defense unit.[5] Her operator directed the pair of *Super Hornets* to investigate the bogeys, but neither pilot saw anything unusual until Fravor looked down at the sea.

"It was calm that day, but the waves were breaking over something that was just below the surface. Whatever it was, it was big enough to cause the sea to churn." Hovering about 50 feet above the agitated water was a whitish, oval craft, some 40 feet long and 12 feet thick. "It had no plumes, wings or rotors," Fravor said, emitted no exhaust, and appeared to violently tumble through the air.

"The craft was jumping around erratically," the *New York Times* continues, "staying over the wave disturbance but not moving in any specific direction. The disturbance looked like frothy waves and foam, as if the water were boiling. Fravor began a circular descent to get a closer look, but as he got nearer, the object began ascending toward him. It was almost as if it were coming to meet him halfway, he said. Commander Fravor abandoned his slow circular descent and headed straight for the object. But then the object peeled away."[6]

The object outmaneuvered the jets to come around from behind on the tail of Slaight's aircraft, then sped off "like a bullet," Fravor said. "It accelerated like nothing I've ever seen, and outran our F-18s."[7] With a top speed of 1,190 mph at 40,000 feet, his F/A-18 Super Hornet could climb 44,882 feet per minute. The *Princeton*'s radar operators calculated that the unknown intruder rose vertically, without accelerating, to 10,000 feet per second, giving it a speed of 6,818 mph. (For comparison, the North American X-15 rocket plane is the world's fastest manned aircraft at 4,520 mph.)

Figure 18.1. Two F-18 *Super Hornets*.

Both men kept the UFO in view for a full five minutes before it sped off in a direction that was followed precisely by the *Princeton's* elaborate sensor systems. Her operator vectored both jets to rendezvous at a cap point sixty miles distant, where they were supposed to intercept the object, although he shortly thereafter radioed Fravor while they were still *en route:* "Sir, you won't believe it, but that thing is at your cap point."

"We were at least 40 miles away," the commander recalled, "and in less than a minute, this thing was already at our cap point."[8] By the time the F-18s reached it, the object had disappeared.

When the pilots returned to their home vessel, they learned that an undetermined number of other UFOs had been detected within the vicinity of supercarrier USS *Nimitz*, one of the largest, most powerful warships afloat, for several hours. "I believe, as the other folks who were on the flight when we visually saw it," retired commander Fravor told Fox News, "that it was something not from this world."[9]

Fravor's confrontation was followed by a somewhat similar one observed the following May 27, in Noble, Oklahoma, about twenty-five miles east of Tinker Air Force Base. Shortly before midnight, a scientist saw:

a triangular craft . . . traversing the sky from north to south at about 20K feet. The sky is very clear. . . .

The craft's speed was about 500 knots [575 mph]. The craft was perfectly silent. Several miles behind the craft was what appeared to be a fighter jet moving very rapidly, 600–700 knots [690–806 mph]. As the jet was chasing the craft they both were flying toward my position. I could begin to hear the engines of the jet at that time.

It appeared as though the triangular craft was toying with the jet in that as the jet got closer to the craft, the craft would speed up somewhat and leave the jet behind. As the craft and jet got nearly directly over my location, the triangular craft made a sharp right hand turn to the west. The jet was unable to make the turn at the same angle as the craft. The jet's turn was much more pronounced and made a much wider loop.

Due to that, the jet lost quite a bit of ground on the craft during the turn, yet again, as both craft began traversing in a straight line toward the west-northwest. . . .

After a few seconds it appeared that the craft accelerated dramatically and left the jet behind. . . . Referencing the wingspan of the jet, two of the lights on the craft were about 50 to 75 feet apart and the third light was approximately 100 to 150 feet from the other two lights. . . .

It should be noted, that the color of the triangular craft lights were an unusual milky white color, nothing like that of the very bright red, green and white lights observed on the jet.[10]

Similar aerial shadowboxing typified the first decade of the twenty-first century, and was particularly well documented on October 11, 2007, by the captain of Olympic Airways flight 266 from Athens to London. At 3:20 a.m., he was distracted by an extremely bright light that appeared abruptly below his starboard wing at about 10,000 feet. It executed impossibly erratic maneuvers and constantly changed its shape west of the Greek capital city. His radio report was visually confirmed by two more Olympic Airways pilots of flight 730 to Kos and flight 700 to Rhodes. At the same moment, employees at the Athens Airport control tower spotted the object moving toward Karystos, a small town on the island of Euboea. It was simultaneously sighted by Hellenic Air Force officers stationed atop Mount Parintha, near Athens, where radar operators tracked the large, oval intruder's spasmodic performance at wildly varying speeds of several thousand miles per hour.

Two F-16s were scrambled and soon after approached the target closely enough for all four crew members to photograph it. The object then shot away in a perfectly vertical climb, vanishing into the night sky. Although these images are still classified, a live recording of conversations between F-16 pilots and Mount Parintha control describing the incident was released to the public. Also disclosed was *Lightning 2*, an official Hellenic Air Force document featuring the original orders that both fighter pilots received that night for intercepting the UFO.[11]

The year 2008 began a two-year period of unprecedented USO encounters, at least one of them fatal. This kind of object had been encountered by Russian naval units on several occasions, but these incidents were unknown to the outside world until post-Soviet disclosure of pertinent records by an investigative group within the Russian Navy itself. Encompassing a fifty-year-period, beginning in the early 1960s, the documents, according to Russia's *Svobodnaya Pressa* news website, deal specifically with USOs. "They are most often seen in the deepest part of the Atlantic Ocean, in the southern part of the Bermuda Triangle," stated the Russian Navy's deputy commander, Admiral Nikolay Smirnov, who spearheaded release of the suppressed archives, "and also in the Caribbean Sea."[12]

Smirnov's colleague, Rear Admiral Yury Beketov (ret.), testified that target-location sonar aboard a nuclear submarine he commanded during early 2008 in Arctic waters repeatedly tracked USOs—one of them almost as long as his own vessel—cruising about 400 feet beneath his keel at an incredible 230 knots, approximately 265 miles per hour. At that speed, the USOs should have generated enough turbulence to tumble the admiral's submarine like a reed in Niagara Falls. Instead, the fast-moving objects passed by at depth without a ripple.[13]

Another atomic-powered Russian Navy submarine was aggressively monitored by six USOs (the same that Beketov encountered?) during underwater maneuvers during that spring in the central Pacific Ocean. Every evasive maneuver the commander executed failed to shake his unidentified pursuers—even crash-diving to nearly 1,000 feet. In desperation, he gave the order to clear the ballast tanks, as the objects kept close pace with his vessel's ascent. Moments after it surfaced, the Russians were flabbergasted to behold all six USOs shoot out of the sea and disappear at what must have been several thousand miles per hour into a clear afternoon sky.[14]

A severely truncated report discovered by Admiral Smirnov's investigators told how an undisclosed number (no more than seven or ten) Russian Navy divers were dispatched for unspecified reasons to Siberia's Lake Baikal. At an estimated 5,387 feet deep, it is the world's deepest lake, as well as Earth's largest fresh-water lake in terms of volume. It was here, according to the abridged document, that the divers encountered "a group of humanoid creatures dressed in silvery suits" at a depth of 160 feet. The report does not explain what took place, concluding only that "three humans died during the ensuing chase."[15]

The Russians were not alone in extraterrestrial experiences at sea. A sailor was aboard a U.S. Navy warship *en route* from Hawaii to its home port of San Diego, after having participated in the Rim of the Pacific Exercise (RIMPAC) during July 2010. This, the largest international maritime warfare exercise of its kind, is held biennially, but this year was unusual, because his vessel, "as well as every other ship in our strike group, experienced strange connectivity and communication issues. An investigation was launched by the strike-group commander under the premise that there was a suspected probe initiated by the Chinese on our entire strike group. I later discovered that the communications and systems phenomenon the ships experienced had no explainable origin and no evidence of an attack from a foreign nation . . . there were other reports of communications failure."

On the night of August 4, the sailor finished his watch in sonar control and went to the smoke deck on the starboard quarter, where he "saw a medium-sized ball of light about 10 or 20 feet above the water, approximately 3 kiloyards away almost as soon as I got there," around 10:15 p.m. "Initially, I thought it was another ship that was also in transit, and continued to observe it, because, to my knowledge, we were alone in transit on our PIM [path of intended movement]. It was mirroring our course and speed almost exactly, with no discernible difference to our own for a period of about 15 minutes. The ball then traveled very rapidly from a forward position relative to my ship to aft, and then changed elevation, and rose vertically, nearly instantly, to an elevation of about 200 feet or so from my perspective. It then appeared to mirror our course and speed from that elevation and follow us" before disappearing into the starry sky.[16]

Soon after the sailor learned that the warship's surface and air-search radar corresponded to his sighting, which had been similarly

Figure 18.2. Various elements of Exercise RIMPAC.

reported by three other witnesses over the previous two days. The object had played havoc with state-of-the-art communications and shipboard electronics systems operated in conjunction by several navies—again, possibly a demonstration of extraterrestrial predominance over human technology.

That same lesson may have been a repetition of the lesson demonstrated at a sighting on April 10, 2010, as two Royal Air Force fighter jets roared low over a West Midlands service-station park at the M5 motorway in central England, closely pursuing a "saucer-shaped craft."[17] Some observers speculated that the test flight of some secret warplane was being mistaken for a confrontation between the RAF and a UFO, but hazardous experimental projects are never carried out in broad daylight at low altitude over civilian population areas.

A more disastrous encounter took place on July 23, 2010, in Alberta. Rehearsing for a featured appearance in the following day's Lethbridge Airshow, Royal Canadian Air Force Captain Brian Bews was practicing with his CF-18 *Hornet,* putting it through a high alpha pass by slowing down the twin-jet fighter to roughly 144 miles per hour as he pitched the aircraft's nose up to 45 degrees. As impressive to see as it is difficult to perform, it was old hat to Bews, who had already executed this maneuver "fifty or sixty times so far in that season," he later said in a broadcast interview, "but something that day went terribly wrong, as you all know."[18]

As Bews advanced the throttle to power away from some turbulence, the nozzle of his left engine suddenly closed, indicating a flameout. Asymmetrical thrust caused by the other, fully functioning engine led to adverse yaw rate and right-wing-down rolling movement, putting the aircraft into an uncontrollable spin. Bews ejected four seconds before the 18½-ton *Hornet* nosed into the ground, exploding in a huge fireball. He survived with compression fractures to his spine. The CF-18 was a Canadian version of America's McDonnell Douglas F/A-18, noteworthy for the exceptional reliability of its General Electric F404-GE-400 turbofan engines, which had never before failed in flight. Accident investigators could determine no specific cause for the incident, surmising only that the electromagnetic circuitry of the *Hornet's* left engine had somehow shorted out.

That day's pre-airshow flight rehearsals were visually documented by several spectators, but a videographer furthest away from the action

Figure 18.3. Moist, warm air is transformed into a surrounding shock wave by the CF-18 *Hornet's* abrupt acceleration from lower to higher speeds as it approaches the sound barrier. Photograph by TMWolf.

captured something the others, too close to the fly-bys, missed. In this two-minute and forty-seven-second clip, a dark sphere drops straight down at high speed out of the partially cloudy sky to vanish just before it would have collided with the ground. When Bews flew over the exact position where the falling object had disappeared moments before, his left engine inexplicably flamed out, causing the jet to crash. In its YouTube presentation, the clip is repeatedly analyzed and re-analyzed through various digital-enhancement filters, which not only establish the images' original authenticity but also define the plummeting article as a solid spheroid.[19]

The close proximity of this object to the CF-18 mishap seems more than coincidental, given the long history of UFOs shorting out aircraft electrical systems. The destroyed *Hornet's* accident investigators did suspect that an electromagnetic problem of some kind caused its left engine to fail. If, as seems likely, extraterrestrials deliberately downed the Canadian warplane, its loss marked a shift from mere demonstration of technological superiority to its destructive application.

Did July 23, 2010, signify the opening of a new, more dangerous phase in Earth's War of the Worlds? That question appears to have been answered by Gubernia TV, a mainstream Russian network and the Far East's largest television station. The station reported an immense object, partially illuminated with two lights, slowly traveling at low altitude in perfect silence over the town of Lesopilniy.

On the night of May 16, 2011, dozens of eyewitnesses observed the 650-foot-wide disk. Many of them tried to document it with their cameras, but, inexplicably, the object wasn't caught on tape. An Italian broadcast about the sighting stated, "The video footage did not show anything, just a black screen." The huge vehicle gradually vanished in the direction of nearby Khabarovsk, a large city nineteen miles from the Chinese border and home for an important base of the Russian Air Force. Lesopilniy residents saw the huge object sporadically reappear in the flash of exploding ordnance, as base defenders "fired artillery shells at the UFO without harming it." Several ground-to-air missiles then streaked toward the craft, which jumped out of harm's way before rising at high velocity into the sky. According to the Gubernia TV story, the UFO was "not detected by radar."[20]

During January 2012, Iran was plagued with a rash of UFO intruders reconnoitering the country's atomic facilities. "According to *Combat Aircraft Monthly*," writes *Forbes* columnist Michael Peck, "Iranian sources described that the UFOs 'displayed astonishing flight characteristics, including an ability to fly outside the atmosphere, attain a maximum cruise speed of Mach 10, and a minimum speed of zero, with the ability to hover over the target.' These craft also reportedly emitted high levels of magnetic energy that disrupted navigation systems and jammed radars."

The "luminous objects," as the Iranians describe them, "used powerful ECM that could jam enemy radars using very high levels of magnetic energy, disrupting navigation systems. An electronic countermeasure (ECM) is an electrical or electronic device designed to trick or deceive radar, sonar or other detection systems, like infrared (IR) or lasers. It may be used both offensively and defensively to deny targeting information to an enemy. . . . The question is this: what kind of aircraft flies at Mach 10? That's ten times the speed of sound, or 7,612 miles per hour (the legendary SR-71 *Blackbird* spy aircraft flew at around Mach 3, or 2,283 miles per hour)." Peck also mentioned "the Air Force X-51 Waverider, which flew at Mach 5 for nearly four minutes last May before plunging into the Pacific."[21]

Determined to put a stop to these unidentifiable intruders, Islamic Republic of Iran Air Force (IRIAF) commanders scrambled an F-16 to intercept and destroy an incoming UFO that had been previously monitoring the Bushehr Nuclear Power Plant. Seconds after takeoff, the jet fighter exploded, killing both crewmen. "Other attempted engagements by the F-4s [McDonnell Douglas F-4 *Phantoms*] and F-14s [Grumman F-14 *Tomcats*] proved futile," writes Peck, "so the IRIAF reportedly ordered an end to flying missions against these 'luminous objects.'"[22]

19

Whispering Devils

I have told several sources about my connections over the years with military officers manning missile silos during the Cold War with the Soviet Union who told me personally of UFOs hovering over their missile sites and disabling the missiles targeting the Soviet Union.

Also, that some of our military missiles were shot down by UFOs during some missile tests from a military station on the California coast. This was rather common knowledge coming from various military officers from years back.

EDGAR MITCHELL,
THE SIXTH ASTRONAUT TO WALK ON THE MOON.[1]

During the night of April 5, 2013, residents in the area of Simonstown, South Africa, sighted "an orange fireball" hovering over False Bay. These observations formed a prelude to events that transpired the following day, when "aggressive firing" at a small naval facility based there was seen and heard by civilians a few miles outside the base between 9:00 and 10:00 p.m. When a law-enforcement officer directed the night-vision lens of his camcorder at Simonstown, he discerned two triangular objects—each one estimated at approximately four miles in length—involved in an armed exchange of some kind. Cape Town reporters covering the incident stated that investigators for the Counter Intelligence Agency confirmed they were analyzing the police officer's original video, which showed no signs of fakery.

South African Navy authorities claimed that no artillery fire of any kind had taken place, but later changed their initial denial, explaining that an artillery exercise did occur at the time. Skeptics were not convinced that practicing cannon fire in the middle of the night was particularly feasible, especially after they learned from an inquiry into Navy log records for April 6 that such a training exercise was neither scheduled nor carried out. When further pressed to account for Simonstown's colossal triangles captured on video, Navy spokesmen suspended all further public briefings.[2]

This was not to be the last mass sighting by civilians. On July 25, 2013, a driver on Parnell Road, in Wauchula, Florida, observed one or more unusual objects in the Friday night sky after sunset. Returning to his home, he saw four "fighter jets flying overhead so low that the windows on my house started to rattle" around 9:00 p.m. "Even the fenders on my car were making a rattling sound." The warplanes were joined by sixteen more, "all in pairs of two" with four each in the north, south, east, and west, while "chasing UFOs that would streak across the sky like falling stars and . . . then turn with pin-point precision, losing the jets in their wide turns. When I saw the first [object], it had a radiant light, and then, as I counted them, I saw that there was some blue, some red, others orange and golden-white, neon colored. I counted fifty-five of these brilliant colored UFOs." He added that "my family and I, along with neighbors, a total of eight of us," saw the objects.

After about ten minutes of aerobatic maneuvers, all but one of the fifty-five craft flew off. It "bobbed out of the way and back to its regular position" at four air-to-air missiles fired by the fighter jets, and was just as successful eluding ground fire directed from the Avon Park U.S. Air Force Range, some sixteen miles to the east. The object "started going in a circular orbital motion, disappearing and reappearing," until it vanished "into thin air."[3]

Florida's midsummer sighting involved more earthly aircraft and otherworldly vehicles together at one time in the same area than any other account of its kind. Did this mass encounter signify a change, or even an acceleration in military encounters with UFOs? Perhaps the extraterrestrials wanted to demonstrate their predominance both in overwhelming numbers and in one-on-one superiority.

One month after Wauchula's aerial display, large black UFOs were spotted patrolling the skies over Syria's civil war, where they are known as *WhissWhasseh,* from *whiss-whass,* mentioned in the Qur'an as a "whispering devil." Syrian UFOs are said to "give off an odd-sounding hum intermittently," according to Ken Oz, writing for the Altheadline website. He quotes Free Syrian Army rebel commanders in Damascus on August 28 as having stated that the WhissWhasseh "are 'hunting down and systematically targeting' innocent locals, using unknown, weaponized technology 'not of this earth,' or anything the fighters have ever seen." A U.S. Army serviceman serving at the time in Syria said the UFOs "appear at the height of battles at night or in danger zones, and they seem to protect the Syrian Army." This lends support to Oz's sources, which define the WhissWhasseh as taking sides against the rebels—untypically, because extraterrestrials have seldom demonstrated apparent partiality in any human conflict.[4]

The WhissWhasseh do, however, take exception to our guided missiles, as evidenced by their manipulation and even destruction of several examples, as long ago as America's post–World War II testing of ex-German V-2s. More recently, an unmanned Russian Proton-M rocket carrying Ekspress-AM4R, the world's most sophisticated communications satellite, failed shortly after liftoff from Kazakhstan's Baikonur Cosmodrome, "erupting into a ball of flames and releasing highly toxic rocket fuel into the air," according to Britain's newspaper the *Telegraph.*[5] Spokesmen for Roscosmos, Russia's space agency, stated that something apparently went wrong with the third stage of the engine, possibly causing the crash. Video analysis of the Proton-M rocket showed another possible reason.

"Forty seconds before the third stage was scheduled to deploy the satellite," writes Michael E. Salla, Ph.D., on the Exopolitics website, "a

UFO is seen intercepting the rocket, and then leaves just as the third stage of the rocket begins to malfunction." May 16, 2014 visual coverage shows a small ball of light in the proximity of Proton-M at an altitude of 49,000 feet. "The UFO intercepts the rocket, and leaves just as the rocket's third stage begins to behave erratically. The conclusion that emerges from the recorded video is that the UFO intercepted and caused the Russian rocket to malfunction just before the satellite was to separate and deploy."[6]

Civilian observers Andrea Finney, her husband, Nigel, and their son witnessed an unusual attempted intercept on March 25, 2015, when they observed several UFOs flying at low altitude over the English town of Bolton. "There were four of them, and they zoomed across the sky," said Mrs. Finney. "They zoomed off after we spotted them, and the craziest thing was that they were then followed by a Ministry of Defense helicopter. We just could not explain it. They were not hot air balloons. They were not Chinese lanterns. They were just something else."[7]

Civilians would again witness government interception of UFO spacecraft when, in January 2016, residents of Bramer, in eastern India, reported seeing illuminated spheres falling from the skies above their village. Less than three hundred miles away, a fast-moving, balloon-shaped contact appeared on radarscopes at Rajistan's Indian Air Force (IAF) headquarters between 10:30 and 11:00 on the morning of the twenty-sixth, sounding a general alert. One twin-jet fighter "was ordered to intercept the object and bring it down," according to a feature article by John Austin in Britain's *Daily Express* based on original reports in the *India Times*. The target was destroyed, though whether the pilot fired his cannon or the warplane's air-to-air missile was not reported.

"Many villagers had claimed that they heard a loud blast over a three-mile radius when the incident took place," writes Austin. "Eyewitness Manoj Singh said he heard the explosion sound five times, and something went down after an aircraft flew by. . . . Debris from the object has been recovered, and subjected to further investigation. The police investigators, who checked the area for debris, reportedly retrieved five, triangle-shaped pieces of a metal object, which were turned over to the IAF."[8]

The aliens would be luckier on their next crusade. On September 1, 2016, extraterrestrials destroyed another missile: the next-generation space rocket for NASA's crew flight in 2017, and carrier of the new Amos-6 Internet-beaming satellite. The Falcon 9 was built by Elon Musk, a South African–born multibillionaire and founder of Space Exploration Technologies Corporation, a U.S. aerospace manufacturer and space-transport services company headquartered in Hawthorne, California. The rocket exploded moments before a test launch, resulting in a massive technological and financial loss for his company.

"Engines were not on and there was no apparent heat source," Musk said. "We have not ruled out that a UFO may have caused the Space X explosion," he confessed one week after video footage from the explosion was publicly released.[9] It shows a black circular or spherical figure passing at very high speed near Falcon 9 only seconds before the incident.[10] Its appearance behind riggings not only rules out all possibilities for a bug on the camera lens, but also enabled analysts to

Figure 19.1. A Falcon 9.

determine how fast the object traveled in between the launch area's left and right towers. The 0.25 second needed for the black spheroid to pass between them gave it a speed conservatively estimated at 3,600 mph, far faster than any insect or bird, as critics initially argued, and certainly faster than foreign enemies or government agents (the favorite hypotheses of conspiracy theorists). Two or more birds appear in the video, but they are obviously not buzzing by Falcon 9 at a much faster speed.

"Others opined," write the UFO-skeptical editors of *Sputnik International,* "that whatever the flying vehicle that may have given rise to the explosion, it appears it was a 'well-planned attack from a competitor.'" The object, however, bears no resemblance to any known existing defense products, none of which are capable of traveling 3,600 mph.

"Particularly trying to understand," said Musk, "is the quieter bang sound a few seconds before the fireball goes off. May come from the rocket, or something else."[11]

Any question concerning "something else" is unequivocally answered by careful scrutiny of the high-resolution video that documented Falcon 9's fate from start to finish. The rocket is sitting on the launchpad, with condensed water vapor steaming off booster tanks filled with liquid oxygen and liquid hydrogen. A dark object streaks in from screen left at low-altitude high speed behind girded steel towers and the missile itself, disappearing off screen right. About a second later, it reverses the same linear course and altitude (around 50 feet) from right to left, but seems to take off from the ground not far to the right of and behind the rocket, flashing off to the left. Two seconds later, it reappears from screen right, heading directly at the rocket, then turns back in a steep climb, all in the blink of an eye. One second after the object loops off screen right, it streams in again from the same direction at approximately 300 feet.

Each pass appears at different distances from the camera, sometimes a bit closer or farther away, but always on the far side of the towers. In its final pass, as it makes straight for Falcon 9, the object appears to shape-shift from a sphere to a teardrop to a jumping-jack configuration to a disk to a winged vehicle back into a sphere—all within the space of around two seconds. When it is about 75 feet from just above the apex of the rocket, the missile's uppermost section erupts into a colossal fireball, over which the object makes a gentle climb to disappear forever at screen left.

A split second before doing so, either sunlight or the flash of the explosion reflects off the surface of the object in a shiny silver-metallic glint.[12] All this is only apparent when slowing down the imagery to use stop-motion examination of its anomalies; otherwise they move too quickly to be properly seen. The unknown intruder made four passes on his target, as though sizing it up, before carrying out a premeditated attack. Because of the high caliber of the video that captured this event, it is perhaps the most convincing visual documentation of an extra-terrestrial sortie so far recorded.

It may be that more people than ever are witnessing extra-terrestrial movement throughout international airspace. The following October 19, hundreds, perhaps thousands, of persons across west-central Saudi Arabia heard a powerful commotion of some kind thundering from the heavens after Wednesday evening prayers. Almost immediately thereafter, observers were horrified by the appearance of a large, intensely bright light, low in the sky. The noiseless blue-green object emitted green flashes as it floated slowly away toward the Yemeni desert, east of Riyadh, the Saudi capital. Before turning south, the vehicle frequently changed its course, as though searching for something over a desert stretching about 220 miles north and slightly east of Al Mukalla.

This is a dangerous area, where Houthi terrorists have been fighting the Yemen government since 2015, and it was here that the slow-moving object was fired upon by an insurgent using a Russian 9K32 *Strela*-2, shoulder-mounted, surface-to-air missile. Staggering under the impact of a high-explosive warhead, the gigantic craft lurched forward and down, falling into the sandy waste.

Saudi government authorities, which had been tracking the UFO on radar, were almost immediately at the crash site, which they cordoned off with armed patrols for ten miles around in each direction.

Figure 19.2. A 9K32 *Strela*-2.

Since then, no further information concerning the incident has been forthcoming.[13]

An exceptionally loud, totally blacked-out "military helicopter" was observed December 2, 2016, at 7:22 p.m., for about a minute flying at treetop level over the small northern Georgia town of Cumming. Only 50 to 70 feet directly ahead of the unmarked chopper was "a tubular-shaped, glowing white object" that it seemed to be chasing.[14]

January 6, 2017, was extraordinary for the public release of perhaps the most credible and unique, if not disturbing, visual evidence of a UFO ever documented. After almost three years of painstaking analysis, an international team of computer and photographic experts found no evidence of "alteration of the video by any computer application in the editing and processing of the images." Alberto Vergara, lead analyst from the Chilean Air Force's photogrammetric department, stated that "the great majority of committee members agreed to call the subject in question a UAP (unidentified aerial phenomenon), due to the number of highly researched reasons that it was unanimously agreed could not explain it."[15]

Analysts ruled out a bird, flying insect, drone, parachute, spy plane, or hang glider as possible explanations. "It can be concluded that the object has all the characteristics to be classified as an unidentified aerial phenomenon," according to Vergara.[16] Under the jurisdiction of the Chilean Air Force, the Comité de Estudios de Fenómenos Aéreos Anómalos (Committee for the Study of Anomalous Aerial Phenomena) convenes committees of world-class astrophysicists, nuclear chemists, military officers, technicians, and academics from many disciplines to investigate unidentified aerial phenomena.

The video in question was taken with unlimited horizontal visibility on the clear afternoon of November 11, 2014, during a routine patrol mission undertaken by a Chilean Navy helicopter flying north along the coast, west of Santiago. At 1:52 p.m., both pilot and observer aboard the French-built Airbus *Cougar* AS-532 visually confirmed the appearance of a "flat, elongated structure, white, with a semi-oval shape," plus a pair of connected, white, circular lights radiating intense heat, traveling west-northwest, approximately 35 to 40 miles off the chopper's starboard side.[17] Both were flying at about 152 mph at an altitude of approximately 4,500 feet. Almost immediately after it was first sighted, the observer began filming the object with his WESCAM MX-15 HD forward-looking infrared camera, used for medium-altitude covert intelligence, surveillance, and reconnaissance.

Meanwhile the pilot contacted two separate radar stations, "one close by on the coast," writes Leslie Kean for the *Huffington Post,* "and the other, the main DGAC Control system (Ground Primary Radar), in Santiago, to report the unknown traffic. Neither station could detect it on radar, although both easily picked up the helicopter. (The object was well within the range of radar detection.) Air traffic controllers confirmed that no traffic, either civilian or military, had been reported in the area, and that no aircraft had been authorized to fly in the controlled airspace where the object was located. The on-board radar was also unable to detect the object, and the camera's radar could not lock onto it. The pilot tried several times to communicate with the UAP, using the multi-national, civilian bandwidth designed for this purpose. He received no reply."[18]

After filming for about eight minutes, the observer was astounded to see the UFO emit a massive plume of gas several times the object's length. Kean explains how "the material came out from two different parts of the object, and then joined in space making one wake. The first was massive and dark in the IR (meaning very hot); the second lighter and semi-transparent. Another, smaller, cooler, white plume streamed from the rear of the craft moments later." The ejected material could not have been water, because "it would have immediately plummeted to the ground, given the warm air temperature. Contrails form at very high altitudes (usually above twenty-six thousand feet), where the air is extremely cold (less than -40°C). The plume ejected from the object must have been some kind of gas or energy, and was not something tangible, like water."[19]

The craft moved forward, away from the lingering plumes, then vanished behind a cloud. Why the object dumped a mixture of two different gasses over a sparsely inhabited area of the Chilean coast is entirely mysterious. No effects to humans, animals, or plants on the ground were subsequently detected, while the nature of the UFO's ejected plume itself defies explanation.

Figure 19.3. Chile's unique UFO.

Just two months later, on January 17, 2015, an unspecified number of large "glowing orbs" began hovering at low altitude over downtown Tehran. When alarm verging on panic spread through the capital, mobile antiaircraft guns were hastily set up around 5:00 p.m. by Iranian Air Force Defense personnel in Enqelab Square, at the city center. Massed artillery discharged exploding shells heavenward, and the surrounding concrete canyons of skyscrapers reverberated with their thunder, as large crowds of pedestrians watched the display of military might. But the gunfire seemed to have no visible effect on the almost stationary targets, which neither took evasive action nor returned fire. Just before Iranian Air Force jets roared in over Tehran, the glowing orbs" speedily disappeared.[20]

Advances in technology allow a kind of monitoring never before available. On January 25, London's *Daily Mail* reported that Google Earth satellite imagery revealed what appears to be an artificial, saucer-shaped structure with an estimated diameter of 217 feet in the polar wastes of Antarctica.[21] Half-obscured by an overhanging ridge, the dark object cast its shadow on the snowy ground.

While much of the visual evidence for UFOs is questionable at best and more often fraudulent, the Google Earth photograph is not privately owned or manufactured, but available for public scrutiny, which so far has not be able to detect any indications of fakery, technical aberrations, or misidentification of natural phenomena. The image was found by members of Secureteam, a YouTube channel based in Cleveland.[22]

Their discovery foreshadowed February 2's "The Impact of Wikileaks on UFOs," an article by investigator M. J. Banias, in which he tells how an impending "massive collection of UFO-related information [was expected to emerge] from Wikileaks" throughout 2017.[23] Part of that classified data concerns renewed military operations carried out by American naval and air commands in the South Polar regions.

Some two weeks after Banias released his preliminary story, *UFO Digest,* widely acknowledged for its careful reporting, republished and updated Doc Vega's "Wikileaks Alleges Secret War with UFOs in Antarctica," on February 17, 2017.[24] The piece derives its title from his statement, "Wikileaks revealed alleged compromised Department of Defense cable communications indicating that U.S. armed forces may be in the midst of a secret war with UFOs."

The documents refer in part to a firefight that allegedly occurred between American and extraterrestrial combatants in the South Polar Sea during 2004. Vega continues:

> Recently, another massive emergence of the unknown objects headed toward the southern tip of South America, and flew over Chile.
>
> Experts say that the immediate threat posed by these huge displays of large numbers, as they launch from beneath the water, is the dangerous wave they generate that is capable of sinking ocean traffic, such as freighters and other vessels. In the most recent appearance of the UFO armada from the Antarctic Southern Ocean, one cruise ship was nearly capsized with one hundred sixty aboard, while another vessel was overturned with a crew of sixty, with only twenty rescued survivors. This story was originally released by *The European Union Times*, which had reported that the Russian president was receiving intelligence briefings indicating that the U.S. was involved in secret military confrontations with massive UFO formations originating from underwater bases in and around the Antarctic oceans.[25]

Travelers would again witness ET activity on February 20. A Jet Airways 777-300 ER, flying from its corporate headquarters in Mumbai, India, failed to respond to appropriate air traffic control frequencies while passing over southwestern Germany. A dispatched Eurofighter *Typhoon* caught up with the foreign passenger plane near Cologne, where the pilot was able to establish contact through emergency radio channels with the airliner pilot, who proceeded to London without further incident.

The intercept was captured almost in its entirety by a video camera operated by the flight crew aboard a British Airways jet approximately one mile behind and above the Indian and German aircraft. The resulting visual documentation clearly shows a dark figure entering from the left in a 45-degree angle toward the northeast, while passing beneath and not far behind the Eurofighter and the passenger plane at a velocity substantially higher than their 562 mph speed. Unenhanced close-up views of the object show it resembling an elongated barrel or stubby cigar. Unlike a drone or any conventional airplanes at high altitude, it emitted no condensation trail. Nor was it the shadow of another, higher aircraft out of camera range, because the object is clearly discerned against both light and dark backgrounds.

"If you notice the video of the jets is played in slow motion," writes commentator Steve Duvall, "and yet the craft is covering three to four times the distance crossing them; it must be doing two to four thousand miles per hour."[26] He was seconded in a comment by Kirk Klosterman who observed, "I've worked in aviation. That is definitely not a plane. If it was, it would be subjected to the same atmospheric conditions and would produce a trail also. The size, speed and flight path don't add up either. I think this is a video of a UFO."[27]

"If you look closely," another commentator added, "it momentarily vanishes, as it goes through the clouds. I don't think shadows do that."[28] Commenter Lam Nguyen affirmed, "UFO definitely. Shade stays the same, no matter what color the cloud is."[29]

More than fifty persons attending a UFO conference in California's Mojave Desert got more than they bargained for when they and their Sunday-night guide, Melinda Leslie, saw "a large, amber-colored light low to the horizon just behind Giant Rock."[30] This is not only the world's largest freestanding boulder, but among the strangest. Towering seven stories high and covering 5,800 square feet of ground near the small, unincorporated community of Landers, Giant Rock has been a gathering point for ufologists since the early 1950s because of the high number of sightings reported there. Around the turn of the twenty-first century, the gigantic monolith, for no apparent cause, fractured in two, revealing an interior of white granite.

From this location on May 21, shortly before 10:00 p.m., Leslie and her companions observed "a large diamond-shaped UFO . . . it appeared

Figure 19.4. Giant Rock.

to be a large, orangish (amber) light, that flew like a bumble bee." Soon after it vanished from view, "three military jets flew over in the direction of the object, now gone from sight, behind the hill . . . we heard the sound of a low-flying jet from behind the hill, and suddenly, clearing the top of the hill and right over our heads, came a very fast military jet chasing a faster, large, red-glowing light. The military jet had both red and white blinking strobe lights and glowing afterburners, and was very loud, as it flew directly above our heads. The large red light had no blinking lights and no sound at all. It became clear to all fifty-plus witnesses, this was no jet." They reported seeing "two UFOs (fast moving lights), flying in perfect, locked tandem with one another."[31]

Observers would again see more than expected as they gathered for an air show at Washington State's Fairchild Air Force Base, located about twelve miles southwest of Spokane. Skyfest's main attraction was an appearance by the famous Thunderbirds, a USAF air-demonstration squadron of four specially marked Lockheed Martin

F-16C/D (Block 52) *Fighting Falcons* flying in aerobatic formation and solo. On July 30, John Whichelow was one among numerous spectators enjoying the show. He noticed nothing unusual in their daredevil performance as he followed it through the viewfinder of his handheld video camera. Only after he returned home did he notice some peculiar streaks flitting across the recorded imagery.

These became clear when he slowed down the action to reveal a bright white object materializing in the sky on the right side of the screen. As the object rises in a low angle at very high speed, it is rapidly orbited by a pair of smaller orbs before exiting at screen left. A moment later, two *Thunderbirds* approach each other head-on from opposite directions at low altitude. After executing their close pass, the camera follows one of the F-16s in its steep ascent to the left. Beneath its contrail, a round, dark (possibly black) object materializes, then goes after the jet in an accelerating climb, but eventually veers away to the left, disappearing off screen.[32]

Both the white and dark globes move about four times faster than the performing *Thunderbirds,* giving the UFOs an approximate speed of 2,000 mph. Whichelow's video was telecast by NBC's Spokane affiliate, KHQ-TV.[33]

Another amateur videographer captured the image of a single UFO at a Texas air show the previous year. His April 23, 2016, YouTube video shows the equally famous Blue Angels, another flight-demonstration squadron, this one with pilots from the U.S. Navy and Marines, rising in a combined, vertical climb. As their *Hornets* ascended into the clear skies over Fort Worth, a bright white sphere shot straight upward through their long contrails to emerge between the jets and disappear far above them. After it vanished at the top of the screen, all six aircraft sparkled repeatedly but briefly with some kind of electric-like effect.[34]

The *Hornets* climbed at 50,000 feet per minute, about six times slower than the white object, meaning that its approximate speed was 3,409 miles per hour. Perhaps, again, its extraterrestrial pilot wanted to demonstrate his vehicle's superiority over Earth's best jets.

AFTERWORD

Conquest or Quarantine?

> *Yet, across the gulf of space, minds that are to our minds as ours are to those of the beasts that perish—intellects vast and cool and unsympathetic—regarded this Earth with envious eyes, and slowly and surely drew their plans against us.*
>
> H. G. WELLS, *THE WAR OF THE WORLDS*[1]

The known history of human contact with intelligent beings from other worlds goes back more than thirty centuries, to a remote time when dynastic Egyptians saw "fire discs" over the Nile Valley. Dated between ten and almost thirty millennia earlier, rock art in France and Australia suggest similar sightings. If so, then our planet has been visited by these distant travelers since, if not before, the birth of modern humanity. In subsequent centuries, their relationship with our ancestors was almost exclusively confined to Close Encounters of the First Kind: visual sightings. After more than 3,000 years of mostly benign observation of and nonintervention in human affairs, this relationship changed drastically during World War I, when for the first time aircraft bore aloft high explosives on an international scale. To demonstrate their displeasure, the extraterrestrials began targeting American munitions factories in 1916, just as they would, decades later, shut down nuclear-warhead guided missiles in both the US and the USSR.

A real surge in their activity paralleled the Third Reich's earliest successful development of rocket-powered missiles capable of leaving the upper atmosphere; at the same historical moment, Americans exploded their first atomic bomb. More alarming still was our willingness to use this weapon without compunction—not once, but twice within three days—against fellow inhabitants of our own planet. Thereafter, we divided it among nine countries in possession, altogether, of 14,900 nuclear weapons—more than enough to kill every living thing on Earth several times over.[2] Meanwhile, 815 million persons, about one in nine people around the globe, do not have enough to eat. Each year, more than three million children under five years of age starve to death.[3] As observed from the coldly objective viewpoint of outer space, our international priorities are clear. They do not favor a species that some more advanced civilization would welcome into what Stanton Friedman calls "their galactic neighborhood."[4]

So long as ignorance kept humanity earthbound, the aliens seemed content to study it and monitor its progress. But as soon as humans learned how to fly and produce nitroglycerin for high explosives, particularly after mastering the atom and space flight, the aliens realized that humans would inevitably reach beyond the stars. The accelerating pace of our technological development should make us capable of intergalactic travel within the next one hundred to two hundred years.

"Once Mars has colonies independent of the Earth," James B. Edson, director of U.S. Army Research and Development, declared as long ago as 1960, "then, if the Earth is destroyed, Man can carry on in this reserve world."[5] In other words, having rendered our God-given home no longer livable, we can relocate to other places and similarly trash them, leaving behind one planetary landfill after another, as we spread our refuse across the universe. The vast slums and blight of cities around the world show how we can transfigure pristine environments. These and similar examples of modern civilization are microcosms of what can be expected from our move into outer space. Our own planet is already orbiting with so much space junk that it has become dangerous for working astronauts, as was dramatized by the 2013 film *Gravity*.

Kraft Ehricke, the chief space consultant at Convair, spoke for many of his colleagues when he remarked, "The solar system, as much of the universe as Man can reach, are Man's rightful field of activity. It is up to us to spread life."[6] Dealing with this not invariably desirable inevitability is the aliens' chief concern, at least regarding our grasp beyond the solar system. Accordingly, they continue to buzz and sometimes disable nuclear facilities, demolish missiles, and down warplanes—apparently less to destroy our military capabilities entirely than to warn us against further deployment of these measures, which must inexorably lead to application in outer space. Even now, despite the aliens' technological wizardry, they are not invincible, as demonstrated in the foregoing pages. How much more at a military disadvantage they may be in years to come must give them pause.

"Over the past year," said Clifford Clift, international director of MUFON (the Mutual UFO Network), in 2011, "we've been averaging 500 sighting reports a month, compared to about 300, three years ago"—an increase of 67 percent.[7] Four years later, MUFON spokesmen stated, "2015 saw a total of 1,353 UFO sightings reported to MUFON from around the world. This represents a 35 percent increase in UFO sightings over July of last year."[8]

Even if just 10 percent of the objects observed can be verified as extraterrestrial vehicles, this would mean that 135 of them visited our planet in 2015. The actual figure was undoubtedly much higher, because most sightings of this kind go unreported, while additional UFOs, maybe a majority, are probably not even noticed. Conservatively, hundreds, up to one thousand or more extraterrestrial visitors arrive here each year. Why? What do their occupants want? Does such a surge in their observed numbers suggest an invasion of sorts? Perhaps their preconceived threshold, once crossed by our technology and our inherent acquisitiveness, will trigger direct, decisive intervention by extraterrestrials, as appears to have happened long ago on Mars. All the engagements between earthly armed forces and alien craft over the last hundred years may have only amounted to nothing more than skirmishes foreshadowing real military campaigns to come.

If humanity runs true to form as Earth's chief despoiler, others with whom we share the universe will look upon us as something less than another intelligent life form and more like a dangerous virus. Should they ever come to regard us as such, they know that pathogens not eliminated can go viral. No doubt, like good surgeons everywhere, they have already pondered prophylactic measures.

We leave hornets alone in the wild, but obliterate those that nest in our homes. Whenever we find a hornets' nest in the attic, we do not attempt to communicate with its creators, for all their sophisticated social organization and architectural skills. We make no effort to have them understand somehow that their natural behavior threatens our well-being, that they should voluntarily remove their dangerous stingers, thereby allowing us all to thrive together peacefully. We do not give a second thought to calling an exterminator or spraying the nest with insecticide. So too, representatives of a civilization as far removed from us as we are from arthropods may be no less hesitant to eliminate pestiferous humans.

Illustration from the original 1898 edition of
H. G. Wells's *The War of the Worlds*.

For most of human history, we seem to have been a species worthy of scientific study by extraterrestrials, like entomologists cataloging caterpillars. That changed the moment we fastened nuclear warheads to ICBMs, just as an entomologist would put aside his microscope for a spray can of insecticide if the docile honeybees he had been examining suddenly morphed into dangerous killer bees. Similarly, beings capable of traversing the galaxy, and possibly beyond, would find little difficulty in dusting off of Earth its anthropic parasite, if they deemed it necessary for their own safety to do so. "They could probably wipe us out," Major Keyhoe stated. "We can do that ourselves, and they may have worse things than H-bombs or germ warfare and poison gas."[9]

If future developments resemble past and present actions, a turning point of some kind might be reached when the militarization of space attains a saturation level unacceptable to alien observers. We may be already about to cross that line, as Reuters analyst David Axe explains:

> Quietly and without most people noticing, the world's leading space powers—the United States, China and Russia—have been deploying new and more sophisticated weaponry in space. Earth's orbit is looking more and more like the planet's surface—heavily armed and primed for war. . . . Widespread orbital destruction could send humanity through a technological time warp. It's hard to say exactly how many weapons are in orbit. . . . Even taking into account the difficulty of accurately counting space weaponry, one thing is clear: The United States is, by far, the world's most heavily armed space power. . . . U.S. companies and government agencies have at least five hundred satellites—roughly as many as the rest of the world combined. At least one hundred of them are primarily military in nature. . . . They join a growing number of space weapons guided by expanding networks of Earth-based and orbital sensors on a new, distant battlefront of a so far bloodless neo–Cold War."[10]

Each one of the ironically or hypocritically named "Peacekeepers" is capable of lofting ten independently targeted nuclear warheads twenty-

America's LG-118A missiles being tested at the
Marshall Islands' Kwajalein atoll.

five times more powerful than the bomb that destroyed Hiroshima along trajectories outside of Earth's atmosphere. David James Paquin's long-exposure photo shows the paths of multiple reentry vehicles deployed by the missile.

All this is no doubt thoroughly appreciated by those "intellects, vast and cool and unsympathetic," watching from afar. Whether or not they will actually draw up plans against us is impossible for us to know in advance, because we cannot second-guess nonhumans who possess technologies beyond our comprehension.

We are nonetheless caught in the double-grip of David Axe's "neo–Cold War," fueled by an internationally paranoid climate, with potential aggression from various quarters, as well as our inherently exploitative nature.

If extraterrestrial agendas are inscrutable, Earth's military position concerning UFOs has always been clear: acquire superior methodologies, mandate the downing of off-world craft, and impose top secrecy. As was described in chapter 2, U.S. government officials have been collecting advanced alien systems since at least 1941. Because the U.S. Office of Foreign Technology continues to regard these specimens of scientific know-how as keys to military predominance by back-engineering them, no one outside the federal cognoscenti is permitted to have access to such innovations.

If increasing incorporation of these captured technologies enables Earth's military to eventually assume levels of parity with otherworldly armed forces, how might alien strategists react? So far, the incidents recounted in the foregoing pages of this history may amount to nothing more than preliminary skirmishes in a real War of the Worlds to come.

References

FOREWORD
ENTERING THE COSMIC ARENA

1. As quoted in *Visions: How Science Will Revolutionize the Twenty-First Century* (Oxford: Oxford University Press, 1999), by Michio Kaku.

INTRODUCTION
CLOSE ENCOUNTERS OF THE EIGHTH KIND

1. *The Bhagavad Gita,* trans. Laurie L. Patton (New York: Penguin, 2008), 11:32; 88.
2. Kenneth Arnold, *The Coming of the Saucers* (Amherst, MA: Amherst Press, 1952), 76.
3. General Hugh S. Johnson, "Keeping Out of War," CBS broadcast, June 22, 1940, www.ibiblio.org/pha/policy/1940/1940-06-22b.html.
4. John E. Brandenburg and Monica Rix Paxson, *Dead Mars, Dying Earth* (Berkeley, CA: Crossing Press, 1999), 101.
5. Frank Joseph, "War on Mars?" interview with John E. Brandenburg, *New Dawn* 150, (May–June 2013), 12.
6. Joseph, "War on Mars?," 13.
7. Joseph, "War on Mars?," 12.
8. Rowena Lindsay, "Universe May Hold Ten Times More Galaxies than We Thought," *Christian Science Monitor,* Oct. 14, 2016, www.csmonitor.com /Science/2016/1014/Universe-may-hold-10-times-more-galaxies-than-we -thought.

9. R. Cedric Leonard, "Fire Circles: A Revised Translation of the Tulli Transcription," www.atlantisquest.com/Firecircle.html (site discontinued).

10. Diodorus Siculus, *Bibliotheca Historica* (London: Andesite Press, 2015), 16:66, p. 33.

11. Plutarch, *Lives* (New York: Delphi, 2013), 97.

12. "Royal Frankish Annals," Wikipedia, last updated Feb. 12, 2018, https://en.wikipedia.org/wiki/Royal_Frankish_Annals.

13. Einhard, *Annales Laurissenses maiores* (New York: Ulan Press, 2012), 44.

CHAPTER 1. ENGAGEMENT WITH EXTRATERRESTRIALS IN WORLD WAR I

1. In Mattweb, "Military UFO Quotes," UFO Evidence: Scientific Study of the UFO Phenomenon and the Search for Extraterrestrial Life website; accessed Oct. 27, 2017, http://www.ufoevidence.org/documents/doc1743.htm.

2. Joe Berger, "German Fighter Ace Red Baron Shot Down a UFO in 1917!" *Weekly World News,* Aug. 31, 1999, 14: https://books.google.com/books.

3. Berger, "German Fighter Ace," 14.

4. Nigel Watson, *UFOs of the First World War: Phantom Airships, Balloons, Aircraft, and Other Mysterious Aerial Phenomena* (Stroud, UK: History Press, 2015), 146.

5. Michael David Hall, *UFOs: A Century of Sightings* (Lakeville, MN: Galde, 1999), 54.

6. Watson, *UFOs of the First World War,* 129.

7. Watson, *UFOs of the First World War,* 131.

8. Watson, *UFOs of the First World War,* 131.

9. Watson, *UFOs of the First World War,* 133.

10. Watson, *UFOs of the First World War,* 135.

11. Watson, *UFOs of the First World War,* 135.

12. Watson, *UFOs of the First World War,* 138.

13. Watson, *UFOs of the First World War,* 138.

14. Watson, *UFOs of the First World War,* 140.

15. Watson, *UFOs of the First World War,* 142.

16. Posted by Info junkies, "William Cooper Aliens UFO's Are a Government Hoax Created for Project Bluebeam Mirror," Dec. 30, 2014, https://www.youtube.com/watch?v=7_g0NIBevWk.

17. Posted by Info junkies, "William Cooper Aliens," https://www.youtube
.com/watch?v=7_g0NIBevWk.

CHAPTER 2. ALLIES AND ETs IN WORLD WAR II

1. Reproduced by Paul Blake Smith, *MO41: The Bombshell before Roswell*
(St. Louis, MO: W & B Publishers, 2016), 93.

2. Ian Topham, "Cresswell UFO (1942)," Mysterious Britain & Ireland, http://
www.mysteriousbritain.co.uk/england/northumberland/ufos/cresswell
-ufo-1942.html (site discontinued).

3. Keith Chester, *Strange Company: Military Encounters with UFOs in World
War II* (Charlottesville, VA: Anomalist Books, 2007), 113.

4. Chester, *Strange Company*, 113.

5. Chester, *Strange Company*, 114.

6. David Clarke, *The UFO Files: The Inside Story of Real-Life Sightings*
(London: National Archives, 2009), 69.

7. Andrew Hough and Peter Hutchison, "UFO Files: Winston Churchill 'Feared
Panic' over Second World War RAF Incident," *Telegraph,* Aug. 5, 2010,
http://www.telegraph.co.uk/news/newstopics/howaboutthat/ufo/7926037
/UFO-files-Winston-Churchill-feared-panic-over-Second-World-War-RAF
-incident.html.

8. Hough and Hutchinson, "UFO Files."

9. Hough and Hutchinson, "UFO Files."

10. Quoted in PRG Quotes website, accessed Feb. 23, 2018: http://www
.paradigmresearchgroup.org/QuotesPage.htm.

11. Hough and Hutchinson, "UFO Files."

12. Hough and Hutchinson, "UFO Files."

13. Smith, *MO41,* 103.

14. Smith, *MO41,* 103.

15. Posted by The Moore Show, "MO41 The Bombshell before Roswell: The
Case for a Missouri 1941 UFO Crash," April 27, 2016, https://www.youtube
.com/watch?v=QUiuFYuvYn4&t=1393s.

16. Smith, *MO41,* 107.

17. Smith, *MO41,* 108.

18. Posted by The Moore Show, "MO41 The Bombshell before Roswell:
The Case for a Missouri 1941 UFO Crash," https://www.youtube.com
/watch?v=QUiuFYuvYn4&t=1393s.

19. Posted by The Moore Show, "MO41 The Bombshell before Roswell: The Case for a Missouri 1941 UFO Crash," https://www.youtube.com/watch?v=QUiuFYuvYn4&t=1393s.
20. Smith, *MO41,* 108.
21. Quoted in Smith, *MO41,* 108.
22. Paul Blake Smith, correspondence with the author, Nov. 15, 2016.

CHAPTER 3. THE BATTLE OF LOS ANGELES

1. George C. Marshall, top-secret memo to the president, in UFO Quotes, MUFON Pennsylvania, West Virginia, Delaware, accessed Feb. 23, 2018, http://mufonpa.com/wordpress/ufo-quotes.
2. Paul T. Collins, "The Battle of Los Angeles," *Fate* 17, no. 322 (July 1987).
3. Dirk Vander Ploeg, "The Untold Story of the Battle of Los Angeles," *UFO Digest,* accessed Oct. 27, 2017, www.ufodigest.com/news/0706/battleofla.html.
4. Joseph Trainor, ed., "Army Gunners Fire at UFOs over Los Angeles," *UFO Roundup* 3 no. 8, February 22, 1998, http://ufoinfo.com/roundup/v03/index.shtml.
5. Terrenz Sword, *The Battle of Los Angeles, 1942: The Mystery Air Raid* (Seattle: CreateSpace, 2010), 121.
6. Collins, "Battle of Los Angeles," 89.
7. Paul T. Collins "World War Two UFO Scare" as cited on Jeff Rense, "1942 'Battle of Los Angeles' Biggest Mass UFO Sighting In History," accessed Feb. 23, 2018, www.rense.com/general93/battleofla.htm.
8. Trainor, "Army Gunners Fire at UFOs over Los Angeles."
9. Marvin Miles, "Army Says Alarm Real Roaring Guns Mark Blackout," UFO Casebook, accessed March 7, 2018, http://www.ufocasebook.com/battleoflosangeles2.html.
10. Sword, *Battle of Los Angeles,* 122.
11. Kevin D. Randle, *The UFO Dossier: One Hundred Years of Government Secrets, Conspiracies, and Cover-ups* (Canton, MI: Visible Ink, 2015), 95.
12. Vander Ploeg, "Untold Story."
13. The Institute for the Study of Globalization and Covert Politics, "Battle of Los Angeles: Recent Testimony," accessed Feb. 23, 2018, https://isgp-studies.com/ufo-1942-02-25-battle-of-los-angeles-picture-recent-info.
14. The Institute for the Study of Globalization and Covert Politics, "Battle of Los Angeles, Recent Testimony."

15. The Institute for the Study of Globalization and Covert Politics, "Battle of Los Angeles: Recent Testimony."

16. Jerome Clark, *The UFO Encyclopedia* (Detroit, MI: Omnigraphics, 1998), 68.

17. Collins, "The Battle of Los Angeles."

18. Philip L. Rife, *It Didn't Start with Roswell: Fifty Years of Amazing UFO Crashes, Close Encounters, and Cover-ups* (Bloomington, IN: iUniverse, 2001), 136.

19. "The Return: The Battle of Los Angeles," *Ancientalienpedia,* https://ancient alienpedia.com/1-6-the-return-the-battle-of-los-angeles.

20. Vander Ploeg, "Untold Story."

21. Posted by gustavo G. F., "UFO Battle of Los Angeles Original Footage and Broadcast February 26, 1942, February 25, 2013, https://www.youtube .com/watch?v=5m7736RMBEg.

22. Littleton, C. Scott. "Eyewitness to History: The Battle of Los Angeles," 24 May 2007, https://www.sott.net/article/132795-Eyewitness-to-History -The-Battle-of-Los-Angeles.

23. Vander Ploeg, "Untold Story."

24. Paul T. Collins "World War Two UFO Scare" as cited on Jeff Rense, "Battle of Los Angeles."

25. Editorial quoted in "Army Says Alarm Real," on Jeff Rense, "Battle of Los Angeles."

26. Quoted in Sword, *Battle of Los Angeles,* 125.

27. Quoted in Sword, *Battle of Los Angeles,* 126.

28. Quoted in Sword, *Battle of Los Angeles,* 126.

29. Rife, *It Didn't Start with Roswell,* 138.

30. Rense, "Battle of Los Angeles."

31. "Battle of Los Angeles," Wikipedia, last updated Jan. 30, 2018, https:// en.wikipedia.org/wiki/Battle_of_Los_Angeles.

32. Bruce Maccabee, "The Battle of Los Angeles Photo Analysis," Feb. 26, 2018, www.bibliotecapleyades.net/ciencia/ciencia_flyingobjects33.htm.

33. Steven Lacey, "Battle of LA UFO: Stunning New Photo Enhancements," Aug. 31, 2005, www.rense.com/general93/batofla.htm.

34. George C. Marshall, top-secret memo to the president, http://mufonpa .com/wordpress/ufo-quotes.

35. Posted by eeasynow, "UFO over Los Angeles 1942: The Witnesses," March 30, 2012, https://www.youtube.com/watch?v=VujrBpvLqko (site discontinued).

36. Posted by eeasynow, "UFO over Los Angeles," https://www.youtube.com /watch?v=VujrBpvLqko (site discontinued).

CHAPTER 4.
FOO FIGHTERS

1. "More UFO Debunkery from the Air Force's Top Generals: Includes UFO quotes from Generals Vandenberg, Twining, Spaatz, LeMay and others," Roswell Proof, last updated on July 24, 2017, roswellproof.homestead.com /ramey_and_ufos.html.

2. Anonymous, "France, Tuesday, June 6, 1944," UFO Hunters, Oct. 30, 2009, https://goo.gl/cUc1MM.

3. Anonymous, "France, Tuesday, June 6, 1944."

4. Randle, *UFO Dossier*, 172.

5. Paul Stonehill, *The Soviet UFO Files* (n.p., UK: Bramley Books, 1998), 72.

6. Stonehill, *Soviet UFO Files,* 73.

7. Hall, *UFOs: A Century of Sightings,* 84.

8. Harre Cowe, "Project 1947, UFO Reports 1944," Project 1947, accessed Oct. 27, 2017, http://www.project1947.com/fig/1944a.htm.

9. Cowe, "Project 1947, UFO Reports 1944."

10. "The Foo Fighters of World War II," Saturday Night UFORIA, accessed Feb. 26, 2018, www.saturdaynightuforia.com/html/articles/articlehtml /foofightersofworldwariipartthree.html.

11. "Foo Fighters of World War II," Saturday Night UFORIA.

12. Chester, *Strange Company,* 92.

13. Chester, *Strange Company,* 137.

14. Jan L. Aldrich, "Updated Draft Catalogue of UFOs/USOs Reported by Seagoing Services—NavCat 2.0," Project 1947, 2013–15, accessed Oct. 27, 2017, www.project1947.com/47cats/usnavydraft1.htm.

15. "USO Research," Above Top Secret, accessed Oct. 27, 2017, www .abovetopsecret.com/forum/thread440363/pg1.

16. "Large Object Emerges from Sea near *The Delarof,*" National Investigations Committee on Aerial Phenomena, accessed Feb. 26, 2018, www.nicap .org/45SUMRaleutianisles_dir.htm.

17. Report #1214, accessed Oct. 27, 2017, www.waterufo.net/item.php ?id=1214.

CHAPTER 5.
CLOSE ENCOUNTERS OF THE AXIS KIND

1. Linda Moulton Howe, "Werner von Braun and Dr. Carol Rosin: False Flag Wars and Exopolitics," Exopolitics, 2004, exopolitics.blogs.com/exopolitics /2006/12/eyeopening_inte.html.

2. Hanna Reitsch, *Flying Is My Life* (New York: G. P. Putnam, 1954), 210.

3. Henry Stevens, *Hitler's Flying Saucers* (Kempton, IL: Adventures Unlimited, 2015), 147.

4. Hall, *UFOs: A Century of Sightings,* 37.

5. Hall, *UFOs: A Century of Sightings,* 37.

6. Stevens, *Hitler's Flying Saucers,* 153.

7. Chester, *Strange Company,* 72.

8. Douglas Botting, *The U-Boats* (Chicago: Time-Life, 1979), 55.

9. "Project 1947 UFO Reports, 1944," accessed Feb. 26, 2018, www.project1947 .com/fig/1944a.htm.

10. Hall, *UFOs: A Century of Sightings,* 41.

11. Hall, *UFOs: A Century of Sightings,* 42.

12. Yves Naud, *U.F.O.s and Extra-terrestrials in History* (vol. 4) as cited by Robert J. Lee, "The German Cylindrical UFO, Interview with a CIC Veteran," 2003, http://www.thelivingmoon.com/47brotherthebig/01archives/A /Bob_Lee_Cylindrical_UFO.htm.

13. "1949 UFO Chronology and the Grudge Report," http://sohp.us/collections /ufos-a-history/pdf/GROSS-1949-July-Dec.pdf.

14. Bryce Barker, "Did the Military Battle with UFOs over Southeast Missouri?" Smokey Mirror, Feb. 12, 2015, www.smokeymirror.com /did-the-military-battle-with-ufos-over-southeast-missouri.

15. "1945: January UFO and Alien Sightings," Think About It, Dec. 12, 2012, www.thinkaboutitdocs.com/1945-january-ufo-alien-sightings.

16. "Korea, 1952: Wonsan-Sunchon Sightings," Project 1947, accessed Feb. 26, 2018, www.project1947.com/fig/korea52a.htm.

17. Hall, *UFOs: A Century of Sightings,* 101.

18. "UFO Sighting Chronology 1939–1945; The World War II Years and 'Foo Fighters,'" National Investigations Committee on Aerial Phenomena, accessed Feb. 26, 2018, www.nicap.org/chronos/1939-1945.htm.

19. "UFO Sighting Chronology, 1939–1945," www.nicap.org/chronos/1939-1945.htm.

20. Chester, *Strange Company,* 94.

CHAPTER 6. THE BATTLE OF ANTARCTICA

This chapter is based on an article published by the author in Melbourne, Australia's *New Dawn* magazine 6, no. 5 (Sept. 2012), 22.

1. General Douglas MacArthur, statement on Japan's surrender, accessed Feb. 26, 2018, http://www.freedomdocuments.com/macarthur.html.
2. David A. Kearns, *Operation Highjump: Task Force 68: Where Hell Freezes Over; A Story of Amazing Bravery and Survival* (New York: Thomas Dunne, 2005), 52.
3. Posted by DasNeueZeitalter, "Mythos Neuschwabenland—Deutsche Vertonung—Vril—Haunebu," June 11, 2011, www.youtube.com/watch?v=znbHUcbKkjk&feature=related.
4. Joseph P. Farrell, *Reich of the Black Sun: Nazi Secret Weapons and the Cold War Allied Legend* (Kempton, IL: Adventures Unlimited, 2004), 184.
5. Lee Van Atta, "El almirante Richard E. Byrd se refiere a la importancia estrategica de los polos," Santiago de Chile, *El Mercurio*, March 5, 1947, 2.
6. Van Atta, "El almirante Richard E. Byrd," 2.
7. Van Atta, "El almirante Richard E. Byrd," 5.
8. Van Atta, "El almirante Richard E. Byrd," 88.
9. Kearns, *Operation Highjump,* 28.
10. "The Secret Land," https://www.youtube.com/watch?v=uB1rSlLR7lM (site discontinued).
11. Peter Duffy, "The Congressman Who Spied for Russia: The Strange Case of Samuel Dickstein," Politico, Oct. 6, 2014, www.politico.com/magazine/story/2014/10/samuel-dickstein-congressman-russian-spy-111641.
12. Posted by DasNeueZeitalter, "Mythos Neuschwabenland," www.youtube.com/watch?v=znbHUcbKkjk&feature=related.
13. Posted by DasNeueZeitalter, "Mythos Neuschwabenland," www.youtube.com/watch?v=znbHUcbKkjk&feature=related.

CHAPTER 7. THE GERMAN CONNECTION

1. "Comments from Key Players," Pegasus Research Consortium: The UFO Files, accessed Oct. 27, 2017, www.thelivingmoon.com/45russel_hamerly/03files/Key_Players_UFU_Files.html.
2. Erich J. Choron, "Operation Highjump and the UFO Connection," accessed

Feb, 26, 2018, www.bibliotecapleyades.net/antarctica/antartica11.htm.

3. Van Atta, "El almirante Richard E. Byrd," 2. Italics added.

4. Posted by DasNeueZeitalter, "Mythos Neuschwabenland," www.youtube
.com/watch?v=znbHUcbKkjk&feature=related.

5. Robert S. Dietz, *Some Oceanographic Observations on Operation Highjump:
Final Report* (Berkeley: University of California Libraries, 1948), 10.

6. Robert Hastings, *UFOs and Nukes: Extraordinary Encounters at Nuclear
Weapons Sites* (Bloomington, IN: Author House, 2008), 29.

7. "UFO Sighting Chronology, 1939–1945," www.nicap.org/chronos/1939-1945.htm.

8. "UFO Sighting over Hanford Nuclear Reactor, Mid-July, 1945," National
Investigations Committee on Aerial Phenomena, accessed Oct. 27, 2017,
www.nicap.org/ncp/ncp-hanford45.htm.

9. "UFO Sighting Chronology, 1939–1945," www.nicap.org/chronos/1939-1945.htm.

10. Posted by TheJamescc, "Aliens Don't Like Baker Nuclear Blasts US
Fifth Nuclear Bomb," March 23, 2010, https://www.youtube.com/watch
?v=jWMM3oIivRI&t=1s.

11. Hall, *UFOs: A Century of Sightings,* 88.

12. Aldrich, "Updated Draft Catalogue."

CHAPTER 8. SEEING IS BELIEVING

1. Quoted in "This Is the Greatest Proof We'll Be Allowed to Share for Now
about the Existence of Alien Life!" Nov. 1, 2016, http://www.lifecoachcode
.com/2016/11/01/controversial-quotes-by-nasa-astronauts-aliens.

2. Alex Mistretta, "Arctic UFO Photographs, USS *Trepang,* SSN 674, March
1971," The Black Vault, June 29, 2017, www.theblackvault.com/casefiles
/arctic-ufo-photographs-uss-trepang-ssn-674-march-1971.

3. Alejandro Rojas, "Navy Arctic UFO Photos Allegedly Leaked by Anonymous
Source," OpenMinds, July 15, 2015, www.openminds.tv/navy-arctic-ufo
-photos-allegedly-leaked-by-anonymous-source/34350.

4. Mistretta, "Arctic UFO Photographs."

CHAPTER 9. PAYBACK AT ROSWELL

1. "RAAF Captures Flying Saucer on Ranch in Roswell Region, Roswell Daily
Record, Tuesday, July 8, 1947," www.angelfire.com/indie/anna_jones1
/daily_record.html.

2. Scott Ramsey, Suzanne Ramsey, and Frank Thayer, *The Aztec UFO Incident: The Case, Evidence, and Cover-up of One of the Most Perplexing Crashes in History* (Wayne, NJ: New Page, 2015), 209.

3. Posted by Abundance of Energy, "Dr. Steven Greer on Shooting Down UFOs and Killing ETs," July 9, 2015, https://www.youtube.com/watch?v=7rmFXOe5Ufg&t=196s.

4. Ramsey, Ramsey, and Thayer, *Aztec UFO Incident*, 210.

5. Frank Scully, *Behind the Flying Saucers* (New York: Holt, 1950), 202.

6. Karl T. Pflock, *Roswell: Inconvenient Facts and the Will to Believe* (Amherst, NY: Prometheus, 2001), 152.

7. Patricia D. Netzley, *Alien Encounters* (San Diego: Reference Point, 2011), 226.

8. Netzley, *Alien Encounters,* 236.

9. Ramsey, Ramsey, and Thayer, *Aztec UFO Incident,* 162.

10. Smith, *MO41*, 41.

11. Stanton Friedman, personal email correspondence with the author, Nov. 17, 2016.

12. Jon Austin, "Does FBI Memo Prove Aliens DID Crash near Roswell and THREE UFOs and Were Covered Up?" Express, October 5, 2015, www.express.co.uk/news/science/610020/Does-FBI-memo-prove-aliens-DID-crash-near-Roswell-and-THREE-UFOs-and-were-covered-up.

13. The Federal Bureau of Investigation, Official FBI Reports on Unidentified Flying Objects Released under the Freedom of Information Act. (Rockville, MD: Wildside, 2008), 33.

14. Tony Brunt, *Secret History* (Auckland, New Zealand: Vailima Press, 2011), 82.

15. Nathan Farragut Twining, AZ Quotes, accessed Feb. 28, 2018, www.azquotes.com/quote/615737.

16. Robert M. Wood, "Validating the New Majestic Documents," Full text of "MJ 12 Documents Ultimate Collection, May 2000, https://archive.org/stream/MJ12Documents20150601/rmwood_mufon2000_djvu.txt.

17. Stanton T. Friedman and Whitley Strieber, *Top Secret/Majic: Operation Majestic-12 and the United States Government's UFO Cover-up* (Boston: Da Capo, 2005), 106.

18. Michael Hall and Wendy Connc, Full text of "UFOs and ETs Collection," accessed Feb. 28, 2018, https://archive.org/stream/UFOsAreReal_201611/UFO%20And%20ETs/Great%20Flying%20Saucer%20Wave%20Of%201947_djvu.txt.

19. Hall, *UFOs: A Century of Sightings,* 83.

20. Hall, *UFOs: A Century of Sightings,* 80.

21. Hall, *UFOs: A Century of Sightings,* 84.

22. Hall *UFOs: A Century of Sightings,* 85.

23. Hall *UFOs: A Century of Sightings,* 85.

24. Hall, *UFOs: A Century of Sightings,* 87.

25. Hall, *UFOs: A Century of Sightings,* 88.

CHAPTER 10. CRASHES—OURS AND THEIRS

1. "Relationships with Inhabitants of Celestial Bodies: The Einstein-Oppenheimer Draft Document, 1947," accessed Feb. 28, 2018, http://www.bibliotecapleyades.net/sociopolitica/esp_sociopol_mj12_3p.htm.

2. David Michael Jacobs, *The UFO Controversy in America* (Bloomington: Indiana University Press, 1975), 162.

3. Edward J. Ruppelt, *The Report on Unidentified Flying Objects* (New York: Doubleday, 1956), 49.

4. Ruppelt, *Report,* 49.

5. Hall, *UFOs: A Century of Sightings,* 161.

6. Harold T. Wilkins, *Flying Saucers on the Attack* (New York: Ace Star, 1967), 177.

7. Ruppelt, *Report,* 50.

8. Hall, *UFOs: A Century of Sightings,* 111.

9. Ruppelt, *Report,* 50.

10. Ramsey, Ramsey, and Thayer, *Aztec UFO Incident,* 200.

11. Hall *UFOs: A Century of Sightings,* 167.

12. Hall, *UFOs: A Century of Sightings,* 167.

13. Ramsey, Ramsey, and Thayer, *Aztec UFO Incident,* 72.

14. Ramsey, Ramsey, and Thayer, *Aztec UFO Incident,* 72.

15. Ramsey, Ramsey, and Thayer, *Aztec UFO Incident,* 73.

16. Ramsey, Ramsey, and Thayer, *Aztec UFO Incident,* 74.

17. Ramsey, Ramsey, and Thayer, *Aztec UFO Incident,* 77.

18. Ramsey, Ramsey, and Thayer, *Aztec UFO Incident,* 78.

19. Ramsey, Ramsey, and Thayer, *Aztec UFO Incident,* 78.

20. Ramsey, Ramsey, and Thayer, *Aztec UFO Incident,* 82.

21. Ramsey, Ramsey, and Thayer, *Aztec UFO Incident,* 82.

22. Ramsey, Ramsey, and Thayer, *Aztec UFO Incident,* 85.

23. Ramsey, Ramsey, and Thayer, *Aztec UFO Incident,* 88.

24. Ramsey, Ramsey, and Thayer, *Aztec UFO Incident,* 93.

CHAPTER 11. CAT-AND-MOUSE ENCOUNTERS

1. Jonathan Leake, "Stephen Hawking: ET Exists," *Times of London,* April 25, 2010, https://www.thetimes.co.uk/article/stephen-hawking-et-exists-66lzlnt0wdt.

2. "The Short Heyday of Sign, 1948," NICAP: National Investigations Committee on Aerial Phenomena, accessed Feb. 28, 2018, nicap.org/docs/loedd/loedd_conclusion.htm.

3. "The Short Heyday of Sign," nicap.org/docs/loedd/loedd_conclusion.htm.

4. "The Short Heyday of Sign," nicap.org/docs/loedd/loedd_conclusion.htm.

5. "24 July 1948 02:45 Montgomery, Alabama, USA," UFO DNA: The Encyclopedia of UFO Sightings, accessed Feb 28, 2018, www.thecid.com/ufo/uf18/uf6/186319.htm.

6. Hall, *UFOs: A Century of Sightings,* 174.

7. "Alfred Loedding and the Great Flying Saucer Wave of 1947," https://rr0.org/time/1/9/9/8/Hall-Connors_LoeddingAndGreat1947Wave/FinalWord.html.

8. Hall, *UFOs: A Century of Sightings,* 178.

9. Hall, *UFOs: A Century of Sightings,* 178.

10. Clark, *UFO Encyclopedia,* 69.

11. Wilkins, *Flying Saucers on the Attack,* 175.

12. Wilkins, *Flying Saucers on the Attack,* 176.

13. William J. Birnes, *The UFO Magazine UFO Encyclopedia* (New York: Gallery, 2004), 24.

14. Bruce S. Maccabee, "UFO Related Information from the FBI File," *The MUFON UFO Journal,* no. 130, September 1979, https://www.scribd.com/document/21256965/The-Mufon-Ufo-Journal.

15. Jacobs, "Debate over Existence of UFOs."

16. Wilkins, *Flying Saucers on the Attack,* 179.

CHAPTER 12. THE KOREAN WAR ERA

1. Burke Josslin, "UFOs No Strangers to Korea," *Korea Herald,* 2000, as reported on http://www.rense.com/general11/NK.HTM.

2. John Timmerman, "Bizarre Craft Hit Soldiers With Debilitating Light Beam," interview with Francis P. Wall, Jan. 1987, accessed Feb. 28, 2018, www.nicap.org/springkor.htm. Bracketed insertion Timmerman's.

3. Timmerman, interview with Wall.

4. Barker, "Did the Military Battle with UFOs over Southeast Missouri?" www .smokeymirror.com/did-the-military-battle-with-ufos-over-southeast-missouri.

5. Barker, "Did the Military Battle?"

6. Pat Pratt, "Poplar Bluff UFO Sighting in 1950 Included in Online Database," *Southeast Missourian* website, Jan. 28, 2015, www.semissourian .com/story/2160533.html.

7. Clark, *UFO Encyclopedia,* 236.

8. Hall, *UFOs: A Century of Sightings,* 183.

9. Jacobs, "Debate over Existence of UFOs."

10. Richard F. Haines, *Advanced Aerial Devices Reported during the Korean War* (Brookfield, CA: Lighting Design, 1990), 183.

11. Birnes, *The UFO Magazine UFO Encyclopedia,* 66.

12. Birnes, *UFO Magazine Encyclopedia,* 66.

13. Haines, *Advanced Aerial Devices,* 187.

14. Donald Keyhoe, *Flying Saucers: Top Secret* (New York: G. P. Putnam's Sons, 1960), 231.

15. Clark, *The UFO Encyclopedia,* 194.

16. Hall, *UFOs: A Century of Sightings,* 169.

17. Kevin D. Randle, *Invasion Washington: UFOs Over the Capitol* (San Francisco: HarperTorch, 2001), 88.

18. Hall, *UFOs: A Century of Sightings,* 54.

19. Posted by ufokonferanse, "UFO/USO sightings during Operation Mainbrace in 1952. By Pia Knudsen." Nov. 9, 2012, https://www.youtube.com/watch?v= qRFUFLWPDDA&t=8s.

20. Posted by Revealing the REAL Truth, "UFOs/USOs—Operation Mainbrace—1952," January 28, 2012, accessed October 27, 2017, https:// www.youtube.com/watch?v=tBXOBAiglIc.

21. Posted by Grossbel1, "USS FDR UFO and USO sightings," July 6, 2015, https://www.youtube.com/watch?v=puVr3ws0mBs (site discontinued).

22. Posted by Grossbel1, "USS FDR Sightings," https://www.youtube.com /watch?v=puVr3ws0mBs (site discontinued).

23. Posted by Grossbel1, "USS FDR Sightings," https://www.youtube.com /watch?v=puVr3ws0mBs (site discontinued).

24. Posted by ufokonferanse, "UFO/USO Sightings," https://www.youtube .com/watch?v=qRFUFLWPDDA&t=8s.

25. Posted by ufokonferanse, "UFO/USO Sightings," https://www.youtube .com/watch?v=qRFUFLWPDDA&t=8s.

26. Posted by ufokonferanse, "UFO/USO Sightings," https://www.youtube .com/watch?v=qRFUFLWPDDA&t=8s.

27. David E. Twichell, *Global Implications of the UFO Reality* (Infinity Publishing, 2003), 70.

28. Jacobs, "Debate over Existence of UFOs."

29. Keyhoe, *Flying Saucers,* 179.

30. Keyhoe, *Flying Saucers,* 181.

31. Keyhoe, *Flying Saucers,* 181.

32. Keyhoe, *Flying Saucers,* 184.

CHAPTER 13. COLD WAR, HOT SAUCERS

1. Susan Wright, *UFO Headquarters* (New York: St. Martin's Press, 1999), 55.

2. "1952, Flying Saucer 'Shoot Down' Stories," Roswell Proof, accessed Feb. 28, 2018, roswellproof.homestead.com/ShootDown_INS_72952.html.

3. Quoted in Frank C. Feschino Jr., *Shoot Them Down! The Flying Saucer Air Wars of 1952* (n.p.: Lulu, 2007), 50.

4. Keyhoe, *Flying Saucers,* 197.

5. Keyhoe, *Flying Saucers,* 199.

6. Clark, *UFO Encyclopedia,* 143.

7. Keyhoe, *Flying Saucers,* 201.

8. Keyhoe, *Flying Saucers,* 208.

9. Stonehill, *Soviet UFO Files,* 77.

10. "UFO Found near 1953 Kinross F-89 Scorpion in Lake Superior," IRAAP, accessed Feb. 28, 2018, http://www.iraap.org/news/sep.htm#ac1b.

11. "The Kinross Air Force Base Incident (Jet Disappears While Chasing UFO)," *UFO Evidence: Scientific Study of the UFO Phenomenon and the Search for Extraterrestrial Life,* accessed Oct. 27, 2017, www.ufoevidence .org/cases/case610.htm.

12. Gordon Heath, "1954 Grouse Mountain USAF F-86 Crash," UFO*BC, accessed October 27, 2017, www.ufobc.ca/kinross/planeMishaps/grouseMtn Crash.html

13. Heath, "1954 Grouse Mountain USAF F-86 Crash."

14. Keyhoe, *Flying Saucers,* 133.
15. Keyhoe, *Flying Saucers,* 133.
16. "Four Die near Utica as Air Force Jet Fighter Hits Auto, Two Houses," *Troy Record,* July 3, 1953, GenDisasters.com, http://www.gendisasters.com /new-york/11705/walesville-ny-jet-fighter-crashes-homes-july-1954.
17. Keyhoe, *Flying Saucers,* 136.
18. Francis Ridge, "The Walesville Incident," National Investigations Committee on Aerial Phenomena, accessed Feb. 27, 2017, www.nicap.org /reports/540702walesville_ridge.htm.
19. "Four Die near Utica," http://www.gendisasters.com/new-york/11705 /walesville-ny-jet-fighter-crashes-homes-july-1954.
20. "Four Die near Utica," http://www.gendisasters.com/new-york/11705 /walesville-ny-jet-fighter-crashes-homes-july-1954.
21. "Four Die near Utica," http://www.gendisasters.com/new-york/11705 /walesville-ny-jet-fighter-crashes-homes-july-1954.
22. Keyhoe, *Flying Saucers,* 139.
23. Keyhoe, *Flying Saucers,* 141.
24. Keyhoe, *Flying Saucers,* 141.
25. Stonehill, *Soviet UFO Files,* 94.
26. Randle, *UFO Dossier,* 230.
27. Wilkins, *Flying Saucers on the Attack,* 152.
28. Wilkins, *Flying Saucers on the Attack,* 152.
29. "CRIFO Newsletter Transcript, June 3, 1955," National Investigations Committee on Aerial Phenomena, Oct. 10, 2006, www.nicap.org/reports /550408rockford_CRIFO.htm.
30. "CRIFO Newsletter Transcript," www.nicap.org/reports/550408rockford _CRIFO.htm.
31. Alfredsson, "Swedish UFO Interception," Deviant Art, Accessed October 27, 2017, http://alfredsson.deviantart.com/art/Swedish-UFO -Interception-16815960.
32. "INS *Dakar,*" Wikipedia, last updated March 20, 2018, https://en.wikipedia .org/wiki/INS_Dakar.
33. "INS *Dakar,*" Wikipedia.
34. "Historique du sous-marin Minerve, accessed March 15, 2018, www.netmarine .net/bat/smarins/minerve/histoire.htm.
35. "The Amazing Story of the K129—Project Azurian," December 2, 2012, archive.is/5ZCSh#selection-127.0-127.47.

36. "Scorpion Crew Remembered," United Press International Archives, May 28, 1988, https://www.upi.com/Archives/1988/05/28/Scorpion-crew-remembered/3914580795200/.

37 "USS Scorpion (SSN-589)," Wikipedia, last updated March 7, 2018, https://en.wikipedia.org/wiki/USS_Scorpion_(SSN-589).

38 "UFO Sightings in 1968," accessed March 20, 2018, http://thecid.com/ufo/chrono/chrono/1968.htm.

39 "UFO Sightings in 1968," http://thecid.com/ufo/chrono/chrono/1968.htm.

40 "UFO Sightings in 1968," http://thecid.com/ufo/chrono/chrono/1968.htm.

41 "Sighting Report # 737 6-??-1968," Water UFO, accessed March 20, 2018, www.waterufo.net/item.php?id=737.

42 "USS Hyades, (AF-28)," Wikipedia, last updated February 25, 2018, https://en.wikipedia.org/wiki/USS_Hyades_(AF-28).

43 "Sighting Report # 737 6-??-1968," Water UFO.

44. Quoted in Brad Steiger, *Project Blue Book* (New York: Ballantine, 1987), 274.

45. John Powell, "Subject: Another Bill English Interview," September 12, 1992, http://mirror.bagelwood.com/textfiles/ufo/UFOBBS/2000/2905.ufo.

46. The Dyatlov Pass incident refers to nine Russian hikers killed and their bodies mutilated, allegedly by extraterrestrial aliens in the northern Ural Mountains, on February 2, 1959. See "When UFOs Kill: Dyatlov Pass Incident," Ancient UFO, July 23, 2015, ancientufo.org/2015/07/when-ufos-kill-the-mountain-of-the-dead-dyatlov-pass.

47. "Human Mutilations: The Case of USAF Sgt. J. P. Lovette," accessed Feb. 27, 2018, www.reocities.com/aliengrip/mutilations/JPLovette56-En.htm.

48. Keyhoe, *Flying Saucers,* 143.

CHAPTER 14.
THE VIETNAM WAR ERA

1. Quoted in Steiger, *Project Blue Book,* 276.

2. John Powell, "Subject: Another Bill English Interview," September 12, 1992, http://mirror.bagelwood.com/textfiles/ufo/UFOBBS/2000/2905.ufo.

3. Milton William Cooper, *Behold a Pale Horse* (Flagstaff, AZ: Light Technology, 1991), 59.

4. Mack Maloney, *UFOs in Wartime* (New York: Berkley, 2011), 137.

5. Maloney, *UFOs in Wartime,* 138.

6. Hall, *UFOs: A Century of Sightings,* 74.

7. "Vietnam UFOs: UFOS in the DMZ," Cosmic Connection, accessed Feb. 27, 2018, http://tvufo.tripod.com/id128.html.

8. Quoted in post by J. Antonio Huneeus, "UFOs during the Vietnam War," Open Minds, Nov. 11, 2009, www.openminds.tv/ufos-during-the -vietnam-war/563.

9. Brent Swancer, "Mysterious Otherworldly Engagements in the Vietnam War," Mysterious Universe, Feb. 10, 2017, mysteriousuniverse.org/2017/02 /mysterious-otherworldly-military-engagements-in-the-vietnam-war.

10. Swancer, "Mysterious Otherworldly Engagements."

11. Jon Wyatt, "HMAS *Hobart* Hit during Vietnam UFO Encounter?" UFO Evidence: Scientific Study of the UFO Phenomenon and the Search for Extraterrestrial Life, April 2003, www.ufoevidence.org/cases/case60.htm.

12. Jim Steffes, "The Sinking of PCF-19 as Seen from PCF-12," last updated Jan. 3, 2009, www.swiftboats.net/stories/pcf19.htm.

13. Ray Fowler, "The Nha Trang Incident: Vietnam, Mid-June 1966," National Investigations Committee on Aerial Phenomena, accessed Feb. 28, 2018, www.nicap.org/reports/660619nhatrang_fowler.htm.

14. Huneeus, "UFOs during the Vietnam War."

15. Huneeus, "UFOs during the Vietnam War."

16. The History Channel, "Norway's Navy Reports an Alien USO," Posted by spaceshipidentified@yahoo.com palm, Dec. 6, 2011, https://www.youtube .com/watch?v=tlK4O0VgiQU&t=13s.

17. "The Worlds [*sic*] Most Active USO UFO Hotspot UFO Documentary," Posted by UFO, June 3, 2015, https://www.youtube.com/watch ?v=ZXxw2DajE6I.

18. Posted by spaceshipidentified@yahoo.com palm, "Norway's Navy Reports an Alien USO," https://www.youtube.com/watch?v=tlK4O0VgiQU&t=13s.

19. See https://www.aftenposten.no/nyheter/iriks/article3444559.ece (site discontinued).

20. Posted by Top5s, "Five Most Mysterious and Unidentified Submerged Objects," Aug. 27, 2016, https://www.youtube.com/watch?v=8U-mocoCkms&t=627s.

21. Posted by spaceshipidentified@yahoo.com palm, "Norway's Navy Reports an Alien USO," https://www.youtube.com/watch?v=tlK4O0VgiQU&t=13s.

22. "Norwegians Decide Submarine Is Real and Drop Depth Charges," *New York Times,* Nov. 26, 1972, http://www.nytimes.com/1972/11/26/archives /norwegians-decide-submarine-is-real-and-drop-depth-charges.html.

23. Posted by Beyond Creepy, "The Norway Fjord Incident," March 24, 2016, https://www.youtube.com/watch?v=_WicY6sBS2U.

24. Posted by Beyond Creepy, "The Norway Fjord Incident," https://www.youtube .com/watch?v=_WicY6sBS2U.

25. Sean Martin and Monika Pallenberg, "Did Aliens Interfere in the Vietnam War? Soldiers give Shocking Accounts," *Express,* updated May 16, 2017, http://www.express.co.uk/news/weird/804778/ALIENS-Vietnam-war -Soldiers-UFO.

26. Mattweb, "Military UFO Quotes," www.ufoevidence.org/documents /doc1743.htm.

27. Stonehill, *Soviet UFO Files*, 88.

28. Pat Otter, "New Revelations on the Watery Fate of Foxtrot 94," *Grimsby Evening Telegraph,* October 8–10, 12–13, 1992, http://www.latest-ufo -sightings.net/2017/11/american-pilot-die-seeing-flying-cone-sky.html.

29. Otter, "New Revelations."

30. Otter, "New Revelations."

31. David D. Schindele, *It Never Happened, Volume 1: U.S. Air Force UFO Cover-up Revealed* (n.p., WA: Edgar Rock, 2017), 125.

32. Maloney, *UFOs in Wartime*, 146.

33. Posted by Sirius Disclosure, "ET Extraterrestrial Structures on the Moon: Sgt. Karl Wolfe," Nov. 29, 2013, https://www.youtube.com /watch?v=_4hycqDNnPE.

34. Posted by Sirius Disclosure, "ET Extraterrestrial Structures," https://www .youtube.com/watch?v=_4hycqDNnPE.

35. Posted by Sirius Disclosure, "UFO Crash Recovery: Sgt. Clifford Stone Testifies," Nov. 4, 2013, https://www.youtube.com/watch?v=1GnGGCaC6P4&t=23s.

36. Posted by dumbbell33, "Phil Schneider 1 of 7 Dulce Alien Confrontation," April 22, 2009, https://www.youtube.com/watch?v=Xs4emKd_fG4.

37. "Alien Firefight at Secret Military Base Reexamined," https://www.youtube .com/watch?v=1wl6PyEhS8M (video discontinued).

CHAPTER 15. CONFLICT IN THE LATE TWENTIETH CENTURY

1. Ronald Reagan, "The Alien Thread," accessed Oct. 27, 2017, www .bibliotecapleyades.net/exopolitica/exopolitics_reagan03.htm.

2. Stonehill, *Soviet UFO Files,* 147.

3. Hastings, *UFOs and Nukes,* 131.

4. B. J. Booth and Richard Hall, eds., "Alien Being Shot Dead by MPs, January 18, 1978 (Ft. Dix and McGuire)," UFO Casebook, accessed Feb. 28, 2018, www.ufocasebook.com/ftdix.html

5. Stonehill, *Soviet UFO Files,* 122.

6. "Testimony of Mr. Don Bockelman, US Army," September 2000, http:// www.hestories.info/disclosure-project-briefing-document-prepared-for .html?page=13

7. Stonehill, *Soviet UFO Files,* 110.

8. Zhang Ke-Tao, *Flying Saucer Review* 44, no. 2 (summer 1999).

9. Stonehill, *Soviet UFO Files,* 117.

10. Stonehill, *Soviet UFO Files,* 115.

11. Anthony Bragalia, "Of Roswell and Rockets: The Secret V-2 Flying Saucer Film," Weird True Stuff, Feb. 28, 2010, https://weirdtrue.wordpress. com/2010/03/01/testimonies-flying-saucers-filmed-by-white-sands-v-2 -rockets-a-possible-roswell-crash-connection/.

12. Jacobs, "Debate over Existence of UFOs."

13. "Col. Ross Dedrickson Testimony," https://www.youtube.com/watch?v =SchsQD88wk&t=497s (video no longer available).

14. Antony Barnett, "US Planned One Big Nuclear Blast for Mankind," *The Guardian,* May 14, 2000, https://www.theguardian.com/science/2000 /may/14/spaceexploration.theobserver.

15. Shar Adams, "Peruvian Jet Pilot Tells of Tangle with UFOs (+Photos)," The Epoch Times, last updated May 4, 2013, www.theepochtimes.com /n3/37316-peruvian-jet-pilot-tells-of-tangle-with-ufo.

16. Stonehill, *Soviet UFO Files,* 76.

17. Stonehill, *Soviet UFO Files,* 78.

18. Stonehill, *Soviet UFO Files,* 78.

19. "Aliens Zapped Russian Soldiers, Declassified CIA Report Claims," Latest UFO Sighting, April 22, 2017, http://www.latest-ufo-sightings.net/2017/04 /aliens-zapped-russian-soldiers-declassified-cia-report-claims.html.

20. "Aliens Zapped Russian Soldiers," http://www.latest-ufo-sightings .net/2017/04/aliens-zapped-russian-soldiers-declassified-cia-report-claims .html.

21. "Aliens Zapped Russian Soldiers," http://www.latest-ufo-sightings .net/2017/04/aliens-zapped-russian-soldiers-declassified-cia-report-claims .html.

22. Posted by Earth Mystery News, "UFO Crash in Peru: Lance Corporal Jonathan Weygandt Testimony," May 29, 2016, https://www.youtube.com /watch?v=SU8alQ3Daaw.

23. Posted by Earth Mystery News, "UFO Crash in Peru," https://www.youtube .com/watch?v=SU8alQ3Daaw.

CHAPTER 16.
FROM IRAN AND SOUTH AFRICA
TO THE GULF WAR

1. Quoted in Leslie Kean, *UFOs: Generals, Pilots, and Government Officials Go on the Record* (New York: Three Rivers, 2011), 253.

2. Quoted in David E. Twichell, *Global Implications of the UFO Reality* (New York: Infinity, 2003), 56.

3. Kean, *UFOs,* 253.

4. Kean, *UFOs,* 255.

5. Kean, *UFOs,* 261.

6. Kean, *UFOs,* 263.

7. Kean, *UFOs,* 265.

8. Kean, *UFOs,* 265.

9. "UFO Crashes on Botswana/South Africa Border," The Night Sky, last updated Nov. 9, 2017, thenightsky.org/kalahari.html.

10. "Speech for Ossette Conference September, 1989," http://www.textfiles .com/ufo/ossette.ufo.

11. Leonard H. Stringfield, *Situation Red: The UFO Siege,* (New York: Doubleday and Company, 1978), 73.

12. "The Kalahari UFO Crash Case History," posted on Facebook by The Truth about Aliens and UFOS, April 27, 2013, https://www .facebook.com/238240472899332/photos/a.351411358248909.86442 .238240472899332/523426397714070.

13. Schwann, "The Kalahari UFO Crash," written comment to "aliens in South Africa," Accessed Oct. 27, 2017, https://groups.google.com/forum/#!msg /alt.alien.visitors/dsvex7qpT0s/b623fNfgLAgJ.

14. "Navy Submarine UFO Encounter," UFO UpDates, October 30, 1998, http://www.ufoupdateslist.com/1998/nov/m08-001.shtml.

15. "USS *Memphis* SSN 691," U.S. Carriers, last modified Oct. 13, 2013, www .uscarriers.net/ssn691history.htm.

16. Maloney, *UFOs in Wartime,* 149.

17. Maloney, *UFOs in Wartime,* 149.

18. Maloney, *UFOs in Wartime,* 153.

19. John Kettler, "UFO Blown To Bits During Gulf War," John Kettler Investigates, Accessed October 27, 2017, www.johnkettler.com/ufo-blown-to-bits-gulf-war.

20. Kettler, "UFO Blown to Bits during Gulf War."

CHAPTER 17.
UFO ESPIONAGE

1. Quoted in Arjun Walia, "Why Are UFOs Shutting Down Our Nuclear Missiles?" Collective Evolution, Nov. 10, 2014, www.collective-evolution.com/2014/11/10/why-are-ufos-shutting-down-our-nuclear-missiles.

2. "UFO Sighting over Nuclear Power Plant, Canada," Latest UFO Sightings, March 31, 2010, http://www.latest-ufo-sightings.net/2010/03/ufo-sighting-over-nuclear-power-plant.html.

3. Coyoteprime, "UFO Casebook: 'Unknown Object Photographed over France,'" April 4, 2010, coyoteprime-runningcauseicantfly.blogspot.com/2010/04/unknown-object-photographed-over.html.

4. Hastings, *UFOs and Nukes,* 108.

5. "Argentina: UFOs Buzz Atucha Nuclear Power Station," Inexplicata: The Journal of Hispanic Ufology, July 6, 2010, http://inexplicata.blogspot.com/2010/07/argentina-ufos-buzz-atucha-nuclear.html.

6. Hastings, *UFOs and Nukes,* 109.

7. Hastings, *UFOs and Nukes,* 110.

8. Hastings, *UFOs and Nukes,* 110.

9. Marc Ambinder, "Failure Shuts Down Squadron of Nuclear Missiles," *The Atlantic,* Oct. 26, 2010, https://www.theatlantic.com/politics/archive/2010/10/failure-shuts-down-squadron-of-nuclear-missiles/65207.

10. CNN Wire Staff, "Object Shot out of Sky above Israeli Nuclear Plant, Military Says," CNN, Dec. 16, 2010, www.cnn.com/2010/WORLD/meast/12/16/israel.negev.shootdown.

11. Posted by masamon, "Top Secret Footage: 'Huge UFO That Appeared in the Fukushima Daiichi Nuclear Power Plant,'" Jan. 18, 2016, www.youtube.com/watch?v=z2y2_Em4cJI.

12. Jon Austin, "New Zealand Earthquake Caused by Large Hadron Collider, UFO

and Supermoon in Crazy Claims," *Express,* Nov. 15, 2016, www.express.co.uk /news/weird/732555/New-Zealand-earthquake-Large-Hadron-Collider -UFO.

13. Michael Persinger and Gyslaine Lafrenière, *Space-Time Transients and Unusual Events* (Chicago: Nelson-Hall, 1977), 22.

14. Robert Hastings, "UFOs Reported Near Malmstrom AFB's Nuclear Missile Sites in September 2012," Nov. 4, 2012, www.ufohastings.com/articles /ufos-reported-near-malmstrom-afbs-nuclear-missile-sites-in-september -2012.

15. "Most Remarkable UFO Sightings in January 2013," Latest UFO Sighting, Feb. 1, 2013, http://www.latest-ufo-sightings.net/2013.

16. Alejandro Rojas, "UFO Buzzed French Nuclear Power Plant Says Director," HuffPost, updated March 30, 2015, www.huffingtonpost.com/alejandro-rojas /ufo-buzzed-french-nuclear_b_6558798.html.

17. Paul Seaburn, "Another UFO over a Nuclear Plant, This Time in Arkansas," Mysterious Universe, Nov. 26, 2014, mysteriousuniverse.org/2014/11 /another-ufo-over-a-nuclear-plant-this-time-in-arkansas.

18. Posted by Latest UFO Sightings News, "UFO during the Last Flight of the Vulcan Bomber in Gloucestershire, England," Aug. 19, 2015, https://www .youtube.com/watch?v=ZwwYMioxRwk&t=17s.

19. "Avro Vulcan," Wikipedia, last updated Jan. 18, 2018, https://en.wikipedia .org/wiki/Avro_Vulcan.

20. Simon Tomlinson, "Has an Alien Corpse Been Found in Russia? Scientists 'Baffled' by Discovery of Tiny Creature with Mysterious Skull, No Neck and Wings near Nuclear Power Plant," *Daily Mail,* Sept. 2, 2015, www .dailymail.co.uk/news/article-3219351/Has-alien-corpse-Russia-Scientists -baffled-discovery-tiny-creature-mysterious-skull-no-neck-wings-near -nuclear-power-plant.html.

21. Alanna Ketler, Collective Evolution blog, accessed Oct. 27, 2017, worldnews .indywatch.org/archiver/worldnews.indywatch.org/resources/timemachine /2015/247/world.html.

CHAPTER 18. INTRUDERS IN THE EARLY TWENTY-FIRST CENTURY

1. Timothy Good, *Need to Know: UFOs, the Military, and Intelligence* (New York: Pegasus, 2007), 221.

2. Jason McClellan, "Military Magazine Highlights Iranian Air Force Encounters with UFOs," Open Minds, Sept. 30, 2013, www.openminds .tv/military-magazine-highlights-iranian-air-force-encounters-with -ufos-1153/23907.

3. McClellan, "Military Magazine."

4. Helene Cooper, Leslie Kean, and Ralph Blumenthal, "Two Navy Airmen and an Object That 'Accelerated Like Nothing I've Ever Seen,'" *New York Times,* Dec. 17, 2017, https://www.nytimes.com/2017/12/16/us/politics /unidentified-flying-object-navy.html.

5. CNN Live, "2017-12-19 New Interview with pilot David Fravor (the USS Nimitz UFO Incident)," Posted by eventimus, Dec. 20, 2017, https://www .youtube.com/watch?v=3w0aXTfDDq8.

6. Cooper, Kean, and Blumenthal, "Two Navy Airmen."

7. Cooper, Kean, and Blumenthal, "Two Navy Airmen."

8. Cooper, Kean, and Blumenthal, "Two Navy Airmen."

9. Posted by secureteam 10, "Pilot Who Chased This UFO Reveals All," Dec. 23, 2017, https://www.youtube.com/watch?v=OQ7l-Fi5nJY&t=527s.

10. "Fighter Jet Observed Chasing a Triangular Craft in Central Oklahoma," UFO Casebook, May 30, 2005, www.ufocasebook.com/oklahoma052705.html.

11. Michael Cohen, "Greece: Amazing UFO Incident Involving Air Force and Airline," UFO Casebook, July 2, 2009, www.ufocasebook.com/2009 /greekairforceairlinesighting.html.

12. "Russian Navy UFO Records Say Aliens Love Oceans," RT, last updated Feb. 17, 2010, www.rt.com/news/russian-navy-ufo-records-say -aliens-love-oceans.

13. "Russian Navy UFO Records," www.rt.com/news/russian-navy-ufo-records -say-aliens-love-oceans.

14. "Russian Navy UFO Records," www.rt.com/news/russian-navy-ufo-records -say-aliens-love-oceans.

15. "Russian Navy Reveals Its Secret UFO Encounters," Fox News, July 28, 2009, www.foxnews.com/story/2009/07/28/russian-navy-reveals-its-secret -ufo-encounters.html.

16. Roger Marsh, "Former Navy Serviceman Reports UFO Monitoring Ship," UFO Chronicles, Feb. 10, 2014, http://www.theufochronicles.com/2014/03 /former-navy-serviceman-reports-ufo.html.

17. "RAF Jets Chase UFO Down M5," *UFO Matrix* 1, accessed Oct. 27, 2017, https://www.scribd.com/document/152272191/Ufo-Matrix-Issue-01.

18. Posted by Calgary Herald, "CF-18 Pilot Describes Spectacular Crash," *Calgary Herald,* Aug. 17, 2010, https://www.youtube.com/watch?v=anz4bBsZ2WM&t=1s.

19. Posted by justa4t, "UFOs Lethbridge, Alberta Airshow before CF-18 Jet Crash July 2010," Aug. 11, 2010, https://www.youtube.com/watch?v=X9aCT3e7cuY&t=17s.

20. Antonio Huneeus, "Russian Military Spooked by UFO," Open Minds, May 27, 2011, www.openminds.tv/russian-military-ufo-696/9926.

21. Michael Peck, "Did Iranian Fighters Battle UFOs?" *Forbes,* January 14, 2014, https://www.forbes.com/sites/michaelpeck/2014/01/14/did-iranian-fighters-battle-ufos/#5d9bd9121a32.

22. Peck, "Iranian Fighters."

CHAPTER 19.
WHISPERING DEVILS

1. Lee Speigel, "The UFOs Didn't Come in Peace! Astronaut Sets Record Straight On ET Nuclear War," HuffPost, updated Aug. 28, 2015, www.huffingtonpost.com/entry/moonwalker-edgar-mitchell-denies-saying-ets-prevented-nuclear-war_us_55d61660e4b07addcb45eb80.

2. "Aggressive Firing on an Apparent Large UFO Caught on Video," Latest UFO Sighting, April 21, 2013, www.latest-ufo-sightings.net/2013/04/aggressive-firing-on-apparent-large-ufo.html.

3. "Fleet of UFO Engage a Fleet of Military Jets—Florida UFO Dog Fight," UFO Casebook, July 25, 2013, www.ufocasebook.com/2013/floridajetsufos.html.

4. Ken Oz, www.altheadlines.com/syria-large-ufo-sighting-8-28-13-13250773 (site discontinued).

5. Reuters, "Unmanned Russian Proton-M Rocket Crashes Just after Launch in Kazakhstan," *Telegraph,* July 2, 2013, www.telegraph.co.uk/news/worldnews/europe/russia/10154076/Unmanned-Russian-Proton-M-rocket-crashes-just-after-launch-in-Kazakhstan.html.

6. Michael Salla, "Did UFO Destroy Russian Proton-M Rocket?" Exopolitics, May 15, 2014, exopolitics.org/did-ufo-destroy-russian-proton-m-rocket.

7. John Shammas, "UFO Sighting: Family 'Gobsmacked' as Four Mysterious Objects Zoomed across Sky during BBQ—Chased by 'MOD Helicopter,'"

The Mirror, March 23, 2015, www.mirror.co.uk/news/uk-news/bolton-ufo-sighting-family-gobsmacked-5388130.

8. "Air Force Jet Shoots Down a UFO?" Latest UFO Sighting, Jan. 29, 2016, http://www.latest-ufo-sightings.net/2016/01/air-force-jet-shoots-down-a-ufo.html.

9. "Elon Musk: 'We Have Not Ruled Out' That UFO Caused Space X Explosion," Sputnik, Nov. 9, 2016, https://sputniknews.com/science/201609101045180070-elon-musk-ufo-spacex-explosion.

10. Posted by USLaunch, "SpaceX—Static Fire Anomaly AMOS-6 09-01-2016 Explosion," Report, Sept. 7, 2016, https://www.youtube.com/watch?v=_BgJEXQkJNQ&t=83s.

11. "Elon Musk: 'We Have Not Ruled Out' That UFO Caused Space X Explosion, https://sputniknews.com/science/201609101045180070-elon-musk-ufo-spacex-explosion.

12. "SpaceX—Static Fire Anomaly—AMOS-6 09-01-2016," https://www.youtube.com/watch?v=_BgJEXQkjNQ&t=83s.

13. "UFO Crashes in Saudi Arabia after Being Hit with Surface to Air Missile," Latest UFO Sighting, October 27, 2016, Accessed October 27, 2017, http://www.latest-ufo-sightings.net/2016/10/ufo-crashes-saudi-arabia-hit-surface-air-missile.html.

14. Roger Marsh, "Georgia Witness Describes UFO Chased by Military Helicopter," OpenMinds, Jan. 18, 2017, http://www.openminds.tv/georgia-witness-describes-ufo-chased-by-military-helicopter/39496.

15. Leslie Kean, "Groundbreaking UFO Video Just Released by Chilean Navy," *Huffington Post,* Jan. 5, 2017, https://www.huffingtonpost.com/entry/groundbreaking-ufo-video-just-released-from-chilean_us_586d37bce4b014e7c72ee56b.

16. Kean, "Groundbreaking UFO Video."

17. Kean, "Groundbreaking UFO Video."

18. Kean, "Groundbreaking UFO Video."

19. Kean, "Groundbreaking UFO Video."

20. "UFO over Tehran, Iran. Allegedly Attacked by the Military 16-Jan-2017," Latest UFO Sighting, Jan. 17, 2017, http://www.latest-ufo-sightings.net/2017/01/ufo-tehran-iran-allegedly-attacked-military-16-jan-2017.html.

21. Ellie Zolfagharifard, "UFO Hunters Claim They Have Spotted an 'Alien Ship' Hidden in an Antarctic Cave in Google Earth Images," *Daily Mail,*

Jan. 25, 2017, http://www.dailymail.co.uk/sciencetech/article-4156592 /UFO-hunters-spotted-alien-ship-Antarctica.html.

22. Posted by Secureteam10, "Large Saucer UFO Found Buried in Antarctica," Jan. 13, 2017, https://www.youtube.com/watch?v=boU8eM_-JO4.

23. M. J. Banias, "The Impact of WikiLeaks on UFOs," Mysterious Universe, Feb. 2, 2017, http://mysteriousuniverse.org/2017/02/the-impact-of-wikileaks -on-ufos.

24. Doc Vega, "Wikileaks Alleges Secret War with UFOs in Antarctica," *UFO Digest*, Jan. 2013, http://ufodigest.com/article/wiki-leaks-alleges-secret-war -ufos-antarctica.

25. For the original story, see "Wikileaks Set to Reveal US-UFO War in Southern Ocean," *European Union Times,* Dec. 13, 2010, http://www.eutimes .net/2010/12/wikileaks-set-to-reveal-us-ufo-war-in-southern-ocean.

26. Posted by Secureteam10, "UFO Appears during Fighter Jet Intercept of Airline 2/20/17," Feb. 20, 2017, https://www.youtube.com/watch?v =6vniiVy76oM.

27. Posted by Secureteam10, "UFO Appears during Fighter Jet Intercept," https://www.youtube.com/watch?v=6vniiVy76oM.

28. Posted by Secureteam10, "UFO Appears during Fighter Jet Intercept," https://www.youtube.com/watch?v=6vniiVy76oM.

29. Posted by Secureteam10, "UFO Appears during Fighter Jet Intercept," https://www.youtube.com/watch?v=6vniiVy76oM.

30. "Night Vision Camera Reportedly Captures US Military Jets Chasing UFOs," Latest UFO Sighting, July 18, 2017, http://www.latest-ufo-sightings .net/2017/07/night-vision-camera-reportedly-captures-us-military-jets -chasing-ufos.html.

31. "Night Vision Camera," http://www.latest-ufo-sightings.net/2017/07/night -vision-camera-reportedly-captures-us-military-jets-chasing-ufos.html.

32. "UFOs Join at Air Show in Washington State," Latest UFO Sightings, Aug. 8, 2017, http://www.latest-ufo-sightings.net/2017/08/ufos-join-air -show-washington-state.html.

33. NBC KHQ, "UFOs Filmed at Washington's Fairchild AFB Air Show," Posted by NowYouKnow, Aug. 1, 2017, https://www.youtube.com/watch?v =JSTcBZo1emw&t=154s.

34. Edun Suoja, "UFO Overtakes Blue Angels at Full Vertical Climb: Fort Worth, Texas," Posted by UFO News, April 23, 2016, https://www.youtube .com/watch?v=3JlfNPKKa7w.

AFTERWORD. CONQUEST OR QUARANTINE?

1. H. G. Wells, *The War of the Worlds* (London: Baronet, 1983), 1.
2. Eric Schlosser, *Command and Control: Nuclear Weapons, the Damascus Accident, and the Illusion of Safety* (New York: Penguin, 2014), 88.
3. The Hunger Project, "World Hunger," accessed Feb. 28, 2018, http://www.thp.org/knowledge-center/know-your-world-facts-about-hunger-poverty.
4. Stanton T. Friedman, *Flying Saucers and Science* (Wayne, NJ: New Page, 2008), 171.
5. Keyhoe, *Flying Saucers,* 129.
6. Keyhoe, *Flying Saucers,* 131.
7. Lee Speigel, "UFO Sightings Increase 67 Percent In Three Years," HuffPost, Aug. 26, 2011, accessed November 7, 2017, www.huffingtonpost.com/2011/08/26/ufos-pilots-history-channel_n_935847.html.
8. "MUFON Statistics Report July 2015," Educating Humanity, Aug. 6, 2015, http://www.educatinghumanity.com/2015/08/ufo-sighting-statistics-july-2015.html.
9. Keyhoe, *Flying Saucers,* 224.
10. David Axe, "When It Comes to War in Space, U.S. Has the Edge," Reuters, Aug. 10, 2015, blogs.reuters.com/great-debate/2015/08/09/the-u-s-military-is-preparing-for-the-real-star-wars.

Index

Page numbers in *italics* indicate illustrations.